Freddie Mercury

A KIND OF MAGIC

MARK BLAKE

Backbeat
Books

An Imprint of
Hal Leonard Corporation

Published in 2016 in the United States by
BACKBEAT BOOKS
An Imprint of Hal Leonard Corporation
7777 West Bluemound Road
Milwaukee, WI 53213
Trade Book Division Editorial Offices
33 Plymouth St., Montclair, NJ 07042
www.backbeatbooks.com

Design and layout © 2016 Palazzo Editions Ltd
Text © 2016 by Mark Blake
Please see picture credits on page 223 for image copyright information.

Created and produced by
Palazzo Editions Ltd
15 Church Road
London SW13 9HE
United Kingdom
www.palazzoeditions.com

Publisher: Colin Webb
Managing Editor: Joanne Rippin
Editor: James Hodgson
Photo Editor: Sally Claxton

ISBN 978-1-4950-3011-6

Library of Congress Cataloging-in-Publication Data
Names: Blake, Mark, 1965- author.
Title: Freddy Mercury : a kind of magic / Mark Blake.
Description: Montclair, NJ : Backbeat Books, 2016.
Identifiers: LCCN 2016018062 | ISBN 9781495030116 (hardcover)
Subjects: LCSH : Mercury, Freddie. | Rock musicians--England--Biography.
Classification: LCC ML420.M389 B53 2016 | DDC 782.42166092 [B] --dc23
LC record available at https://lccn.loc.gov/2016018062

10 9 8 7 6 5 4 3 2 1

Colour reproduction by XY Digital Ltd
Printed and bound in China by Imago

Page 1: Freddie Mercury, Masonic Temple, Detroit, 11 February 1976.
Pages 2–3: Freddie flies the flag, Wembley Stadium, London, 12 July 1986.

Contents

'I mean, why do we use anything? It doesn't necessarily mean I studied demonology. I just love the word "Beelzebub".'

FM, c. 1976

'It would be so boring to be seventy.'

FM, 1987

The last time I saw Freddie Mercury was on 9 August 1986. He was wearing a crown and coronation robes and promenading across the stage at Knebworth Park while the National Anthem blared in the background. Nobody knew it at the time, but this would be his final concert with Queen.

The band had played all the hits – they *always* played the hits – including 'Bohemian Rhapsody' which, as the lyrics promised, came with thunderbolts and lightning, but also so much dry ice it looked as if the stage was on fire. Queen's mission statement when performing live was very simple: 'blind 'em and deafen 'em'. But my abiding memory is of the crown and the robe, and Freddie's knowing grin, as if to suggest, 'Yes, of course I look ridiculous, but isn't it brilliant!'

The first time I saw Freddie Mercury was on TV in winter 1975. He was just a hazy black-and-white image – all hair and teeth – in the video for 'Bohemian Rhapsody'. My ten-year-old brain could not process all those 'Galileo Figaro!'s and 'Bismillah! No!'s. But then growing up in the seventies and

Previous: Little devil, Marquee, London, 3 February 1973.
Opposite: Killer queen, June 1974.
© Mick Rock 1974, 2016
Right: Heir to the throne, Wembley Stadium, July 1986.

eighties, you couldn't avoid Queen. As the years passed I fully discovered the music. No two Queen albums ever sounded the same; in fact, no two Queen *songs* sounded the same. But they always immediately sounded like Queen, and that was much to do with Freddie.

Over time, my impressionable young mind boggled to early Queen curios such as 'The Fairy Feller's Master-Stroke' and 'Stone Cold Crazy' – songs that sounded like Led Zeppelin in ballet tights and a tutu. Later came 'Bicycle Race', perhaps the most peculiar pop song of 1978, and almost certainly (if the story is true) the only hit single ever inspired by a romantic tryst with a Tour de France rider. Later still, came the Queen/David Bowie musical summit 'Under Pressure', a track that sounds like several different songs fused together. It doesn't make sense but it remains inexplicably, indisputably magnificent.

By then, though, there had been two public versions of Freddie Mercury. There was the old one with the long hair and the teeth, and the new one with the short hair, the moustache and the teeth. Both made me laugh. But what they both brought to the music was a knowing wit and a craftsman's skill as a writer and interpreter of songs. The other members of Queen wrote songs – often great songs – but it was Freddie who sold them.

'I thought, I'm going to do exactly as I please, do as many multi-layer harmonies as possible, go well over the top and, you know, didn't give a shit about anybody else.'

FM ON 'BOHEMIAN RHAPSODY', c. 1977

It was the same on stage: whether at Knebworth, Wembley or any of the other venues in which they blinded and deafened me. Queen were always ridiculous and brilliant, and no one more so than Freddie Mercury. As he sang in the Queen song 'Let Me Entertain You', 'to thrill you I'll use any device'. He took the business of being Freddie Mercury seriously, but was aware of how absurd it all was. Look again at his performance at Live Aid. He can barely keep a straight face.

Offstage it was sometimes a different story. Freddie's life was complex, troubled, shrouded in secrecy and, ultimately, tragic. He died far too young. But even now, twenty-five years later and on the eve of what would have been his seventieth birthday, his music remains inescapable. It's everywhere.

Since 1998 I have interviewed his band mates Brian May and Roger Taylor many times and have also spoken to around a hundred other people who knew Freddie during his forty-five years on the planet. Some of them knew him only as Farrokh Bulsara, or later Fred Bulsara, the person he was before Queen. Others knew him

only as a world-famous rock star. All of them shed some light on his story.

This book, then, is the story of the man Freddie Mercury was and the man he became. It's a celebration of his humour and showmanship, but also of a musician and songwriter whose talents were sometimes lost behind that larger-than-life persona.

I sometimes wonder what Freddie Mercury would be doing now had he lived. Still singing with Queen? Judging a TV music talent show? Writing hits for other artists? Scoring a West End musical? Vacuuming the house in a short PVC skirt and high heels? Or enjoying a quiet life, but donning the crown and coronation robes whenever the mood took him? Whatever he would be doing, I hope it would still be as ridiculous and brilliant as ever.

Left: Always brilliant, Hammersmith Odeon, November 1975.
Opposite: Conquering the world, Live Aid, 13 June 1985.

THE GOLDEN BOY

'Accomplished boxer, good singer, outstanding pianist, unbeatable table-tennis player, thoroughly mediocre cross-country runner.'

FM'S SCHOOL REPORT, c. 1959

Opposite: Freddie Mercury, when he was
still Farrokh Bulsara, 1958.

'He never talked about his background at all. But he did dress weirdly: middle-aged jackets and strange drainpipe trousers that weren't quite long enough.'

ADRIAN MORRISH,
EX-ISLEWORTH POLYTECHNIC STUDENT, 2010

Below left: Freddie's boarding school in Panchgani, India.
Below right: Seventeen-year-old Freddie Mercury (far right) helps carry a drunken college friend, Isleworth, London, 1965.

TIMELINE

1946

5 September: Born Farrokh Bulsara in the then-British protectorate of Zanzibar.

1954

Sent to a British boarding school, St Peter's, in Panchgani near Bombay (now Mumbai), India, where he starts piano lessons. Around this time he begins to call himself 'Freddie'.

1958

Forms his first band in school, the five-piece Hectics, in which he plays piano. They play a basic rock 'n' roll repertoire at school dances and local fêtes.

1963

February: Having finished school, moves back to his parents' home in Zanzibar.

1964

March: Due to political unrest in Zanzibar, the Bulsaras move to England where they settle in Feltham, Middlesex.

September: Freddie enrols at Isleworth Polytechnic where he studies art.

1966

Summer: Leaves Isleworth Polytechnic with a GCE A Level in art.

'Mercury isn't my real name, dear. I changed it from Pluto.'

FM, 1974

It was March 1964 when the plane from Zanzibar's Kisauni Airport landed at London Heathrow with Freddie Mercury on board. Back then, Queen's future lead singer was seventeen years old and still known by his birth name of Farrokh Bulsara.

Since January of that year, Zanzibar had been torn apart by violent civil unrest. The Bulsara family, fearing for their lives, fled for England, bringing little more than their precious British passports and all the belongings they could cram into a couple of suitcases.

Entering the arrivals lounge at Heathrow, thousands of miles from the warmth and comfort of Zanzibar, the Bulsaras must have wondered what their new life had in store. For one family member, though, Zanzibar was already a past life. Britain was where his future belonged.

The man who would become Freddie Mercury, one of the most famous rock stars in the world, was born on 5 September 1946 in Zanzibar City. His father, Bomi, and his mother, Jer, had both been born in Bombay (now Mumbai), India. The family name was derived from the southern Gujarat town of Bulsar. The Bulsaras made their home on the East African island of Zanzibar, while maintaining strong familial ties with India.

The family were Parsee Indians, devotees of Zoroastrianism, one of the oldest religions in the world, with its roots in ancient Persia. According to Freddie's sister, Kashmira, born six years after him, their faith instilled in her brother

many of the qualities he later applied in his musical career: 'perseverance, a work ethic, and the desire to follow your dreams,' she said.

Zanzibar had been a British colony since the nineteenth century, and Bomi Bulsara worked as a High Court cashier for the British governor. In later interviews, Freddie tended to be guarded about his childhood and background, rarely speaking in any detail about Zanzibar, and often referring to himself as Persian. In reality, Bomi's civil-service job afforded his family a comfortable, middle-class lifestyle. The Bulsaras were not rich, but they wanted for very little. 'Have I got upper-class parents who put a lot of money into me? Was I spoilt? No,' claimed Freddie in 1974. 'My parents were very strict.'

Jer Bulsara recalled her son showing an interest in music at a young age: 'He used to love playing records all the time and then sing – any sort of music, folk, classical or Indian music.' But it wasn't until Freddie was sent to boarding school in India, aged eight, that his musical talent became obvious.

Freddie made the ten-day journey from Zanzibar to India by ship. He stayed with his maternal aunt and grandmother in Bombay, before making a second journey by train to St Peter's Boy's School some 150 miles north in the hill town of Panchgani in the state of Maharashtra.

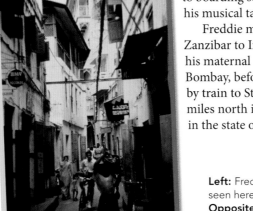

Left: Freddie's place of birth, Zanzibar City, seen here in 1965.
Opposite: Photographs outside the Bulsara family's former home in Zanzibar City.

St Peter's fashioned itself on a traditional British boarding school, with the emphasis on discipline, sporting prowess and academic achievement. It was a Church of England school, but many of its pupils were Hindu, Muslim or Parsee Indian, and it observed Indian religious holidays.

The school insignia still depicts a phoenix rising from the flames with an olive branch clenched in its beak. In the same way, the Latin school motto – '*Ut Prosim*', meaning 'That I may serve' or 'That I may be useful' – remains unchanged.

St Peter's is still a thriving educational establishment, built on tradition and constancy. However, it was here that the young Farrokh took the first step towards changing his identity, insisting that his peers call him by a new adopted first name: Freddie. 'The masters called all the boys by their surnames, so they still called him Bulsara,' recalls fellow pupil Bruce Murray, who would go on to sing in Freddie's first group. 'But to his friends, he was always Freddie.'

In his less circumspect moments, Freddie would admit to 'feelings of rejection' during those early years at St Peter's. But being on a different continent from his family, he did what he would do again later in England: he learned to fend for himself and found another 'family'.

Keith Wilson was among Freddie's earliest school friends. 'We immediately bonded as we were both shy and timid boys,' said Wilson in 2013. He was quick to notice how self-conscious Freddie was about his prominent front teeth, accentuated for a time by a painful brace.

The problem was caused by four extra teeth at the back of Freddie's mouth, which forced the others forward. According to some, he acquired the nickname 'Bucky' on account of his teeth; others deny this, and claim he was known by the less insulting sobriquet 'Buckwheat'. Whatever the truth of the matter, there were times when Freddie would become the butt of jokes or fall foul of the pecking order that inevitably developed in the boarding school's hot-house environment.

Remembered by one teacher as 'a thin, intense boy … and very effeminate', Freddie later took to calling his friends 'Darling', regardless of their gender. While this led to some boys making fun of him, he became adept at laughing it off or embracing the joke, a deflecting tactic he deployed later in life, especially when interviewers quizzed him about his sexuality.

'I liked Fred because he was sensitive and caring and not a jack the lad. You could tell that he had come from a cultured background.'

PATRICK CONNOLLY, EX-ISLEWORTH POLYTECHNIC STUDENT, 2010

Sport was a huge part of the curriculum at St Peter's. School reports claim that Freddie was a good high jumper and sprinter, a great boxer and a fantastic table-tennis player.

His ping-pong skills were refined during the epic voyages to and from Zanzibar for the Christmas holidays. Subash Shah, the only other St Peter's pupil from the island, made the trip with Freddie and the lengthy journey with stopovers in the Seychelles and Mombasa gave them both plenty of opportunity to practise.

'We were travelling third class, and ping pong was one of the few games we had,' recalled Shah. 'It was a great way to kill time.' When the ship's captain heard about the boys' skills, Freddie and Subash were allowed to mix with the first- and second-class passengers, who had access to better games and activities.

At school, the shyness and timidity Keith Wilson remembers wasn't enough to stop Freddie competing in the boxing ring, despite his mother writing to plead with him to stop fighting. There were bigger and stronger boys at St Peter's, but the bantamweight Freddie quickly learned how to, as Subash Shah puts it, 'really give it to them'.

Freddie's approach was born out of necessity: his teeth made him vulnerable, and all it took was one well-aimed blow and his lip would split. His solution was to hit first and harder and not give up. Bruce Murray remembers being in the corner for one especially brutal bout, when Freddie, despite bleeding profusely, refused to let him stop the fight: 'He had this incredibly steely look in his eye. He wasn't giving in.'

Away from the ping-pong table and the boxing ring, Freddie also showed a flair for art and music. His aunt identified his talents when he stayed with her during a school holiday. She bought him paints and canvases, and also suggested his parents pay for piano lessons. The headmaster at St Peter's, Oswal D. Bason, later wrote to the couple suggesting the same. Freddie, like most of his classmates, already sang in the school choir, where he was remembered as 'a wonderful soprano'. But soon after, he was taking extra music lessons.

By the late 1950s, pop music had infiltrated St Peter's, just as it had every school in Britain. Each week, Freddie and his friends crowded around the radio to listen to a rundown of the latest pop charts in a programme sponsored by the Indian toothpaste company Binaca.

But just as it was impossible to avoid hearing the toothpaste adverts breaking up the sounds of the Everly Brothers' 'All I Do Is Dream' or Cliff Richard's 'Move It', it was also hard to ignore the Hindi pop played on Vividh Bharati, India's national radio station, Arab contralto Oum Kalthoum, whose records filled the school music library, or the celebrated Indian singer Lata Mangeshkar, whom Freddie saw in concert in Bombay in 1959.

Several evenings a week, after dinner, Freddie and his friends would listen, rapt, to recordings of operas and Shakespearean plays. This fusion of classic English drama, opera, hymns, Western pop, Arab and Indian music and even radio jingles would find an outlet later in his music. The wild eclecticism of his songwriting with Queen – from the countless 'Galileos!' in 'Bohemian Rhapsody', to the Elvis pastiche of 'Crazy Little Thing Called Love', to the Eastern drones in 'Innuendo' – had their roots in the multicultural soundtrack at St Peter's.

Inevitably, then, Freddie was soon playing music. By the time he was thirteen, he had become the pianist in a group called the Hectics.

Opposite top: The boys in the band. Freddie with fellow Hectics Victory Rana (left) and Bruce Murray (centre).
Opposite bottom: St Peter's School, Panchgani, India.
Above: Oum Kalthoum, an Arab contralto singer and early influence on Freddie.

Left: Stonetown, Zanzibar, where Freddie returned for his final school year in 1963.
Opposite: Cliff Richard, the 'English Elvis', an early source of inspiration for Freddie, shown here in 1959.

His band mates were four fellow pupils from the school's Ashlin House dormitory: guitarist Derrick Branche, drummer Victory Rana, bass player Farang Irani (whose 'bass' mimicked those used in British skiffle groups and comprised a tea chest, a broom handle and a piece of wire) and lead singer Bruce Murray.

While it might seem odd to consider the future Freddie Mercury as a sideman rather than a lead vocalist, it made sense at the time. 'Believe it or not, Freddie wasn't one for putting himself forward back then,' says Murray. 'He could still be shy, and his thing was still the piano.'

When the Hectics played at school dances and fêtes, Freddie manned the upright piano, grinning away Little Richard-style, while Murray sang lead vocals on a repertoire that usually included the Coasters' 'Yakety Yak' and Fats Domino's 'Whole Lotta Lovin'.

The Hectics' guitarist, Derrick Branche, would move to England in the 1960s and become an actor, later appearing in the defining Anglo-Asian comedy drama *My Beautiful Laundrette*. Branche remembered that, despite having only a sideman role, Freddie always buzzed with a nervous energy that reminded him of Dean Martin's wisecracking comedy partner Jerry Lewis: 'Those hands were never still. Always being waved around with high intensity to emphasise whatever point he was making at the time.' The hands were just as restless when he later appeared on stage with Queen.

Freddie brought a similar intensity to his roles in the school drama productions, once taking great umbrage when another actor accidentally jabbed him in the backside with a toy sword. 'He slapped the poor boy across the face,' recalled Branche.

However, what everyone noticed early on was Freddie's uncanny ability to hear a piece of music and then reproduce it note-perfect on the piano. 'He had this knack of listening to a radio broadcast and, even though his knowledge of Hindi was limited, he would listen to Indian songs and somehow capture the rhythm on the piano,' says Subash Shah. 'What always impressed me about Freddie was how focused he could be.'

It was a focus he would bring to bear on any subject that interested him, but less so on those that didn't. Music, art and drama benefited from Freddie's intense scrutiny, other subjects did not, and by 1961 his grades had fallen.

In the years after his death in 1991, some ex-pupils would claim Freddie was having a homosexual relationship which led to him leaving St Peter's before he had taken his exams. His band mates in the Hectics insist this was never the case. However, Freddie himself, playing cat and mouse with the press as was his custom, later talked of being avidly pursued by a schoolmaster and described himself as an 'arch poof'.

For whatever reason, come spring 1961 Freddie was back in Zanzibar with Subash Shah. 'Both our parents independently decided not to send us back to the boarding school,' explains Shah, who only discovered this when Freddie walked into his class at their new school in the Stone Town district of Zanzibar City. 'I never really discussed with him why he'd left India. He was academically bright, but he hadn't passed the exams he needed to, and we were both here to finish our education.'

Freddie may not have excelled academically in India, but he'd returned to Zanzibar with an impressive quiff modelled on Cliff Richard's and a fascination with British pop music that, being stuck on an East African island, he could never fully satisfy.

Instead he did the best he could: obsessively listening to the BBC World Service and ordering music papers from England, which would take weeks to arrive. 'For a boy like him there wasn't much for him to do,' said Jer Bulsara. 'He was always looking at magazines which came from overseas and wanting to know what it would be like to be there.'

Subash Shah remembers this final year in Zanzibar fondly. There was school, but there were also beach parties, bike rides, pop music and girls. However, political unrest would make a sudden and dramatic impact on their lives. In December 1963, Britain handed control of the island to the Arab-led Zanzibar and Pemba People's Coalition Party. Their first ruling was to ban all opposition parties, the strongest of which, the Afro-Shiraz Party, rallied its supporters and on 12 January 1964 began violent street protests.

Under the leadership of Field Marshall John Okello, the African rebels proceeded to overthrow the new government. The brief but bloody 'Zanzibar Revolution' resulted in a new African-led ruling party and the deaths of thousands of Arabs. Okello and his supporters regarded civil servants such as Bomi Bulsara as traitors for having colluded with the British to allow the Arabs control of the island.

For a time after the coup, Freddie and Subash continued their daily ritual of strolling around Stone Town every afternoon after tea, but now they observed a strict 7.30 p.m. curfew. 'We'd seen so much death on the island,' says Shah. 'It was terrifying.'

Some years later, Freddie would tell an English college friend that the rebels had threatened to execute his father. Eventually, fearing for their safety, the Bulsaras left Zanzibar for England in March 1964. They took as much as they

Above: People on streets. The military coup which led to the Zanzibar Revolution, January 1964.
Opposite: Previously unpublished pictures of Freddie with his first friends in England, Isleworth Polytechnic, west London, 1965.

could carry; everything else was left behind. 'England's the place we ought to go,' Freddie told his mother, who vividly recalled his excitement at the move.

For his parents it was a huge upheaval. They were now immigrants, facing prejudice and discrimination in a new country. After living for a short time with relatives, the family moved into a three-bedroom terraced house at 22 Gladstone Avenue in Feltham, west London, barely three miles from Heathrow Airport.

Bomi's days as a senior civil servant were now over, and he found a job as an accountant for a catering company. Jer, meanwhile, was employed as a shop assistant. For their teenage son, though, London offered endless possibilities.

Despite Freddie's later claims to have acquired several O Level qualifications, his early departure from St Peter's and the revolution in Zanzibar seriously affected his education. His parents wanted him to study for a professional career as a lawyer or an accountant, but Freddie insisted that he wanted to pursue art.

It didn't take him long to discover that Ealing College of Art and Technology, better known by all as 'Ealing art school', where Pete Townshend of the Who had recently been a student, was a thirty-minute bus ride from Feltham. To get a place at Ealing, though, he needed an art A Level. To achieve that, Freddie persuaded his parents to let him enrol on an art foundation course at nearby Isleworth Polytechnic.

'I think he was lonely at first. He told me what luxuries his family had in Zanzibar, and how much he missed the sun and the lifestyle.'

PATRICK CONNOLLY,
EX-ISLEWORTH POLYTECHNIC STUDENT, 2010

Fellow student Patrick Connolly remembers meeting Freddie soon after he enrolled. With his now rather outmoded quiff and a slightly-too-small maroon-coloured blazer from Zanzibar, he was hard to miss. 'He was lovely and enthusiastic, and you could tell he'd come from a cultured background,' said Connolly. 'We knew his real name was Farrokh. But we never called him that. It was always Fred. He changed it because he wanted to be more anglicised.'

Adrian Morrish was also one of a clique of students who welcomed Freddie into the fold. 'I do remember that Freddie was self-conscious about his teeth,' he recalled, 'and he had a habit of slipping his top lip over them or covering his face with his hand when he smiled. In some ways he seemed incredibly naïve. But he also just slotted into the pop culture of the time. He wanted to belong.'

Freddie joined the college choir and also acted in the drama society's Christmas 1964 production of Arnold Wesker's *The Kitchen*. Encouraged by his new friends, he grew out the quiff and was soon combing his hair down into a more fashionable Beatle-style fringe. 'To start with, it looked like he was wearing a toupee,' recalls Morrish.

Freddie and Adrian were captured on film in June 1965 when a mutual friend bought a cine camera into the college. The silent footage depicts the pair and other students fooling around in the college grounds. With his hip haircut and clothes, Morrish looks like a potential member of the Who or the Yardbirds; Freddie resembles a rather gauche schoolboy. 'You would never have looked at Fred then and thought, "That's a pop star,"' admitted Morrish.

At weekends, though, Freddie would join his new friends at the Eel Pie Island Hotel on the River Thames at Twickenham. Eel Pie had previously been a stronghold for trad jazz bands, but was now the place to watch emerging blues-based performers such as Zoot Money, Alexis Korner, Long John Baldry and Baldry's sidekick, a young, unknown singer named Rod Stewart. Freddie saw them all, but sometimes ducked out of the Sunday evening sessions early, in order to keep his promise to his mother that he would practise the piano.

As Patrick Connolly recalled, Freddie's artistic pursuits were soon overshadowed by performing and music. 'Fred was no great artist,' he told me. 'But that was the thing about Isleworth Polytechnic – you didn't have to be very good. Fred showed an interest in the subject. That was enough. It was always music with Fred – singing and being on stage.'

Connolly worked as stage manager for a college production of a comedy and music revue, and saw how much his friend loved performing: 'He was full of energy and enthusiasm.'

Just like Freddie's friends before at St Peter's, Connolly and Morrish soon witnessed his extraordinary powers of musical mimicry. At lunchtimes, he would park himself at an upright piano in the assembly hall and play the hits of the day, including the Beach Boys' 'I Get Around', after just one listen on the radio.

'He'd play these songs,' said Connolly, 'but then he'd go, "But we can do this, or we can do that" and start improvising to make it sound better.'

'The thing I treasure most is meeting people. I like being sociable, and generally I'm likeable, I think.'

FM, 1974

In early 1966, Freddie decided to go one better and form a group of his own. Patrick Connolly was tasked with producing posters advertising auditions for the group, which were then plastered all over the Polytechnic and neighbouring schools and pubs.

For Connolly it was an exercise in guerrilla marketing decades before the term was invented. And it worked. On the day, some forty or fifty potential musicians queued up outside the assembly hall to be auditioned. 'Freddie knew what he wanted. He took control,' recalled Connolly. 'He was telling them all, "You stand there … You do this … You do that."'

For all Freddie's drive and enthusiasm, the planned group never came to fruition. But he would not be deterred. Connolly would often join him at the Bulsara family home. While his 'charming mother' plied them with cups of tea, Freddie would play the piano and order him to sing along. He couldn't sing, but Freddie wouldn't take no for an answer,

and eventually, with enough encouragement, Connolly would agree: 'And Fred would say, "Look, Patrick, you can do it, you can sing!"'

It was an early example of the power of persuasion and unstinting belief that Mercury would apply to himself and his band mates in Queen. Nothing was impossible, he maintained, if you put your mind to it.

Soon after, Freddie would apply the same ethos to passing his art A Level. He was going to Ealing art school, whatever it took. And what it took was Patrick Connolly helping him to pass. Freddie's exam project was a painting of the Crucifixion. He had managed to paint the figure of Jesus nailed to the Cross. But the Roman centurions at the foot of the Cross were proving problematic. 'Freddie was never very good at doing figures,' says Connolly, who reluctantly admits that he ended up painting the soldiers for him.

The deception paid off. Freddie Mercury left Isleworth Polytechnic with the qualification he needed to be accepted at Ealing. It was summer 1966, the Who's new single 'I'm a Boy' was rarely off the radio, and Freddie was following in the footsteps of the song's writer, Pete Townshend. If there was a time to daydream about becoming a rock star it was now. Queen's future lead singer was about to take the crucial step that would bring him closer to turning his dreams into reality.

Opposite: Friends will be friends. The first known photograph of Freddie (third right) in England, with Patrick Connolly (fourth right) and Adrian Morrish (far right) on the art foundation course, Isleworth Polytechnic, autumn 1964.
Above: Previously unpublished stills from the summer 1965 film of Freddie at Isleworth Polytechnic.

INSATIABLE AN APPETITE

'The biggest influence on Freddie was Freddie himself.'

BRIAN MAY, 2011

Opposite: Are you experienced? Freddie pretending to be Jimi Hendrix with a T-square for a guitar, Ealing art college, 1969.

'It's surprising, really, that we had so much confidence even in those days, when absolutely nothing was happening. I suppose we always had a good time.'

FM, 1974

TIMELINE

1966

September: Freddie is accepted on Fashion Design (later, Art and Graphic Design) course at Ealing College of Art and Technology.

1967-1968

Through bass player Tim Staffell, a fellow student at Ealing, he meets guitarist Brian May and drummer Roger Taylor, and keyboard player Chris Smith, who are rehearsing with Staffell in his band Smile.
Begins writing songs with Chris Smith, while acting as a very informal roadie for Smile.

1969

June: Leaves Ealing College.

Summer: Moves into a flat with Roger Taylor, and opens a second-hand clothes stall in Kensington Market with him.

13 August: Meets Liverpool-based three-piece band Ibex, who are in London trying to make a name for themselves, and begins rehearsing with them as vocalist.

23 August: Debut appearance with Ibex at the Octagon Theatre, Bolton.

October: At Freddie's instigation, Ibex change name to Wreckage. At same time, drummer Mick Smith is replaced by Richard Thompson, the former drummer in Brian May's band 1984.

31 October: First gig as Wreckage, at Ealing College.

1970

January: Back in London after Wreckage break-up, Freddie answers a 'Vocalist Wanted' ad in the *Melody Maker* and becomes lead singer with Sour Milk Sea.

20 March: Final gig with Sour Milk Sea, before they disband.

April: When Tim Staffell leaves Smile, Freddie joins Roger Taylor and Brian May as lead singer, changing the band's name to Queen. He also adopts the stage name 'Freddie Mercury'.

'He sounded like a powerful bleating sheep.'

ROGER TAYLOR ON FM'S
EARLY VOCAL STYLE,
2008

Ealing art school's 'Noisy Common Room' was so called because of the incessant clatter of its table football games. On the evening of 31 October 1969, there was another noise besides the celebratory shouts of 'Goal!' It was Freddie Mercury, lying flat on his back, wailing into a microphone.

The performance by Freddie's group Wreckage was advertised with a flyer promising 'free booze'. Spirits were high, then, but some of the audience preferred table football to the band. It didn't help that there wasn't a stage, and Wreckage had to set up their drum kit and amps on the common room floor.

Undeterred, Freddie did whatever he could to get everyone's attention. He'd already turned up wearing a shocking-pink chiffon scarf and a white suit. Whenever Wreckage's guitarist took a solo, on one of their own songs or a messy version of Elvis's 'Jailhouse Rock', Freddie struck a pose. He'd throw his head back, like a matador challenging a charging bull, play imaginary guitar, or drop to his knees, as if in the grip of some strange reverie.

All the moves Freddie Mercury performed with Queen at Live Aid in 1985, he first tried out on the floor of the Noisy Common Room sixteen years earlier. At Live Aid, though, Freddie had a 72,000-strong crowd hanging on his every move. At Ealing, half the audience wasn't paying attention, and the other half didn't like what they were hearing. Some were even laughing. In the end, Freddie took his microphone off its stand, lay flat on his back and began wailing with the mic almost jammed into his mouth.

Former Ealing Student Union president Aubrey Malden booked Wreckage to play that night. 'They really weren't very good,' he told me. 'In fact, Freddie was crap. He had the moves, but he couldn't sing. It was extraordinary to see how much he changed.'

Malden would later embark on a career in marketing. So inspired was he by Fred Bulsara's transformation, he dedicated a chapter to him in his 2012 book *Things the Brand Gurus Don't Want You to Know*, citing the singer, with his determination and ability to reinvent himself, as a shining example of brand power and awareness.

Future Queen drummer, Roger Taylor, and guitarist, Brian May, also saw Wreckage play live and were unsure about Freddie's vocal technique. 'Freddie's role in Wreckage was to run around and scream his head off,' observed Brian. 'He was so in your face and loud and insistent.' But they spotted something. 'Freddie was a product of his own enormous energy,' said Roger. 'A tribute to the idea that if you believe in something hard enough you can make it happen.'

Free booze! A flyer for Wreckage's debut gig, 31 October 1969, Ealing art college.

'I'm going to be a pop star!' – 'Freddie baby' with Ealing graphics student Tony Catignani, c. 1968.

Freddie Mercury became a student at Ealing Art College in September 1966, and spent the next five years before forming Queen trying to 'make it happen'. For the first year, he was one of just two male students studying fashion design. Former fashion students remember him making a voguish patchwork leather jacket and stealing one of his mother's silk tablecloths and turning it into a shirt.

To supplement his grant, Freddie spent one summer holiday working as a baggage handler at Heathrow Airport. But manual labour didn't suit him. When he discovered the college's evening life-drawing classes required models, Freddie signed up, stripped off and earned £5 a time. 'You were given a towel to protect your modesty,' recalled a fellow model, who wondered how many elderly ladies sketched a near naked Freddie Mercury in the late 1960s.

But, just as at Isleworth, it didn't take long for Freddie's love of music to eclipse his studies. He had an epiphany that winter, when he saw Jimi Hendrix at what his old college friends believe was either Hendrix's official London debut at Soho's Bag O'Nails club in December 1966 or his second show at the same venue the following January. 'Fred loved Jimi so much,' said Roger Taylor. 'I think he saw him nine

nights in a row at pubs all round London' – a run that began with the second Bag O'Nails date and included performances at the Speakeasy, the Seven and a Half club, and the Refectory in Golders Green.

It wasn't difficult to understand Hendrix's appeal. His musical virtuosity was one thing, but his showmanship was quite another. Except for the Who's Pete Townshend, whom Freddie saw smash his guitar on stage at a school hall in Hayes, most British guitarists, such as Eric Clapton, just stood still and played.

Hendrix, with his Afro hair and chiffon scarves, played guitar with his teeth or tongue, behind his head and, later even set his instrument on fire. Hendrix was also part African-American. Like Freddie, he wasn't the typical white rock star.

Before long, Freddie had taped a picture of Hendrix next to his bedroom mirror for inspiration. He acquired a guitar and a black felt hat, just like Jimi's, and could be seen miming the solo in Hendrix's big spring 1967 hit 'Purple Haze' whenever it came on the radio. '[Hendrix] is my idol,' Freddie said later.

Within a year of Freddie's enrolment at Ealing, though, the college authorities had noted his poor attendance. Freddie persuaded the college principal to let him stay on, but switched from studying fashion to graphic design. This had less to do with the subject and more to do with there being several musicians on the course.

'Freddie had this incredible energy.
It was like little sparks were coming off him.'

TONY CATIGNANI, EX-EALING ART COLLEGE STUDENT, 2009

Opposite: Two thirds of Smile – Brian May (third left, seated on car) and Tim Staffell (third right) – with friends, 1969.
Right: Brian May's pre-Smile group, 1984, with Brian (second right) in 1964.
Below: Smile banner designed by Freddie in 1969 and drumskin, pre-dating the Rolling Stones' lips-and-tongue logo by two years.

Among them were keyboard player Chris Smith and budding vocalist and bass guitarist Tim Staffell. Freddie first encountered his future band mate Brian May when May and Staffell's group 1984 played the college ball at Christmas 1967. 'Fred and I went along to see them,' Chris Smith told me. 'We were both very impressed, particularly by the guitarist.'

However, Freddie made no great impression on Brian May until several months later. By then, 1984 had split. But Brian, who was now studying physics and astronomy at London's Imperial College, wanted to form a new group with Tim Staffell.

In autumn 1968, May and Staffell recruited Chris Smith to play keyboards, and placed an advert on the Imperial College noticeboard looking for a 'Ginger Baker-style drummer'. Baker was the powerful drummer alongside Jack Bruce and Eric Clapton in Cream, and was held in the highest possible regard by all aspiring rock groups.

Among those who answered the ad was dentistry student Roger Taylor, who had been drumming in bands around his hometown of Truro, Cornwall, since he was a boy. May, Taylor, Staffell and Smith called themselves Smile and played their debut gig at Imperial College in October 1968. In the audience was Freddie Mercury.

Chris played a few shows with Smile, before they carried on as a three-piece. But he could see Freddie was desperate to join, even then: 'Brian and Roger were loyal to Tim, though. It wasn't going to happen.'

Instead, Freddie did the next best thing and followed Smile around, even working, in the loosest sense of the term, as an occasional roadie. This involved Freddie carrying a drum or a guitar to the stage before stopping to tell Brian and Roger where they were going wrong and what they should be doing instead. 'Fred had this enormous drive and charm,' recalled Roger. 'I think in his mind he was always plotting to join up with us. It just took us a while to realise it.'

For some of his fellow students, Freddie Bulsara was a man of mystery and contradictions. Nobody ever called him Farrokh. He was Fred or Freddie. He rarely spoke about India or Zanzibar, and either claimed to be Persian or gave the impression of having been born in England.

Despite his occasional outbursts of bravado, Freddie could still be very shy. Fellow student John Gotting remembers him at Ealing as this 'incredibly quiet,

reserved chap in a sports jacket and jeans'. The 'complete transformation' Gotting witnessed at Wreckage's gig in the common room left him stunned.

Others, though, saw that transformation coming. One student glimpsed Freddie's recently renewed passport and saw he'd listed his profession as 'musician'. Why? They asked. 'Because I'm going to be a musician,' he replied.

Besides graphic design, Chris Smith was also studying music. At first, Freddie was coy about his musical ability. But as his confidence grew, he let his guard down. Smith and others had long been used to seeing Freddie's Hendrix impersonations; he used either a steel ruler or a T-square as a makeshift guitar. Now, though, Freddie started playing the piano and a real guitar in front of Smith: 'He started showing me things he'd picked up. He had a good ear. He was quick.'

When Tim Staffell and Brian May began writing songs together, Freddie was jealous. Soon after, he and Smith starting messing around with song ideas of their own. Their inspirations were Smile's composition 'Step on Me' and the Beatles' 'A Day in the Life', the bridge of which they used to link their ideas together.

Above: Freddie with friends and Ibex bandmate Mick 'Miffer' Smith (far right), August 1969.
Opposite: Freddie's second public performance as lead singer with Ibex, Queen's Park, Bolton, 24 August 1969.

Smith remembers Freddie bringing in one idea which he christened 'The Cowboy Song'. Its opening lyric was 'Mama, just killed a man' – a line that five years later would be immortalised in Queen's 'Bohemian Rhapsody'. The problem was, though, that even after dropping in the theme from 'A Day in the Life' they could never finish the song. More than once, Freddie ended up with his head in his heads, frustrated, says Smith, because 'Tim and Brian could write a song and he couldn't.'

Undeterred, Freddie carried on telling everyone he was going to make it as a musician. 'I remember him saying, "I'm going be a pop star!" – and we all laughed,' admits Aubrey Malden. It was something 'Freddie Baby' – as some of his classmates called him – said all the time.

When Malden booked the new blues-rock group Free to play a college rag ball, Freddie hung around afterwards to talk to them, avidly listening to everything they said as if taking notes.

When an unknown singer-songwriter named David Bowie arrived to play a lunchtime gig in the college refectory in April 1969, Freddie was waiting at the college gates, and offered his services as a roadie. 'There wasn't a stage in the canteen,' remembers Chris Smith. 'And Bowie really wanted a stage. So Freddie and I made one for him by pushing some tables together.' What nobody could have predicted was

that Free's lead singer, Paul Rodgers, would end up singing Freddie's songs as a guest vocalist with Queen in the mid-2000s, or that in 1982 Bowie and Queen would have a hit together with 'Under Pressure'.

By summer 1969, 'the quiet, reserved chap in the sports jacket and jeans' had blossomed. Freddie had grown his hair long and gone shopping in Carnaby Street for a pair of velvet trousers, as worn by Jimi Hendrix. Among his other accessories was a fluffy pom-pom of the kind waved by American high school cheerleaders.

Smile were regularly playing live, opening for Pink Floyd, the Troggs, Yes, and even Jimi Hendrix. But, like many bands, they played their heavy blues-rock while wearing T-shirts and jeans. Brian May's idea of stagecraft was to look at the floor or close his eyes while playing a solo. Freddie had different ideas.

'Freddie thought we should be much more outgoing,' said Brian. When he told Smile what they should be doing,

he flicked his pom-pom at them, as if using it to punctate his sentences. Looking back, the pom-pom was almost a metaphor for how the unfussy blues-rock of the late 1960s would be succeeded by the flashier glam-pop of the early 1970s. At the time, though, it was just Freddie being Freddie.

Mercury's wish to join a band finally came true in July 1969. Comprising guitarist Mike Bersin, bassist John 'Tupp' Taylor and drummer Mick 'Miffer' Smith, Ibex were a trio from Merseyside who had moved to London for the summer hoping to get more gigs and even a record deal. Their girlfriends had already made the trip and were studying at a teacher training college in Kensington, where Brian May's future first wife, Chrissie Mullen, was also a student.

Smile, Ibex and their respective entourages lived in various student flats close to a pub on Elsham Road called the Kensington, where they met one night for a birthday celebration. It was a fortuitous meeting. 'Freddie told us he was a lead singer, but he didn't have a band,' recalled 'Tupp' Taylor. What Freddie neglected to mention was that he'd never sung as a lead singer in any band before.

However, with his chichi fur-collared jacket and jet-black hair, he *looked* like a rock star. And that was enough. 'At the time I was singing and so was Mike,' 'Tupp' told me. 'I wasn't the best singer in the world and neither was Mike. Neither of us was a frontman, which is where Freddie came in.'

Freddie made his debut with Ibex on 23 August 1969 at Bolton's Octagon Theatre, performing again the day after at an outdoor festival in the city's Queen's Park. College friend Paul Humberstone joined the band on their trip up from London, and photographed the Octagon show.

'At Ealing we were used to seeing Freddie do his Hendrix impersonation with the ruler,' said Humberstone, 'and we were used to hearing him telling everyone he was going to be a star. But now he was actually doing it.'

It's believed that the first song Freddie ever sang as a lead singer on stage was 'Jailhouse Rock'. Humberstone remembered Freddie singing in what he tactfully calls 'a high falsetto'. 'Tupp' Taylor, however, recalled Freddie's voice as 'pretty awful'. Others, including guitarist Mike Bersin, are certain he sang the first few numbers with his back half-turned to the audience, too shy to face the crowd.

By the second gig in Queen's Park, though, he'd gained confidence. When Bersin closed his eyes to play a solo, he opened them a few seconds later to find Freddie kneeling in front of him and urging him on. To Freddie's delight, a photo of him in full vocal flight appeared in the next day's *Bolton Evening News*.

Ibex played again a month later at Liverpool's Sink club on a stage so small Freddie performed on the floor in front of it. The gig was recorded by a roadie. Heard now, it's testament to the band's enthusiasm rather than its talent. Freddie is often out of tune and yelps his way through Led Zeppelin's 'Communication Breakdown', before offering a whispered 'Thank you' to the few in the audience who bother to clap. 'Freddie lacked vocal technique,' admitted Roger Taylor, who attended the gig along with Brian May. 'But he had power.'

While still living at the Bulsara family home, Freddie now spent most of his time at the band flats in Kensington. His parents, especially his father, struggled to understand his obsession with music, making it more appealing for him to stay away from home. However, a boarding-school education and a doting mother had left Freddie lacking in domestic skills. One night he marched into the flat, announced he was hungry and wanted a boiled egg. He emerged from the kitchen several minutes later and sheepishly admitted he didn't actually know how to boil an egg. On another occasion Freddie made a cup of tea, unaware that one of the flat's occupants had stashed his dope in the tea caddy. Freddie spent a disorientating few hours giggling to himself in the living room and listening obsessively to Frank Zappa and the Mothers of Invention's album *We're Only in It for the Money*.

Feeding himself might have been a problem, but dressing himself was easier. Somehow, despite spending many nights sleeping on floors and sofas, he maintained high sartorial standards. Freddie appeared to own one outfit: a white long-sleeved T-shirt and a pair of black trousers. But both were always clean and neatly ironed. 'My mother couldn't get over the creases in those trousers,' marvelled Roger Taylor.

He was both a part of the crowd and also apart from it. Freddie didn't share some of his friends' enthusiasm for alcohol and dope, and was always the first out of bed – or off the sofa – while others slept off their hangovers. While they snoozed, he quietly strummed a guitar and tried to work out how to play songs off the Who's new album, *Tommy*.

When Freddie wasn't learning other people's songs, he badgered Mike Bersin into writing songs with him. Among them was a ballad entitled 'Green'. A rough recording of the song was made at Smile's shared house in Barnes. During the recording, Freddie can be heard giving instructions to his band mates. 'Musically, Freddie was way ahead of us,' admitted Bersin.

What Freddie wasn't doing, though, was studying at college. Official accounts of Queen's history claim he graduated from Ealing with a diploma in art and design. In fact, he dropped out before completing his diploma, but, feeling intimidated by his band mates', especially Brian May's, qualifications, he invented one for himself.

After Freddie had quit Ealing, his musical ambitions stalled in October 1969 when most of Ibex moved back to Liverpool. However, he refused to admit defeat, first persuading Aubrey Malden to book the band for the 'Noisy Common Room' gig and then paying Mike Bersin's train fare back to London. A friend of Brian May's, Richard Thompson, replaced departing drummer 'Miffer' Smith.

With Thompson on board, Freddie suggested changing the band's name to Wreckage. He told each band mate the others had agreed to the change. They hadn't. But the deceit worked. Ibex became Wreckage, a name Freddie thought more in keeping with that of his new favourite group, Led Zeppelin, whom he'd just seen play at London's Lyceum Theatre. When Thompson almost passed out with exertion during Wreckage's first rehearsal, Freddie took it as a good sign.

Despite their inauspicious Ealing college debut, Wreckage would play several gigs in the winter of 1969, including one at a girls' grammar school in Widnes, Merseyside. According to Queen legend, it was here the base fell off Freddie's mic stand, a mishap he'd turn into a gimmick with Queen.

Opposite: Freddie at Roger Taylor's shared flat, Sinclair Gardens, Shepherd's Bush, London, 1969.
Below: Freddie takes a hands-on approach to designing a packet of biscuits, Ealing art college, 1969.

'*Before Fred and I went out together, he'd always look in the mirror, preening himself, pumping up his hair.*'

ALAN HILL, EX-EALING ART COLLEGE STUDENT, 2010

FAMILY ENTERTAINMENT

BRIGHT LIGHTS, SOUR MUSIC..

Without the heavy base to weigh it down, the stand would replace the ruler and the T-square as Freddie's fake guitar. In years to come it would become a recognisable motif. 'All your most famous rock stars work as silhouettes,' pointed out Mike Bersin. 'Slash, Buddy Holly – and Freddie Mercury with his sawn-off microphone stand.'

By January 1970, though, no amount of self-belief could keep Wreckage together. Freddie was, again, a singer without a band. Dogged as ever, he answered a music press advert and found a new group.

Sour Milk Sea, like Ibex, were a blues-rock act in need of a lead vocalist. Cream had split up; power trios were passé, and every band wanted a lead singer like Led Zeppelin's Robert Plant. Dressed entirely in black velvet, Freddie swanned into his Sour Milk Sea audition at a youth club in Dorking, Surrey, looking as if he'd already got the job. He also told the group's manager his name was Fred Bull. It was some time before they discovered the truth.

According to ex-Sour Milk Sea guitarist Chris Chesney, Freddie dazzled them with his enthusiasm, and landed the gig on the spot. Freddie was twenty-four years old; Chesney was eighteen and impressionable. 'I felt an immediate camaraderie with him,' he told me. 'I came from a very conventional middle-class background in Oxford. Freddie, however, seemed to have total freedom. He dressed me, he styled me. I welcomed it.'

Before long, Chesney started spending more and more time with Freddie at Smile's house in Barnes, and noticed that as much as Smile and their entourage adored Freddie, they didn't take him seriously. 'In his milieu he was almost a laughing stock,' he said. 'I had the impression they thought he was a joke. That he was trying too hard.'

Freddie brought showmanship and fun to Sour Milk Sea, but also a broader musical palette. He loved Hendrix's *Electric Ladyland*, *Led Zeppelin II*, the Who's *Tommy* and the Beatles' 'White Album', set texts in late-1960s rock circles. But he also adored 1950s rock 'n' roll, including Cliff Richard, and raved about the Jackson 5 and Marvin Gaye.

These disparate influences would help Queen break out of the confines of early-1970s rock. But before then,

'It was the days when the market had a lot of character. Every stall was individual. Each stall had its own character. It was like a bazaar.'

FM, 1974

they impacted on Sour Milk Sea. Chris Chesney describes Freddie's musical approach as 'a pop sensibility … and big harmonies'. Many of Freddie's song ideas were leftovers from Wreckage, and one would become 'Liar', a song that featured on Queen's debut album. Chesney was happy to let 'Freddie throw out all my lyrics and write his own', but his other band mates weren't so accommodating and resented the singer's growing influence.

Sour Milk Sea lasted until April 1970, long enough for them to support Black Sabbath, the heaviest of the new heavy rock groups, at a gig in Soho. Chesney stuck around, and would later audition to become a second guitarist in Queen. But it wasn't to be.

Besides being Smile's greatest fan, Freddie had become good friends with Roger Taylor. They shared not only an admiration for Zeppelin and Hendrix, but also a lively sense of humour and a love of dressing up. As the drummer later remarked, 'If there were shenanigans and good times, Fred and I would be there.'

By now, the pair were running a stall selling art and antiques at Kensington Market. With the hip Biba fashion store and Chelsea's equally hip Kings Road nearby, the three-storey indoor market was a magnet for the beautiful people of late-1960s London. Fashion models and pop stars, including members of Led Zeppelin, Yes and the Rolling Stones, were frequently to be seen there.

When customers proved scarce, the pair switched to selling clothes, acquiring bags

of what Brian May called 'dreadful old tat' from charity shops and attempting to sell it on. 'We were terrible salesmen,' admitted Roger, 'and Freddie was particularly bad with money.'

A year later and with Queen in its infancy, a fellow stallholder employed Freddie to sell shoes for him. David Bowie, who was now an established star, rocked up one afternoon to try on a pair of fancy leather boots. As he eased Bowie's feet into the boots and clucked approvingly, Freddie chose not to mention the time he had helped build a stage for him at Ealing art school. Instead he told Bowie that he, too, was a singer. Bowie listened politely.

Sour Milk Sea wasn't the only group to break up in spring 1970. After two years of gigging, Smile were no closer to a breakthrough, and Tim Staffell was disillusioned. Staffell loved rhythm 'n' blues and soul and the notion of pure musicianship without the flamboyance and showmanship beloved of their pom-pom-wielding number-one fan.

At one of Smile's frequent gigs on Roger Taylor's home turf of Cornwall, Freddie had jumped on stage with the band to sing a couple of numbers. After all, Freddie knew their songs almost as well as they did. Soon after, Staffell announced he was leaving Smile. There were no hard feelings, no lingering animosity. But seeing his opportunity, Freddie pounced, and suggested he take over.

'We took it on faith somehow,' marvelled Brian May. 'We didn't see a great singer or musician first of all – he was very wild and unsophisticated. We just saw someone who had incredible belief and charisma, and we liked him.'

Two years earlier, Chris Smith remembered seeing Freddie, Brian and Roger strolling down Ealing Broadway, laughing and joking on their way to a music shop. 'And I remember thinking, "That's it, that's the band right there,"' he said. Now, Brian and Roger could recognise what others had seen all along.

Opposite: 'He brought big harmonies.' Freddie with Sour Milk Sea in the *Oxford Mail*, March 1970.
Right: You're my best friend. Freddie's flatmate, Roger Taylor. As well as sharing a flat, Freddie and Roger also ran a second-hand clothes stall in Kensington Market.

THE MIGHTY TITAN AND HIS TROUBADOURS

'Queen wanted the world – and they wanted it no later than teatime on Friday.'

MICK ROCK, 2004

'I used to get the bus with Freddie after he'd joined Queen, and he'd say, "God! I hope this band takes off. I don't know what I'm going to do if it doesn't."'

EX-SMILE KEYBOARD PLAYER CHRIS SMITH, 2009

TIMELINE

PLAYBILL
URIS THEATRE

1970

27 June: The first appearance of Queen, at the City Hall in Truro, Cornwall, with Mike Grose on bass guitar.

18 July: First London appearance of Queen, at Imperial College. Grose leaves the band shortly afterwards.

23 August: First gig with Grose's replacement, Barry Mitchell – back at Imperial College.

1971

18 January: Queen's first gig at London's Marquee Club.

February: Queen settle on John Deacon as their permanent bassist.

2 July: Queen's debut gig with John Deacon in line-up, at a college date in Surrey.

December: Queen begin recording demo tapes at the newly built De Lane Lea Studios, Wembley, London.

1972

24 March: Concert at Forest Hill Hospital's nurses college is attended by Barry Sheffield, co-founder of Trident Studios, who is impressed.

June–November: Recording of debut album takes place at Trident Studios, London.

November: The band sign recording, publishing and management deal with Trident.

20 December: First London Marquee appearance with John Deacon on bass.

1973

5 February: Queen record for the BBC *Sound of the Seventies* radio programme.

6 July: Queen's debut single, 'Keep Yourself Alive', released.

13 July: Debut album, *Queen*, released in UK.

24 July: First TV airing of a Queen song, 'Keep Yourself Alive', on BBC's *Old Grey Whistle Test*.

August: Second album, *Queen II*, recorded at Trident Studios, London.

4 September: *Queen* released in United States.

12 November–14 December: First major UK tour, supporting Mott the Hoople.

3 December: Second Queen session for BBC's *Sound of the Seventies*.

1974

21 February: First appearance on BBC TV's *Top of the Pops*.

1 March–2 April: First UK tour as headliners.

8 March: *Queen II* released.

9 March: 'Seven Seas of Rhye' becomes Queen's first UK chart entry, peaking at #10.

23 March: *Queen II* enters UK chart, peaking at #5.

30 March: Debut album, *Queen*, enters UK chart, peaking at #24.

16 April–5 May: First US tour, supporting Mott the Hoople.

7–11 May: Queen play six shows at New York's Uris Theatre.

July–September: Queen record third album, *Sheer Heart Attack*, at AIR, Rockfield, Trident and Wessex Sound studios.

21 October: 'Killer Queen' from *Sheer Heart Attack* released.

26 October: 'Killer Queen' enters UK singles chart, peaking at #2.

8 November: *Sheer Heart Attack* released, peaking at #2 in the UK chart.

'His hair is cormorant black, he flashes ebony eyes and his smile reveals a row of pearly white teeth which look ready to plunge into a meal of little girl burgers.'

MELODY MAKER, DECEMBER 1974

Several years ago Roger Taylor rediscovered his diaries from the early 1970s. He found them stashed away in his mother Winifred's house after her death. 'One entry from April 1970 reads, "We have decided the best name for the band is Queen,"' Roger told me.

A few entries earlier, though, the group was considering another name, Build Your Own Boat, for which Roger had designed a logo. The drummer shook his head at the memory. 'Thank God that idea was abandoned.'

However, when Freddie Mercury joined Roger, and Brian May in spring 1970, the band was still Smile, and had bookings to fulfil. One of these was a fundraiser for the Cornish branch of the Red Cross, of which Winifred Taylor was an organiser. Roger assured his mother that Smile would still play, despite the loss of Tim Staffell. He told her that Freddie Bulsara, he of the perfectly creased trousers, would be taking over.

Smile were booked to play Truro City Hall on Saturday 27 June. As well as proposing a name change to Queen, Freddie suggested the others ditch their traditional stage uniform of denim jeans and insisted black velvet was the way forward.

With Staffell gone, Queen recruited a new bass player, Mike Grose, a friend of Roger's from Cornwall, who moved to London on the promise of pop stardom. 'We all dressed in black crushed velvet trousers, black T-shirts and stack-heeled boots,' recalled Grose in 2011. After Mike accidentally ripped his first pair of velvet trousers, Freddie provided another. His skill in fashion design proved fortuitous; that and his ability to beg, borrow or steal clothes from his female friends.

Kitted out in their new stage outfits, Queen rehearsed in a lecture theatre at Imperial College, working up a repertoire of Smile songs, Led Zeppelin covers and Freddie's composition, 'Stone Cold Crazy', a frantic hard rock song later covered in the 1990s by heavy metal giants Metallica.

Dolled up in velvet and with Freddie's wrists jangling with bracelets and bangles, Queen looked like stars when they strode on stage at Truro City Hall. Their view from the stage was less impressive, though, as only around fifty people had shown up.

Mike Grose remembered the group's performance as 'pretty rough', not least Freddie's habit of pulling the microphone away from his mouth when he couldn't hit a high note. That said, Freddie still 'jumped about all over the place, a bit like Mick Jagger', shocking Winifred Taylor who'd never seen this side of his personality before.

Despite the poor attendance, Queen/Smile pocketed £50. Grose drove them back to London the following day. Sitting in the back of the van, Freddie chattered excitedly about what they should do next, what songs they should play, how they could make the show better …

Shortly after, Smile officially became Queen. Having been asked about the origins of the group's name more times than they care to remember, Brian May and Roger Taylor have well-rehearsed answers, which can be summarised thus: 'Freddie wanted us to sound regal.' Mike Grose, though, admits to having reservations – calling a band Queen in the early 1970s was 'considered a bit risky … however ridiculous that might seem forty years on'.

The march of the black Queen: Freddie and Brian May, Imperial College, London, 2 November 1973.
© Mick Rock 1974, 2016

45

'*The name was very different. Partly it was the regal thing, partly it was the camp thing. A lot of people have tried to get us to change it, but we've stuck to it. We like it.*'

FM, 1974

The gay connotations of the name might have bothered some in those times. But in 1970 it had not occurred to many people that Freddie might be homosexual. His camp demeanour was considered a pose, an affectation, and one that worked well both on stage and behind his stall at Kensington Market.

Part of the reason nobody gave any thought to Freddie's sexuality was that he'd had several girlfriends since art school. Indeed, by the time he formed Queen he was in a relationship with Mary Austin, the beautiful nineteen-year-old receptionist at the iconic Biba fashion shop in Kensington Church Street.

After instigating the band name change, Freddie took the most significant personal decision of his life. From now on he wanted to be called Freddie Mercury. Brian May pinpointed the decision to a line from Freddie's song 'My Fairy King': 'Oh, Mother Mercury, look what they've done to me.' Freddie, however, said he just took the name from Mercury, the Roman messenger of the gods.

For a rock singer to use a stage name was hardly new. But, in Freddie's case, the name change marked the end of one chapter of his life, one in which he had been a shy

schoolboy in India and Zanzibar, and the beginning of another, in which, as he had told his art-school friends, he was going to become a superstar –bigger than Hendrix.

As with the change from Smile to Queen, Brian and Roger offered little resistance to the singer's new name. Smile had briefly had a record deal and released an unsuccessful single. They had nothing to lose in going along with Freddie's schemes, even the madcap ones. Along with the velvet stage costumes and the regal band name, the arrival of 'Freddie Mercury' was just another part of the package.

Nevertheless, the formation of Queen coincided with Brian and Roger reaching crucial points in their education. Roger had abandoned dentistry in favour of trying to become a pop star. To appease his mother, he had agreed to study biology as a contingency. However, Brian was now working on his PhD and had been identified by his professors as someone who could secure a prestigious scientific career.

Meanwhile, Freddie still worked at Kensington Market, and took on freelance illustrating jobs to top up his paltry earnings. One commission was to illustrate a book about World War Two aircraft, another to design an advert for

Opposite: Queen pose for a 1974 photo shoot in Freddie's Kensington flat, round a table that holds an incongruous tea set and a magazine article about Freddie's idol Liza Minnelli.

women's underwear. But he wouldn't seriously contemplate a career in anything other than rock music.

Inevitably, then, there was friction between Freddie and his parents, who struggled to understand what he was doing with his life. 'Freddie talked to me about being Parsee Indian and about his family,' said Roger, who was soon sharing a flat with the singer in Kensington's Sinclair Road. 'But it was all very private stuff. The Parsee culture was very different, and he felt that he wasn't part of that culture. His mother was always wonderful to him, but he knew there was an immense gap in lifestyles.'

Undeterred, Freddie and Queen spent the remainder of the year dodging aggrieved parents and playing pubs, clubs and college halls, anywhere and everywhere, hoping they would be noticed. But stardom was not forthcoming. On Christmas Day, Roger and Freddie were so penniless their festive dinner consisted of a packet of bread sauce. 'We used to dream of a can of beans,' said Roger. 'We were very broke, but we still managed to ponce around and appear rather grand.'

Mike Grose, however, didn't share his band mates' self-belief and soon moved back to Cornwall and a steady job. His replacement, Barry Mitchell, made his Queen debut in August 1970 at a gig at Imperial College, London.

Mitchell, a part-time park keeper whose idea of stage wear was the same jeans and T-shirt he'd had on all day, was alarmed to see Freddie painting his nails black and teasing his hair with heated tongs before the performance. Mitchell liked Queen but told me he thought their music sounded 'too much like Yes and Led Zeppelin'. He stayed until January 1971 before quitting, convinced Queen were going nowhere.

In February, a chance meeting at the teacher training college where Brian May's girlfriend was studying introduced Queen to bass player John Deacon. Deacon, a nineteen-year-old electronics student from Leicester, whose girlfriend was also attending the teacher training college, was a fine musician. But he was as unassuming as Mercury, May and Taylor were the opposite and was soon given the nickname 'Easy' Deacon. The man who would later write major hits including 'Another One Bites the Dust' and 'I Want to Break Free' fitted in to Queen partly because he didn't challenge the others.

'Freddie's personality was ... like the volume button on the radio. There are not a lot of people who can walk into a room and there's something they bring into it which makes it warm and genial. And then, when they leave, it goes.'

MARY AUSTIN, 2013

John Deacon's arrival coincided with an upswing in Queen's fortunes after eight months of pub and club gigs and very little record company interest. Former Mercury Records A&R man John Anthony had produced Smile's single and had been observing their progress. When he first saw Queen, he recognised Freddie as the dandy he had spotted promenading up and down Kensington High Street, and was impressed. 'He was much better than Tim Staffell,' Anthony told me. 'Freddie had presence.'

Anthony had left Mercury Records to form a production company with producer Roy Thomas Baker. He told Queen he was interested in helping them get a deal, but was busy working with other bands and it would take time. In the interim, Queen recorded a demo at a new studio, De Lane Lea, in Wembley, northwest London. The studio engineers needed a band to test the new facility, and Queen volunteered. The band walked away with a professional demo, which they hawked around the record companies, but to widespread indifference. As one band associate recalled, 'Everyone said Queen sounded too much like Led Zeppelin.'

John Anthony and Roy Thomas Baker heard something else, though. At a gig in Forest Hill, south London, in March 1972, Freddie wowed the pair with an outrageously camp version of Shirley Bassey's 'Big Spender'. For all the Led Zeppelin comparisons, Queen were still willing to go off-piste. Like their other unexpected cover of Cliff Richard and the Shadows' 'Please Don't Tease', it showed a wit and imagination beyond most of the copycat rock bands of the time.

Off the back of the gig, Anthony and Baker's associates, Trident Audio Productions, offered Queen a deal. The company was run by brothers Norman and Barry Sheffield, who owned the high-tech Trident Studios in Soho. Queen would now have access to the finest recording equipment, and Trident would pay for studio time, a new PA, instruments and stage clothes. However, Trident would also be responsible for Queen's song publishing and management. The Sheffields allocated Queen a business manager, Jack Nelson, to handle their day-to-day affairs. But Nelson was accountable to Trident. It was a classic conflict of interest, and would have enormous ramifications. But, at the time, it was the best deal Queen could find.

Trident offered the band wages of £20 a week, and agreed to fund the recording of a debut album, which they would then pitch to record labels. However, Queen could record at Trident only when paying acts were not using the studio. According to the album's co-producer John Anthony, 'They were given that mysterious time, at eleven o'clock at night or two and three in the morning when no one else is around.'

'The owners of the studio, in a sense, owned us,' said Brian May. 'They were our managers, but they didn't want to spend any money.' At the time, David Bowie was at Trident producing Lou Reed's *Transformer* album. 'So if David finished a session at three o'clock [in the morning], we'd get a phone call.'

Despite these setbacks, John Anthony realised Freddie was a tireless ideas man with a strong vision of what he wanted. Anthony was used to bands showing up in the studio with just a bag of dope to fuel their creativity. Freddie arrived brandishing a copy of the glossy fashion magazine *Queen*, its pages filled with glamorous images, and told the producer he wanted their album to be the aural equivalent: 'I'd never met a musician who thought like that before.'

Now Queen were finally making an album, Freddie's perfectionism came to the fore. He was a hard taskmaster, but he was hardest on himself. 'The first time it struck me was in the studio, when Freddie was listening to his voice come back, going, "No, that won't do," and just working and working,' recalled Brian May.

Brian and Roger shared doubts about Freddie's voice to begin with. But as Brian explained, they were amazed by how quickly he improved: 'There was a very quick period, you could almost have blinked and missed it, where he learned to harness his technique.'

Freddie made such an impression at Trident that he was asked to sing on another project. A version of the Beach Boys' 'I Can Hear Music' was released as a single under the name Larry Lurex a year later. The recording also featured Brian and Roger and sounded nothing like Led Zeppelin. 'I Can Hear Music' sank without trace, but was early evidence of Freddie's flair for pop as well as rock.

Queen's eponymous debut album was completed in November 1972. It had been a long haul. John Anthony was forced to duck out of the project and leave Roy Thomas

'And it was really the dandy thing we were into: dressing up, fooling around. Even in those days we knew we'd make it.'

FM, 1974

Previous: Love of my life. Freddie and girlfriend Mary Austin, spring 1974.
© Mick Rock 1974, 2016
Right: 'We worried we'd missed the boat.' Queen's glam rock nemesis David Bowie as Ziggy Stardust.

Baker in control. Baker and Queen clashed over the mixing of many tracks, including the first single, 'Keep Yourself Alive'. Nevertheless, it was the start of a working relationship that would come to define Queen's sound in the 1970s.

After much deliberation, Trident signed a deal with EMI Records who finally released *Queen* in July 1973. 'Freddie wasn't the best-looking bloke in the world,' EMI's then A&R director Bob Mercer told me. 'But he was charismatic and, of course, he had that voice.'

Nevertheless, the time lapse between recording the album and EMI releasing it had cost Queen. They'd stopped playing live and now worried that other bands had overtaken them. David Bowie's recent *Ziggy Stardust* and *Aladdin Sane* albums and his futuristic stage show had re-created him as an alien pop star, a big leap from the hippie singer-songwriter who had once asked Freddie to build a stage for him in the Ealing art school refectory. Then there were Roxy Music and Cockney Rebel, two bands who shared Queen's taste for high camp. 'I thought, "We'd better look out for them,"' admitted Roger Taylor, 'especially Cockney Rebel, who were also signed to EMI.'

Queen's debut was full of fine hard rock songs, but was partly rooted in the Smile and Wreckage era. Smile had even recorded 'Doing All Right', and Freddie's song 'Liar' dated back to Wreckage. Another track on the album, 'My Fairy King', was set in a fantasy world populated by airborne dragons, and horses with eagles' wings, and sounded like a cross between Led Zeppelin's *Lord of the Rings*-inspired 'Ramble On' and Robert Browning's classic poem *The Pied Piper of Hamelin*. This was not the Freddie Mercury of 'Crazy Little Thing Called Love'. 'By the time the album came out, we'd written new songs,' Brian May told me. 'It wasn't so representative of where we were anymore.'

At the time, though, Queen were determined that everyone should hear and appreciate their album. While working as a teenager in a Mayfair record shop, the British music writer and broadcaster Danny Baker witnessed Queen's determination at first hand. One afternoon the band arrived with an early pressing of their debut album. Freddie declared, 'We want you to play our record – constantly! You can fucking play this and nothing else for six weeks!' After one listen of the single 'Keep Yourself Alive', the shop's manager told them he hated the song and had no intention of playing it again.

Recalling the incident in his 2012 memoir *Going to Sea in a Sieve*, Baker claimed the band were so outraged that 'Freddie stood at the door and bellowed, "Attention shoppers! If you have a scintilla of taste, you will never buy a thing in this dreadful shop."'

Neither the album nor 'Keep Yourself Alive' was the big hit Queen and Trident had hoped for. The *NME* in the UK likened the release to a 'bucket of stale urine'. *Rolling Stone* in the US was cautiously complimentary, praising Freddie's 'air of cocky, regal arrogance'. To Freddie's chagrin, though, rock superstardom was still some way away. Months later, he was still shuttling between his Kensington flat and Trident Studios on a Number 9 bus rather than in a chauffeur-driven limousine. Friends recall Freddie sitting in the same front seat on the top deck, gazing at the streets below, assuring his travel companions and, no doubt, himself, that Queen were still going to make it.

By summer 1973, Queen were back at Trident recording a second album. *Queen II* would be split between the 'White Side', comprising Brian and Roger's material, and the 'Black Side', which featured Freddie's compositions. Among these were the Tolkien-influenced 'Ogre Battle' and 'The Fairy Feller's Master-Stroke', inspired by a painting of the same name by Victorian artist Richard Dadd. Just as Freddie had shown John Anthony copies of *Queen* magazine as visual reference for the first album, now he took Roy Thomas Baker to the Tate Gallery to view Dadd's mysterious painting with its intricately detailed figures in a fairy-tale forest.

Freddie even carried a postcard of the painting, like a lucky talisman – although, showing a pernickety eye for detail, he complained to anyone who would listen that the picture was printed back to front. 'I'm very intricate and delicate,' he told *Melody Maker* later that year. 'You can see that in my paintings. I love painters like Richard Dadd, Mucha and Dalí.'

'Oh, he was obsessed with that painting,' recalled Roger Taylor. 'But I did wonder where some of Freddie's mystical references came from. I never saw Freddie with a book, ever. He was not a well-read man. But he was like a magpie, taking ideas from everywhere.'

With its multiple harmonies and overdubs, *Queen II* sounded bigger than its predecessor. And few songs were bigger than Freddie's. However, one song stood out. Besides Freddie's pontificating about 'the mighty titan and his troubadours', 'Seven Seas of Rhye' had a galloping guitar riff and a nagging chorus and, at a trim two minutes forty seconds, didn't outstay its welcome. This was the rock and pop sides of Queen condensed. This was the sound of their future.

Sealing the deal on *Queen II* was a cover photograph that would become the band's defining 1970s image. Queen approached photographer Mick Rock primarily because he had photographed David Bowie. 'I first met Queen at Trident, not long after I'd shot the cover of David's *Pin Ups* album,' Rock told me. 'Queen played me their new record, and I remember saying, "Ooh, it's *Ziggy Stardust* meets Led Zeppelin." But they seemed to like that. I was impressed that a band who hadn't sold many records had persuaded EMI to pay for a gatefold sleeve, even though *Queen II* was only a single album. Queen didn't behave like a new band. They had this incredible confidence.'

Rock showed them a classic photograph by George Hurrell of Marlene Dietrich in the 1932 movie *Shanghai Express*, and explained he wanted to achieve something similar. The resulting regal band portrait for the cover could not have suited the music inside any better. But Freddie, hands folded, chin raised, gazing imperiously into the lens, was the most regal of them all. 'Freddie was the visual director in Queen,' explained Rock. 'It was clearly a democracy, but he had a bit more heft because he'd been to art school.'

Straight away, though, Freddie confided in Mick about his biggest insecurity, his teeth: 'He had that overbite because of the extra teeth at the back of his mouth. So we worked carefully to try to cover it. Years later I said, "Look, Freddie, you've got all this money, why not fix them?" But he wouldn't. He thought if he had any teeth taken out it would mess with his voice.'

Rock would go on to become a regular visitor to the Kensington flat Freddie shared with his girlfriend, Mary Austin. Here he witnessed a less flamboyant aspect of Freddie. 'I would pop round for afternoon tea and Freddie would be wearing his slippers and dressing gown,' he said. 'It was all very domesticated. But that was the side of his personality people didn't always see. Offstage he was this sweet, shy guy.'

With their second album complete and awaiting release, Queen were booked to open for Mott the Hoople on their UK tour in late 1973. Mott had been together since the late 1960s, but without great success until their hit single 'All the Young Dudes', written by David Bowie, had propelled them into the front line of glam rock the previous year.

Above: Freddie's obsession, Richard Dadd's painting *The Fairy Feller's Master-Stroke* (1855–64).
Opposite: The royal family – Mick Rock's band portrait for the *Queen II* album sleeve. © Mick Rock 1974, 2016

Left: Queen appear on BBC's *Top of the Pops* in November 1974.
Opposite: Spread your wings. Freddie in his Zandra Rhodes-designed tunic, June 1974. © Mick Rock 1974, 2016

The tour boosted Queen's profile, and proved to be an illuminating experience for both groups. Mott the Hoople were most amused to see Freddie turning up for rehearsals in his full stage costume, including a single leather glove, as if he was permanently 'on duty'. 'Freddie was larger than life, even then,' said Mott's frontman, Ian Hunter.

Queen, meanwhile, noticed the ease with which Mott the Hoople bridged the barrier between themselves and their audience. Mott was a people's band, with no time for aloofness. In contrast, Freddie sometimes appeared detached and a little frantic on stage. But he never gave up trying to win over an audience. On stage at Birmingham Town Hall, Freddie fell over and landed on his backside to a chorus of jeers. Undeterred, he carried on until even his most vocal critics had been silenced or won over. It was a lesson learned from the headliners, who had taken more knocks than most. 'Ian Hunter was the wise old sage of rock, even then,' recalled Brian May. 'Mott taught us a lot.'

Queen II arrived in March 1974 and outperformed its predecessor by reaching number five. The first single, 'Seven Seas of Rhye', meanwhile, cracked the top ten, thanks to Queen's appearance on BBC's *Top of the Pops*. At first, Freddie refused to appear on the show. After all, Led Zeppelin never performed on *Top of the Pops*. But then Led Zeppelin never released singles. He was eventually persuaded. The press, however, remained unconvinced. A review in *Record Mirror* described *Queen II* as 'the dregs of glam rock', which stung after the praise heaped by the paper on rivals Roxy Music and Cockney Rebel.

For some music critics, there was another issue besides the music. Queen were launched in a blaze of publicity and seemed to have arrived out of nowhere. In the parlance

of the times, 'they hadn't paid their dues'. It was 1974 but a hangover from the 1960s lingered. Queen also didn't disguise their intelligence or middle-class roots or affect the stoned nonchalance of their peers. 'We were a reaction against all that,' insisted Roger Taylor. 'We were ambitious.'

Interviewed by the *NME* in March, Freddie posed with a daffodil outside Buckingham Palace and had previously confided in his interviewer, Julie Webb, that he was 'as gay as a daffodil'. But elsewhere he was guarded and defensive: 'We're a sitting target because we gained popularity quicker than most bands … [I'm] middle class … musicians aren't social rejects anymore.' Elsewhere, Freddie admitted to being 'very highly strung … very temperamental'. Webb gently suggested to her readers that the singer 'has an unfortunate way with him during interviews' that left him 'wide open to mickey-taking'.

Part of the problem was that the only thing the twenty-seven-year-old Freddie Mercury wanted to do was become a pop star, and twenty-seven was almost middle-aged in 1970s pop years. Anything that stood in his way, including sceptical journalists, put him on edge. He was impatient, desperate, even. Freddie believed in himself and wanted the rest of the world to believe in him as well.

To support *Queen II*, the band was booked to headline its own shows in March, including London's Rainbow Theatre. Freddie sweet-talked EMI into paying for new stage costumes. All four members would have outfits made for them by the up-and-coming fashion designer Zandra Rhodes. In Freddie and Brian's case, this meant matching satin tunics.

'I knew they'd want something flamboyant,' said Rhodes in 2012. 'I did some sketches for them and we agreed on these pleated "winged" designs in heavy white satin.' 'Easy' Deacon wore his Rhodes-designed outfit occasionally. But Roger abandoned his, as it was too hot to drum in. Instead, Freddie and Brian became the visual focal points of Queen in their matching pleated tunics.

'It was about being dramatic and working all the senses at once,' said Brian. 'But what we were doing was considered very unfashionable. Showbiz was a dirty word at the time. It was fashionable to eschew having an "act", even though most bands did, including Led Zeppelin. Queen wanted to change all that.'

'I did some sketches for them and we agreed on these pleated "winged" designs in heavy white satin. I had them made up, I finished them off and then I had them delivered. I obviously charged them, but I can't remember how much. Then I went as a guest of Queen to see them at Earls Court. The place was absolutely packed. And the designs looked fantastic under the lights.'

ZANDRA RHODES, 2011

'God, the agony we went through to have the pictures taken, dear. Can you imagine trying to convince the others to cover themselves in Vaseline and then have a hose turned on them?'

FM ON THE *SHEER HEART ATTACK* COVER SHOOT, 1974

Queen's homecoming show at the Rainbow on 31 March 1974 was a triumph. 'Suddenly there was this flood of people at the show who looked like us and dressed like us,' recalled Brian. They would surely not have matched Freddie's white Zandra Rhodes tunic, the pleats of which he fanned out at key moments during the show like a peacock on parade. 'There can be few who have not been impressed by the power of Mercury's performance and the charisma surrounding him,' admitted *Melody Maker*.

In mid-April, Queen flew to Denver for the opening show on their debut US tour. Once again, they were supporting Mott the Hoople. And once again, it was a learning curve. Brian May once described Freddie as 'living like a gypsy' during Queen's early years. While Brian struggled with being away from his home comforts ('I was all at sea,' he confessed), Freddie took it in his stride. The singer's self-sufficiency, forged during his years at boarding school, proved an asset on the road. But as the tour wound on Freddie became aware of how alien Queen, with their sexually ambiguous name and image, seemed to the good folks of, say, St Louis, Missouri. Ian Hunter had to 'talk Freddie down' several times as he sulked in the dressing room after playing a show in which Queen had been heckled by the audience.

However, when the tour reached New York the shows became a magnet for the city's underground tastemakers. Drag artists, transvestites and members of the then unknown glam-rock act Kiss flocked to the Uris Theatre to see the English rock band who had dared call themselves Queen. At last, America was taking notice. But Queen's victory proved to be short-lived, when Brian May woke up after the final New York show to find his skin had turned yellow.

Brian had contracted hepatitis and was smuggled on a plane back to England, wrapped in a blanket to disguise the severity of his condition. Back at Trident Studio, recording Queen's next album, he collapsed and was hospitalised with

a duodenal ulcer. 'It was a terrible time,' Brian recalled. 'I was worried they would have to continue without me.' Day after day, the other members of Queen trooped into Kings College Hospital and gathered round his bed to play him recordings of their new music. 'Freddie, God bless him, was very kind, and said, "Don't worry, darling. We can't do it without you."'

Queen's third album, *Sheer Heart Attack*, was completed in just three months during the summer of 1974, with Brian dragging himself from his sick bed to overdub the guitar parts. Studio engineer Gary Langan recalled that no matter what time of day they were recording, Freddie always arrived dressed and groomed immaculately. 'The fingernails on one hand were always painted black,' Langan told me, 'and the hair was always just right.' Freddie's skin-tight trousers, however, were not designed with long hours in the studio in mind. He would usually undo the top button if sitting down for long periods of time, and hoped no one would notice.

Perverse, as ever, Queen thrived under pressure. Brian's 'Brighton Rock' and 'Now I'm Here' were superlative heavy rock songs. But Freddie's compositions showed a stylistic breadth beyond anything on the earlier albums. His songs swung between explosive hard rock ('Stone Cold Crazy'), grand ballads ('In the Lap of the Gods') and a pastiche of 1920s ragtime jazz ('Bring Back That Leroy Brown'). But best of all was 'Killer Queen', a maddeningly catchy hard-rock-meets-pop song in which the singer serenades a fictional femme fatale. With its multi-tracked guitar solo, sumptuous harmonies and elegant piano, it sounded like Noël Coward jamming with the Beach Boys and Yes.

'Killer Queen' emerged as a single in October 1974. Suppressing their dislike of the show, Queen gamely appeared on *Top of the Pops*. Freddie, clad in a downy fake fur jacket, and holding his mic stand vertically up in the air, preened, primped, pointed and posed for the TV cameras. Nobody watching could ignore Queen or their extraordinary lead singer.

Among those watching was Adrian Morrish, Freddie's old friend from Isleworth Polytechnic. 'There was something about the singer I recognised,' said Morrish. 'Something familiar. But it took a while to work it out.'

Finally, he realised: it was Fred Bulsara. Except Fred Bulsara had become, most definitely, Freddie Mercury.

Previous: Caped crusaders. Freddie and Brian May, Imperial College, London, 2 November 1973. © Mick Rock 1974, 2016
Opposite: An outtake from the *Sheer Heart Attack* cover shoot, London, September 1974. © Mick Rock 1974, 2016

I'M JUST
A POOR BOY

'Queen were every bit as good – and demanding – as we'd anticipated.'

NORMAN SHEFFIELD,
CO-FOUNDER OF TRIDENT STUDIOS, 2013

Opposite: 'Hello, my beauties.' Raising a toast on tour, 1976.

'We have this black-and-white theme that we carry out in England and it's very strong. It has even got to the point where the audience dress and look like me to a tee. They're very faithful and it's beautiful.'

FM, 1975

TIMELINE

1974

23 November–13 December: Queen's first European tour, co-headlining with Lynyrd Skynyrd, visiting Sweden, Finland, Germany, Holland, Belgium and Spain.

1975

5 February–6 April: The band's first North American tour as headliners.

19 April–1 May: Tour of Japan.

29 March: 'Killer Queen' is Queen's first US singles chart entry, peaking at #12.

5 April: *Sheer Heart Attack* enters US Billboard chart, peaking at #12 and earning a gold record for sales of over 500,000.

May: Freddie presented with Ivor Novello Award by the Songwriters' Guild of Great Britain for 'Killer Queen'.

Summer: John Reid becomes Queen's manager in place of Trident.

August–November: Recording sessions for *A Night at the Opera* at various studios including Rockfield, Roundhouse, Sarm East and Scorpio Sound.

31 October: 'Bohemian Rhapsody' from *A Night at the Opera* released as single.

14 November–24 December: UK tour promoting *A Night at the Opera*.

21 November: *A Night at the Opera* released, Queen's first UK #1 album.

29 November: 'Bohemian Rhapsody' becomes Queen's first UK chart-topping single, holding the #1 spot for nine weeks.

December: Queen named Band of the Year by leading UK music paper *Melody Maker*.

1976

January: Freddie receives second Ivor Novello Award, this time for 'Bohemian Rhapsody'.

24 January: *A Night at the Opera* enters US chart, peaking at #4.

7 February: 'Bohemian Rhapsody' enters US chart, peaking at #9.

11–22 April: First tour of Australia.

July–November: Recording of *A Day at the Races* at the Manor, Sarm East and Wessex Sound studios.

18 September: Queen play free concert in London's Hyde Park to a crowd of over 150,000.

December: Girlfriend Mary Austin ends seven-year relationship with Freddie after he admits to affair with David Minns. Freddie and Mary remain close friends for the rest of his life.

10 December: *A Day at the Races* released, becoming another UK #1.

'For me, it's the bigger, the better ... in everything!'

FM, 1985

In November 1974 Queen toasted the success of 'Killer Queen' with two more sold-out shows at the Rainbow Theatre, Finsbury Park. But they soon came back to earth after joining American rockers Lynyrd Skynyrd for a co-headline tour of Scandinavia and Europe, which started just three days later. Skynyrd's image was defined by cowboy hats, confederate flags and scarred knuckles from the fights they'd had the night before. Their recent hit single 'Sweet Home Alabama' was a tribute to America's Deep South. Queen and Lynyrd Skynyrd could not have been a more mismatched bill.

At the show in Munich's Brienner Theatre, filled with GIs from local US military bases, Queen walked on stage to see banners that read: 'Queen Sucks!' According to Roger Taylor, Skynyrd's record label, MCA, was behind the protest: 'They were outraged, confused and a little frightened, because the four nancy boys were giving them quite a run for their money.' It was a reminder, though, that Queen's pomp-rock and showy image did not always go down well with audiences.

Come the new year, Queen were back touring America, where 'Killer Queen' and *Sheer Heart Attack* had both broken into the top twenty. The memory of their last jinxed US tour was foremost in their minds. So when Freddie was diagnosed with nodes on his vocal cords and doctors advised him to rest, he refused to stop. When his voice did give in, several shows had to be cancelled. For every step forward, Queen seemed to take another back.

The strangeness of their situation was underlined as soon as they returned to Britain. Queen shared a song publisher with the successful hard rock band Deep Purple. Word filtered back to EMI that Queen were now outselling Purple in Japan. A Japanese tour was booked for April. 'Can't wait,' Freddie told *NME*. 'All those geisha girls ... and boys.'

Queen arrived at Tokyo's Haneda Airport to a swarm of fans, screaming, crying and brandishing homemade banners that read, 'Love Queen!' The contrast in reception with Munich couldn't have been greater.

Bodyguards escorted a shocked Freddie and the band through the crowd, as fans tugged at their hair and clothes (Brian May lost one of his trademark clogs) and showered them with gifts, including toy penguins, as Brian had casually mentioned a fondness for the bird in a recent interview. Queen sold out all eight of their concerts in Japan, including tour-opening and closing dates at Tokyo's 14,000-capacity Budokan arena.

A month after the Japanese tour, the Songwriters' Guild of Great Britain presented Freddie with an Ivor Novello Award for 'Killer Queen'. But all the wider acclaim couldn't compensate for the band's continuing dire financial situation. Queen had long been unhappy about their deal with the Sheffield brothers. They were now having hits and filling Japanese arenas, but Trident were still paying them the same modest weekly wages.

The band's living conditions were equally austere. Freddie and Mary Austin's Kensington flat had what estate agents call 'a good address', but there was damp rising up the walls. Brian May's situation was even worse. The bathroom of his dingy basement flat in Earls Court was covered in fungus.

The White Queen: *A Night at the Opera* tour, winter 1975.

Their manager Jack Nelson had grown used to hearing Queen's complaints. But Nelson answered to the Sheffields. Earlier that year, a soon-to-be-wed John Deacon requested an advance for a deposit on a house, which Norman Sheffield refused. He insisted Queen would get a big payday when their royalties were due at the end of the year. A house was one thing, but when Sheffield turned down Freddie's request for a new grand piano, the singer lost his temper.

'When I turned him down, he banged his fist on my desk. "I have to get a grand piano!"' recalled Sheffield. When he told Freddie to be patient, that the money was coming, the singer answered, 'But we're stars! We're selling millions of records.'

In 2009, Norman Sheffield told me Trident had invested nearly £200,000 in Queen, a sum now equivalent to over £2 million. The money was spent on equipment, stage clothes, promotional videos and wages. 'Queen owed us,' he said. 'But that didn't seem to register with Freddie.'

Sheffield maintained it was Freddie who had wanted Trident to manage Queen and look after both their publishing and record deals. The resulting conflict of interests made it 'impossible for me to negotiate with myself', as Sheffield pointed out. Others, including John

Above: The Mad Hatter and friends. Queen in Japan, April 1975.
Opposite: Flick of the wrist. Winter Gardens, Bournemouth, UK, 23 November 1975.

Anthony, back up Sheffield's claim that Trident invested a fortune in Queen, but suggest the 'big payday' should have reached them much sooner than it did.

By summer 1975, Queen had appointed a lawyer to negotiate them out of their Trident deals. The lawyer, Jim Beach, would later become Queen's business manager, a position he holds to this day. In the meantime, Beach looked for a way out, while Queen looked for new management.

Several 'name' managers, including Don Arden, ELO's formidable handler (and Sharon Osbourne's father), were approached before Queen signed a three-year deal with Elton John's manager, John Reid. 'Elton had become a fan of Queen and Freddie was almost out of the closet,' recalled EMI's Bob Mercer. 'So Freddie got to know John Reid, and John could see a major worldwide band and he pursued them.'

Reid gave Queen some simple advice: go away and make the best album you can and let me worry about everything else.

So Queen extricated themselves from their Trident deals. But at a price. The Sheffields walked away with £100,000 severance pay funded by Queen's new publishing deal, and a one per cent cut of royalties on their next six albums. 'It was what we deserved,' insisted Norman. After Norman's death in 2014, Brian May wrote on his personal website: 'We had our differences … but, in the grand scheme of things, all the water had long since flowed under the bridge.'

In 1975, though, those differences were still fresh in everyone's mind. Queen's next album, *A Night at the Opera*, would include a song written by Freddie about Sheffield – 'Death on Two Legs (Dedicated to …)' – that was so scathing Norman threatened to sue the group and EMI, resulting in an out-of-court settlement. Freddie was not ready to forgive or forget.

Most of *A Night at the Opera* was recorded at Rockfield Studios, a converted farm near Monmouth in the Welsh borders. 'The studio is the most strenuous part of my career,' a dramatic Freddie explained. 'It's so exhausting, mentally and physically. I sometimes ask myself why I do it. After *Sheer Heart Attack* we were insane and said, "Never again."'

Some of Freddie's stress this time round could be attributed to one particular song. 'Bohemian Rhapsody' would not only define Freddie Mercury and Queen but would also become the third best-selling UK single of all time (behind Band Aid's 'Do They Know It's Christmas?' and Elton John's 1997 rerecording of 'Candle in the Wind' for the funeral of Princess Diana). Before Queen went to Rockfield, Freddie played part of the song on the piano to Roy Thomas Baker, warning the producer there was 'an opera section' to come. No one, however, was prepared for the scale and impact of that section.

Brian May later described 'Bohemian Rhapsody' as 'Freddie's baby … We just brought it to life.' The birthing process began at Rockfield in August 1975. The band recorded a backing track with piano, bass and drums and a sparse vocal. Freddie informed his band mates that all the gaps would be filled later. Each day he arrived at the studio waving sheets of paper with tiny notes only he could decipher scribbled over them.

'There was no demo. It was all in Freddie's head and on lots of little pieces of paper, which he used to make notes on,' recalled Brian May. 'Freddie had the framework in his head. Then we set about embroidering it.' But there was meaning behind all those seemingly random doodles. Before Queen, Roy Thomas Baker had worked with the English light opera company D'Oyly Carte. 'I was probably one of the few people in the world who knew exactly what Freddie Mercury was talking about,' he said. As Freddie later described to *NME*: '"Bohemian Rhapsody" didn't just come out of thin air.'

Opposite: 'The studio is the most stressful part of my career.' Freddie at Rockfield Studios, Monmouthshire, during the sessions for *A Night at the Opera*, summer 1975.
Below: Queen at Rockfield, summer 1975.

Under their singer's direction, Queen were soon plugging the gaps in the track with harmonies, harmonies and more harmonies. They worked seven twelve-hour days adding endless 'Mama Mias', 'Galileos' and 'Figaros' until the tape was wearing thin and an emergency copy had to be made. It would take three weeks and an unprecedented 180 vocal overdubs at several studios in London for the band to finish 'Bohemian Rhapsody'.

Engineer Gary Langan worked with Queen on *Sheer Heart Attack* and was familiar with the band's exacting standards. But 'Bohemian Rhapsody' took it all to a new level. 'It was made in thirds in studio,' he told me, 'the start, the middle and the end – and it was worked on in that fashion. It wasn't until the final day when it was all mixed and we all sat back and listened to it we realised what we'd done. We sat there in the control room and thought, "Ye gods." It was a seminal moment.'

With the song finished, Queen had to battle John Reid and EMI for permission to release it as a single. There was nothing unusual about five-minute songs in the era of wordy progressive rock. But they were confined to albums. Queen presented a mostly united front and insisted the song be released, unedited, as a single. Only John Deacon thought they should compromise.

EMI's hand was partly forced by Kenny Everett, then a DJ for London's Capital Radio. Freddie and Kenny met in 1974 when the singer was a guest on Everett's show, and had become close friends since. Everett visited Queen in the studio and acquired a tape of the song, having promised not to play it on his breakfast show. No sooner was he on air than Everett broke his promise. 'I'm woken up by the sound of "Bohemian Rhapsody" blaring through the ceiling from my upstairs neighbour's apartment,' recalled Brian May. 'I thought I was going mad.'

When EMI learned that listeners had called the radio station asking to hear the song, they gave in. 'Bohemian Rhapsody', the single, arrived in October, with *A Night at the Opera* following a month later.

'The whole group is aiming for the top-slot. We're not going to be content with anything less. That's what we're striving for. It's got to be there. I definitely know we've got it in the music, we're original enough ... and now we're proving it.'

FM, 1974

Piano man. Hammersmith Odeon, London, December 1975.

Brian May later described *A Night at the Opera* as 'our *Sgt Pepper*'. The comparison made sense. In 1968, Fred Bulsara spent hours at the piano in Ealing art college, playing the middle section from the *Sgt Pepper* track 'A Day in the Life'. He was using the Beatles for inspiration while trying to turn his lyric 'Mama, just killed a man' into a song. With 'Bohemian Rhapsody', Freddie Mercury finished the job Fred Bulsara started.

The final 5:54-minute track was a piano ballad, a pseudo-opera *and* a flat-out rock song. But some of its influences went back beyond Freddie's art school days. There were echoes of the classical music he and his friends listened to during those post-dinner sessions at boarding school in India. Years later, some who attended his funeral thought they heard some of Freddie in the chanting and harmonies of the Parsee priests overseeing the service.

Listeners have spent forty years analysing 'Bohemian Rhapsody' and wondering whether its central character – a suicidal murderer in mental turmoil? – was a metaphor for something. And if so, what? Not that Freddie gave anything away. 'I think people should just listen to it, think about it, and then make up their own minds,' he suggested.

'Freddie was a very complex person,' said Brian May, 'flippant and funny on the surface, but he concealed insecurities and problems in squaring up his life with his childhood. He never explained the lyrics, but I think he put a lot of himself into that song.'

'I do think Freddie enjoyed the fact there were so many interpretations of the lyrics,' Brian added in 2015. 'I think it's beyond analysis. That's not me trying to be evasive. I have my own ideas and feelings about "Bohemian Rhapsody" – but I hate talking about it, and I generally refuse.'

'A lot of my songs are fantasy. I can dream up all sorts of things. That's the kind of world I live in. It's very flamboyant, and that's the kind of way I write. I love it.'

FM, 1974

Besides 'Bohemian Rhapsody', Freddie's contributions to *A Night at the Opera* spanned the charming 'Seaside Rendezvous' and the vicious 'Death on Two Legs (Dedicated to …)'. The latter, a protracted rant about 'a sewer rat', 'an old barrow boy', prompted that threatened legal action from Norman Sheffield.

When recording the track, the engineers noticed blood running down Freddie's face after he removed his headphones. His ears were bleeding. 'He'd worked himself up into such a state,' recalled Gary Langan. 'The track in his headphones was so loud.'

Elsewhere, though, Freddie could be as tender as he was caustic on 'Death on Two Legs'. The romantic ballad 'Love of My Life', which would become a fixture of Queen's live shows, was written specifically for Mary Austin.

Above: A day at the races. Freddie and Mary Austin, Kempton Park Racecourse, 23 September 1976.
Opposite: You take my breath away. Masonic Temple, Detroit, 11 February 1976.

While Freddie kept his private life private, it would soon come under great scrutiny. At the end of November 1975, 'Bohemian Rhapsody' reached number one in the UK, assisted by a video that brought Mick Rock's *Queen II* cover image to life. Freddie Mercury, with his hair and his teeth and his 'Galileo Figaros', would soon be recognised by everyone, everywhere.

A Night at the Opera followed 'Bohemian Rhapsody' to number one in the UK. The album also reached number four in America, the first time they had cracked the US top ten. Even some critics were now on side. 'You can feel the colossal effort which went into every second of this long album,' declared British weekly music paper *Sounds*. 'The *Meisterwerk*, the magnum opus even …'

With the success of the single and album came bigger money. And having struggled for so long, Freddie had no qualms about spending it. His auction house visits and shopping expeditions were soon the talk of the recording studio and the Kings Road clubs. Before long, word spread that *A Night at the Opera* had cost EMI an eye-watering £40,000, which made it at the time the most expensive album ever. Queen have always disputed this figure. But the rumour stuck.

Left: 'Mama, just killed a man …' Performing 'Bohemian Rhapsody', September 1976.
Opposite: Pirouetting at Toledo Sports Arena, Ohio, 15 February 1976.

the writing credit" – and that became very much the norm.'

A Night at the Opera turned Queen into superstars, and Freddie into the superstar's superstar. On the winter 1975 tour, the band's staff now included Freddie's personal masseur and Pete Brown, a personal assistant whose tasks included removing the thorns from the roses Freddie tossed into the audience. The BBC broadcast Queen's Christmas Eve show at London's Hammersmith Odeon, and captured them in all their grandeur. Freddie, in a ruffled satin jumpsuit cut away to the midriff, addresses the audience as 'darlings' and conducts himself like a Hollywood grande dame.

Freddie's onstage persona was a creation, and one he never took entirely seriously; something which became obvious in the 1980s. But in 1975, when that persona extended to interviews with the press it often gave a distorted, and not always flattering, impression of Queen's lead singer. 'I thought it was hilarious because it was a complete wind-up,' said Roger Taylor. 'You know – "Fuck 'em. If they don't like me I'll be even worse than they expect."'

Those close to him also knew Freddie's over-the-top demeanour masked many of his insecurities – and he was especially insecure about his sexuality. A year earlier, on Christmas Day 1974, Freddie had presented Mary Austin with a ring and proposed to her. She was surprised, but accepted the offer. Some months later, during which time nothing more had been said, Mary brought the subject up only for Freddie to tell her he'd changed his mind. 'I was disappointed,' she admitted. 'But I had a feeling it wasn't going to happen. The atmosphere between us was changing a lot.'

With money, though, came conflict. Roger Taylor's song 'I'm in Love with My Car' was the B-side of 'Bohemian Rhapsody', against most of his band mates' wishes. When the single spent nine weeks at the top of the charts, the drummer cashed in. 'I made just as much money as Freddie did for writing "Bohemian Rhapsody",' Roger admitted. 'That's not right, is it?'

John Deacon's 'You're My Best Friend' gave Queen a follow-up UK top ten and a US top twenty hit in May 1976. But Deacon, Mercury and Taylor hadn't created these songs alone. Brian May had played the climactic guitar solo on 'Bohemian Rhapsody' and contributed to its 180 vocal overdubs. They all worked on each other's songs. Queen's decision to credit songs to their main writer only would become the cause of many bitter arguments within the group.

'Freddie started all this with "Seven Seas of Rhye",' Brian told me. 'There was a snippet of it on the first album, and then the whole song was on the next album. It was very much a group development. But when it came to the credits, Freddie said, "No, those are my words. I wrote the fucking song! So I'm taking

*'I didn't realise just what we had and how special Freddie was –
how he could galvanise audiences by sheer force of will.'*

ROGER TAYLOR, 2013

'Little things spark me off. Lots of filthy ashtrays about the place. It sounds big-headed but I am a perfectionist, I suppose, and people's inefficiency upsets me. I think that because I'm a Virgo I have to put my foot in it. I can't be left out of any major event that's going on. I'm always trying to be the belle of the ball, I'm afraid.'

FM, 1974

At first Mary blamed those changes on Freddie's punishing workload. Then she suspected he was having an affair. He was, but it wasn't with another woman. Freddie and David Minns, a twenty-four-year-old music publisher, shared a mutual friend, which is how Minns found himself in a club one evening listening to Freddie moaning about how long it was taking Queen to finish their new album. A few weeks later, Freddie invited him to the studio to hear a playback of 'Bohemian Rhapsody'. Soon after, the two men became lovers. But it would be some time before Freddie admitted what was happening to his girlfriend or his family. Homosexuality, although decriminalised in the UK in 1967, was not acceptable in the Parsee faith.

'I know he was tormented by some form of guilt that he had about his past life,' said Minns in 1992, 'and that included both his family and, of course, Mary.' He realised how tormented Freddie was when he met Mary at the flat they still shared, and noticed there was only one bed.

Freddie was also prone to tantrums and violent outbursts. Minns soon observed how he had to psych himself up before a show: 'He had to pit himself against an imaginary foe to get the adrenalin going.'

In April 1976, Queen embarked on their first Australian tour, which included eight dates in Perth, Adelaide, Sydney, Melbourne and Brisbane. After a delayed journey from their hotel to Sydney's Hordern Pavilion, Freddie threw a tantrum backstage and smashed a mirror over his personal assistant Pete Brown's head. The story has developed a life of its own, since neither party is still alive to confirm or deny it. Ex-roadies recall the incident, but insist the mirror was very small. On that night in Sydney, though, Brown became Freddie's 'imaginary foe'. The sleeve for Queen's next album would include the credit: 'Freddie Mercury – vocals, piano, choir meister, tantrums'.

In Queen, a band used to fighting, as Freddie said, 'over the very air we breathe', his behaviour was a little different. 'Freddie never changed one bit for us,' insisted Roger Taylor. 'It was only his lifestyle that changed. To us, it was just Fred being his usual outrageous self.'

'Bohemian Rhapsody' was Freddie being his 'usual outrageous self' in the studio. But such indulgence wasn't confined to his activities with Queen. David Minns was now managing a new singer-songwriter named Eddie Howell. In summer 1975, Freddie produced Howell's single 'The Man from Manhattan' and racked up hours of costly studio time in his quest for perfection. Nothing less would do. 'The Man from Manhattan' turned out to be an expensive flop, prompting Freddie to suggest, only half jokingly, that Howell sue the record company for failing to deliver a hit. 'Freddie gave me a taste of what it was like when money was no object,' said Howell. But when the expensive studio sessions and nightly restaurant visits were over, Howell returned to obscurity and Freddie to Queen.

When Queen went back to the studio, Freddie had even more opportunity to indulge himself. Work on the follow-up to *A Night at the Opera* began in July 1976 at Virgin Records boss Richard Branson's Manor studio in Oxfordshire. For the first time, Queen were working without a pressing deadline and without Roy Thomas Baker.

Asked why they were producing themselves, Freddie replied: 'Roy's been great, but we felt it was now or never.'

In the studio, Baker could match Queen for over-the-top ideas, but he was also a good mediator. After a fraught day at Rockfield, it was Baker who suggested everyone calm down, come to his room and watch a film together on his new-fangled video player. The movie, the Marx Brothers' *A Night at the Opera*, defused the tension and gave Queen an album title.

Groucho and his siblings would give them another title the following year. Queen's fifth album appeared in December 1976, named after the Marx Brothers' 1937 comedy *A Day at the Races*. Some of the songs had been premiered at Queen's free concert in London's Hyde Park in September.

That night, Freddie, in a skin-tight ensemble that made

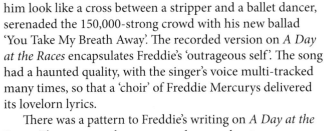

Above: Freddie at the Hyde Park concert, September 1976.
Opposite: Freddie with boyfriend David Minns, inspiration for 'Good Old-Fashioned Lover Boy', 1976.

him look like a cross between a stripper and a ballet dancer, serenaded the 150,000-strong crowd with his new ballad 'You Take My Breath Away'. The recorded version on *A Day at the Races* encapsulates Freddie's 'outrageous self'. The song had a haunted quality, with the singer's voice multi-tracked many times, so that a 'choir' of Freddie Mercurys delivered its lovelorn lyrics.

There was a pattern to Freddie's writing on *A Day at the Races*. These were rather mannered songs about romance and glamour, far removed from Queen's hard rock roots. The future hit single 'Somebody to Love' was a rollicking gospel number, closer to Aretha Franklin (of whom Freddie was a great fan) than Led Zeppelin. Its lyrics were a plea for someone, anyone, to rescue Freddie from the daily grind.

Some might wonder how much of a grind it was being the lead singer in a successful pop group. But, said Roger Taylor, '"Somebody to Love" really did come from his heart.'

Elsewhere, 'The Millionaire Waltz' was an ornate ballad, on which Brian May made his guitar sound like a small orchestra, and 'Good Old-Fashioned Lover Boy' a ragtime number inspired by David Minns. Here, Freddie talked of 'dining at the Ritz' and invited his amour to 'sit on my hot-seat of love'.

Nick Kent, the *NME* reviewer who had compared Queen's debut album to 'a bucket of stale urine', was equally unimpressed by their fifth. 'I hate this album,' Kent wrote. 'These songs with their precious impotent Valentino kitsch mouthings on romance … make my flesh creep.' Even so, Freddie's songs about romantic yearning and upscale London hotels found their mark. *A Day at the Races* gave Queen another UK number one and a US top five album.

Queen seemed unstoppable and untouchable. But Freddie's superstardom couldn't spare him from the growing turmoil in his personal life. After having to explain another of his late-night absences, Freddie finally confessed to Mary Austin that he thought he was bisexual. She told him he was wrong, and to accept he was gay. 'It was a relief really to hear it from him,' she said. 'To know that I had more or less guessed right. I felt that a great burden had been lifted.'

Whatever heartache Mary would suffer, she would never give up on their friendship. Nor did Freddie want her to. The couple simply redefined their relationship. Mary continued to accompany him to public events and private dinner parties. He, in turn, trusted and confided in her in a way he never would with anybody else. When they eventually agreed to live apart, Freddie moved into a flat in Holland Park and bought Mary an apartment nearby; so near, in fact, that she could see his flat from her bathroom window.

'All my lovers asked me why they couldn't replace Mary,' said Freddie, 'but it's simply impossible … To me, it was a marriage. We believe in each other, and that's enough for me.'

'The great irony of Freddie's life,' ventured Mick Rock, 'is that, though he was essentially gay, his greatest relationship was with a woman.'

'His greatest relationship': Freddie at home in Kensington with Mary Austin, c. 1976.

WE'LL GIVE YOU PIECE DE RESISTANCE

'Darlings, we're the most preposterous band that's ever lived.'

FM, c. 1975

'I hate pockets in trousers. By the way, I do not wear a hose. My hose is my own. No coke bottle, nothing stuffed down there.'

FM, 1974

Calling all girls. Queen with fans and Mott the Hoople's Ian Hunter (centre) and producer Roy Thomas Baker (right), Montreal Forum, 26 January 1977.

TIMELINE

1976

1 December: Queen scheduled to appear on TV show *Today*, but after cancelling at last minute are replaced by the Sex Pistols, who give the notorious interview that helps launch them.

1977

13 January–18 March: Tour of US and Canada to promote *A Day at the Races*.

5 February: Sell-out concert at New York's Madison Square Garden.

8–19 May: *A Day at the Races* tour of Europe.

23 May–7 June: *A Day at the Races* 'Jubilee' tour of UK.

6–7 June: Sell-out dates at Earls Court Arena, London.

July–September: Recording of *News of the World* at Sarm West and Wessex Sound studios, London.

7 October: Release of 'We Are the Champions' backed with 'We Will Rock You', both from *News of the World*.

18 October: 'Bohemian Rhapsody' wins Britannia award for best British single of the previous twenty-five years.

28 October: *News of the World* released, peaking at #4 and #3 in the UK and US charts respectively.

11 November–22 December: *News of the World* North American tour.

1978

12 April–3 May: *News of the World* European tour.

6–13 May: Five-date UK *News of the World* mini-tour includes three nights at the Empire Pool, Wembley.

Summer: End of Queen's three-year management deal with John Reid. They now decide to manage themselves with lawyer Jim Beach.

June: Queen relocate to Montreux, Switzerland.

July–October: Recording of *Jazz* at Mountain Studios, in Montreux, and Super Bear Studios, Berre-les-Alpes, France.

28 October–20 December: *Jazz* North American tour.

31 October: *Jazz* pre-release launch party held in New Orleans.

10 November: *Jazz* released.

'Let's face it, he has got more and more preposterous.'

ROGER TAYLOR, 1978

On 1 December 1976, Freddie Mercury visited a dentist for the first time in fifteen years. It was a momentous decision in a way he could never have imagined. Queen had been due to appear on the British TV news show *Today* hosted by Bill Grundy. When they cancelled, EMI offered its new signing, a 'punk rock' group from London called the Sex Pistols, as a replacement. Twenty-four hours later, the Sex Pistols had become a household name, after an expletive-strewn interview in which they'd called Grundy 'a dirty bastard' and 'a fucking rotter' – all at teatime on national television.

Forty years on, the Sex Pistols' schoolboy swearing seems almost quaint. In 1976, though, the group and punk rock were seen as a threat to the nation's youth and morals. As the *Daily Mirror* warned: 'Punk rock groups and their fans despise "establishment" pop stars and specialise in songs that preach destruction.'

Few groups fitted the description 'establishment pop stars' as well as Queen. In truth, once you saw past the manufactured aggression, punk bands such as the Damned and the Clash were simply making records that stripped rock music back to its bare bones. There weren't any multi-tiered vocal harmonies or songs about dining at the Ritz here. As Queen's manager John Reid observed, 'It was anarchy on one side, and monarchy on the other.'

The Clash summed up punk's philosophy in the lyrics to their song '1977': 'No Elvis, Beatles or Rolling Stones'. They could have added Queen to the list. Yet in June 1977, while the Sex Pistols were racing up the UK charts with their anti-monarchy tirade 'God Save the Queen', Queen, the band, were still filling arenas across the globe. Their latest acquisition was an enormous crown-shaped lighting rig, which rose from the stage amid undulating clouds of dry ice. Freddie's new stage garb was a copy of one of celebrated Russian ballet dancer Vaslav Nijinsky's costumes. Queen were as un-punk as any band could be.

'I used to see all the punk bands,' said Roger Taylor. 'I loved the Sex Pistols. The Damned were hilarious. But nothing changed for us. The irony is we became more popular.' But asked if he thought *A Day at the Races* had been a little overblown, Roger admitted, 'Yes, some of it was.'

Queen would never give in to punk, but changes were underway when they joined co-producer Mike Stone at North London's Wessex Studios in July 1977. Stone had worked closely with Roy Thomas Baker on Queen's earlier albums, and the band trusted him to help them create a new sound. 'We could see what was happening, and felt the need to strip it down,' admitted Roger.

Opposite: 'A little silhouetto of a man'. Ahoy Hall, Rotterdam, Netherlands, 17 May 1977.
Right: Queen in front of their crown-shaped lighting rig, Earls Court Arena, London, 6 June 1977.

Left: 'Flash!' Taking a Polaroid picture, 1977.
Opposite: Freddie and John sample the backstage catering, Montreal Forum, 26 January 1977.

'We'd gone as far as we could in the other direction.' *A Day at the Races* had sold as well as *A Night at the Opera*, but no better than that. Remaining static was anathema to Queen.

The band's new back-to-basics approach would go only so far. Roger Taylor rocked up to Wessex first and spent two days with his roadie perfecting his drum sound. For Wessex's eighteen-year-old assistant engineer Andy Turner, working with Queen was quite an experience. When a set of top-of-the-range speakers blew up in the first week, another set was installed without a second thought. 'I couldn't believe how much money they'd spend in a studio that cost £200 an hour,' he said.

Nothing was too expensive, nothing too much trouble, and everything had to be perfect – including Freddie's choice of food. Andy Turner had the daily task of buying him a box of almond slices from the local bakery. When Brian May helped himself to one without asking, the singer reacted with an extraordinary outburst. 'He said, "No one, no one, is allowed to touch my almond slices … apart from Andy,"' recalled Turner. 'I was a young, naïve eighteen-year-old in my first job. This was all new.'

One of Queen's new songs, the Roger Taylor track 'Sheer Heart Attack', was actually a leftover from the sessions for the album of the same name. It had a driving guitar riff, and was quite unlike, say, 'The Millionaire Waltz' on *A Day at the Races*. As if on cue, while Queen were working on 'Sheer Heart Attack', the Sex Pistols arrived at Wessex to finish their debut album, *Never Mind the Bollocks … Here's the Sex Pistols*.

It was a very us-and-them moment: the Pistols in their leather jackets, Freddie Mercury apparently wearing ballet pumps. Roger Taylor remembers having a perfectly civil conversation with the Pistols' guitarist Steve Jones and drummer Paul Cook; Brian May the same with lead singer Johnny Rotten: 'I had a few conversations with John, who was always respectful. We talked about music.'

But not all of the Sex Pistols were as amenable. Queen's road manager Peter Hince was in the control room with Freddie when bassist Sid Vicious burst in. Freddie had been interviewed in the *NME*, and had out-Freddied himself by predicting that ballet would soon become a major influence in rock music. 'It sounds so outrageous and so extreme,' he declared. 'But I know there's going to come a time when it's commonplace.'

'Sid was rather the worse for wear and said, "Oi, Freddie, have you succeeded in bringing ballet to the masses yet?"' recalled Hince. Freddie seized Sid by the lapels on his leather jacket and pushed him out of the room: 'I think I called Sid Vicious, Simon Ferocious or something and he didn't like it at all,' explained the singer. Later, Freddie claimed to have offered to sing on the Pistols' album and for the Pistols to sing on Queen's. But Vicious and co. turned him down.

Freddie refused to be intimidated, but his ego had taken a knock. The *NME* interview in which he'd extolled the virtues of ballet had come with the headline, 'Is This Man a Prat?' In the interview, Freddie defended Queen's flamboyant image, but bridled at any criticism and sneered at interviewer Tony Stewart: 'I would have thought since the last time I met you … you should have become editor of *The Times* or something.'

'Freddie was intense and strong-willed in the studio, but always focused.'

QUEEN PRODUCER ROY THOMAS BAKER, 2005

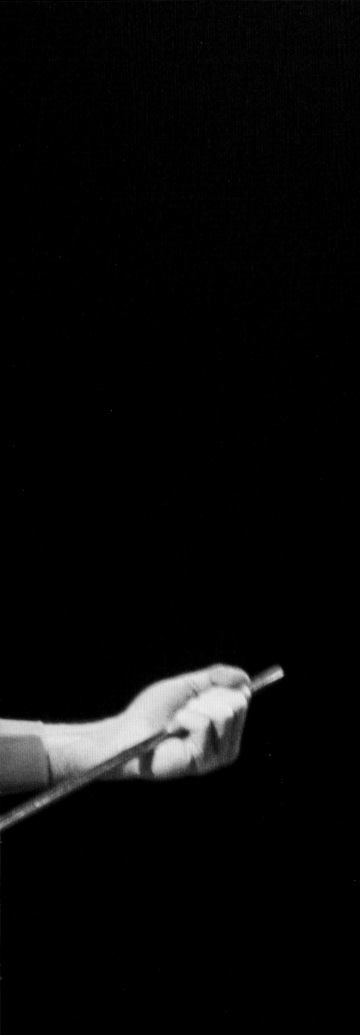

To Queen's critics, their singer's attitude was more fuel to the fire. To Queen it was just 'Fred being Fred'. 'Freddie's attitude was "Take it or leave it,"' said Roger Taylor. 'Freddie didn't want to make himself that available to the press.'

In the studio, the punk-like 'Sheer Heart Attack' wasn't a complete anomaly. Most of Queen's new music was stripped back. Brian May's latest composition, 'We Will Rock You', was as blunt and to-the-point as its title. The only instrument heard on the song was an electric guitar, its now world-famous rhythm created by Queen, their engineers and even the studio tea lady stamping their feet and clapping their hands. 'Mike Stone had all the staff at Wessex up on these drum risers with the band doing the stomp and the clap,' recalled Andy Turner.

Queen's new album, *News of the World*, would include only three Freddie songs, instead of his usual four or five. But one in particular was as overblown as anything he had composed before. '"We Are the Champions" was the most egotistical and arrogant song I've ever written,' he admitted. It was bespoke songwriting, music made for 20,000-seat arenas. With a once-heard, never-forgotten chorus, it depicted Freddie as a downtrodden individual who'd fought impossible odds, but survived and thrived. 'We Are the Champions' is impossible to listen to with a straight face. 'We were all mildly shocked, because it sounded so arrogant,' admitted Brian May.

Brian and Roger claim the 'we' in 'We Are the Champions' referred to Queen's audience as much as the band itself. Freddie described it as 'a winner's song'. But to begin with, the person it focused on most clearly must have been Fred Bulsara, and his transformation into the winning Freddie Mercury.

'What do you know about showbiz?'

FM TO TONY STEWART, *NME*, 1977

Court jester: Madison Square Garden, New York, 1 December 1977.

'We Are the Champions', with 'We Will Rock You' on its B-side, arrived as a single in early October 1977, and reached number two in the UK and four in the US. *News of the World* followed at the end of the month. *A Night at the Opera* and *A Day at the Races* came in white and black covers respectively, with a regal crest on each. Like the music inside, the artwork for Queen's latest release was very different. The American sci-fi artist Frank Kelly Freas's sleeve showed a giant metal robot attempting to clasp the members of the band in its giant metal hand, but with Roger Taylor and John Deacon falling to the ground. It was a garish and most un-regal image.

News of the World reached number four in the UK. It wasn't a failure, but it must have hurt when *Never Mind the Bollocks …* romped to number one instead. 'The whole punk thing was a tough phase for us,' admitted Freddie later. 'But if there is a challenge we embark on it, and that's what keeps us going.' Where Queen were going next was yet to be decided.

Interviewed in April 1978, Roger Taylor had this to say about Queen's lead singer: 'Freddie has absolutely no idea about money … He knows once he didn't have it, but I think the only time he'd know he didn't have any money again would be if a machine chewed up his credit card – and he still wouldn't understand.'

News of the World hadn't sold so well at home, but it was different in America, where the Sex Pistols hadn't made such an impact. The money was still flowing in – and, for Freddie, it was much more than ever. He traded in his Daimler for a Rolls-Royce Silver Shadow (chauffeur-driven, naturally) and splashed out £20,000 in an afternoon at Sotheby's auction house. Freddie decorated the walls of his Holland Park pied-à-terre with antique Japanese woodcuts, and treated two hundred guests at his birthday party to lobster, caviar and Cristal champagne. 'I'm the one member of the band for whom money isn't very endearing,' he said. 'I'm the one who spends it straight off.'

Besides champagne, caviar, Rolls-Royces and antiquities, Freddie now lavished money on his friend the Jamaican-born actor and singer Peter Straker. Straker had come to prominence in the London production of the musical *Hair* in 1968. The pair moved in the same circles, and became friends after attending a fancy dress party where guests were invited to come as 'a famous person' and Freddie came as himself.

Freddie was determined to turn Straker into a star. He signed him to his new production company, Goose Productions, for a three-album deal, and enlisted Roy Thomas Baker to help produce his 1978 debut, *This One's on Me*. Like Eddie Howell before him, Straker was impressed by Freddie's generosity and attention to detail. But his album failed to sell, despite Freddie sinking thousands of pounds of his own money into the project.

If Freddie wanted to keep spending, he had to keep earning. And that meant more touring. They were back in America in November 1977, where 'We Will Rock You' and 'We Are the Champions' proved perfect for the nation's 'cattle shed' arenas. 'I was thinking about football when I wrote ["We Are the Champions"],' said Freddie. 'I wanted a participation song, something the fans could latch on to.'

'Elton's a good old cookie ... He's like one of those last Hollywood actresses of any worth.'

FM, c. 1986

Audiences responded to the communal message, whether they were in New York, Los Angeles or Atlanta, Georgia. It was the same when Queen played the UK the following spring. In keeping with a song that would unite sports fans worldwide, Freddie's stage garb now included a pair of punishingly tight silk shorts. Though 'I seriously doubt if Fred had ever played football,' ventured Peter Hince.

In fact, the only sport Freddie now played was tennis, as a guest at west London's exclusive Hurlingham Club – at least, until his attire prompted a quiet word from the management. 'We received an edict from the club's governing body requesting that those "two young men" should wear longer shorts,' recalled Freddie's tennis partner, Peter Straker.

Queen were going through major changes, and not all were musical. Their three-year management deal with John Reid Enterprises was drawing to a close. 'Things went very well with John in the beginning,' said a diplomatic Brian May in 2007. 'But it started to wear a little thin after a while. He related more to Freddie than the rest of us. His organisation as a whole tended to centre themselves around Freddie.'

Part of the reason for this may have been that Reid and many of those who worked with him were gay. On Queen's 1977 North American tour, Freddie met up with an old art-school friend, Mark Malden, whose brother, Aubrey, had booked the ill-fated Wreckage gig in 1969. Mark was now living in Montreal. Freddie told him how supportive Elton John had been during Queen's early days with John Reid. Being with Elton and Reid's organisation was, Freddie said, 'like joining a private club, where everyone thinks the way you do … like coming home'.

But when Queen's career took off, tensions rose. 'The relationship with John Reid went south because of Elton,' asserted EMI's Bob Mercer. 'Managing Elton John and Freddie Mercury at the same time would obviously end in tears.'

Reid described his split with Queen as 'the most amicable' of his career, and was highly amused when Freddie insisted they sign the severance papers in the back

seat of his new Rolls-Royce. Queen now planned to manage themselves, but with their former lawyer Jim Beach handling their business affairs.

Beach's appointment came at a fortuitous time. In 1978, James Callaghan's Labour government introduced a top tax rate of ninety-eight per cent on unearned income (and eighty-three per cent on already earned income). 'Jim rearranged everything and protected their money from Callaghan's government,' said Mercer. 'One of the first things he did was to have them domiciled overseas.'

Queen would become tax exiles, living and working outside the UK for most of the year. For Brian May and John Deacon, who were both married, with John already father to two young children, this was an upheaval. Less so for the band's resident playboys, Roger and Freddie.

Queen's tax exiledom began in Montreux, Switzerland, in June 1978, after Brian's wife Chrissie gave birth to their first child, James. One of the band's vans travelling from England to their new destination was now stuffed with children's toys and disposable nappies alongside musical instruments.

The following month Queen began recording their next album, *Jazz*, in Mountain Studios in Montreux, overlooking Lake Geneva. For the first time since *A Night at the Opera*, they reunited with co-producer Roy Thomas Baker. 'At the end of *A Night at the Opera*, we'd felt that Roy was drifting off,' said Brian. 'But with *Jazz* he came back incredibly focused, and we thought it might re-ignite the flame within the band.'

There were more exciting places for a rock group to work than Montreux, where even the English-style local pub closed early. But, money-wise, it made sense. Queen would make another shrewd financial decision when they purchased Mountain Studios a year later. In the meantime, they took over the 'Salon' a vast cordoned-off area of Montreux's Grand Casino arena, and filled it with drum kits, guitars, Freddie's grand piano and miles of electrical cable.

The studio's control booth was on a different level from the Salon itself. Closed-circuit TV was installed so Freddie could observe Roy Thomas Baker's face while he recorded his vocals. Freddie learned long ago that a smile, a frown or a raised eyebrow could communicate Baker's thoughts almost as well as words.

Baker came to the project having just produced a huge US hit album for the Boston new wave group the Cars. 'New wave' was a catch-all term for the sharp, snappy pop-rock that had grown out of punk. New wave meant 'current', and Queen wanted to remain current. 'Roy had done the Cars album in a few weeks,' said Brian, 'and it had been a huge hit, which made us think.'

Left: 'Like joining a private club'. Elton John with his manager, John Reid, who also managed Queen from 1975 to 1978.
Opposite: Body language. Brian back to back with Freddie in 'punishingly tight shorts', 1977.

Previous: Casino Royale. Queen at Mountain Studios, Montreux, Switzerland, during the Jazz sessions, 1978.
Opposite: World of leather. Freddie on the Jazz tour, 1978.

Queen and Baker's meticulous standards remained high. When the band finished in Montreux, they moved to Super Bear Studios in Berre-les-Alpes, near Nice. On arrival, Baker declared the studio sound 'too dead' and demanded the carpets be removed to expose the marble floor. When the sound didn't improve, he insisted the carpets be returned. *Jazz* was completed after a gruelling marathon run of late-night sessions. The band needed the album out in time for another US tour.

Inspiration had struck in the unlikeliest of places. Two of *Jazz*'s standout songs were Freddie's 'Bicycle Race' and Brian's 'Fat Bottomed Girls'. Both appeared on a double-A-side single released at the end of October 1978, accompanied by a launch party and rather crass promo video in which sixty-five naked women were seen cycling around Wimbledon Stadium. 'It was Freddie who instilled in us the belief that we had to make people gasp every time,' said Roger. Halfords, the bike retailer who had loaned Queen the bicycles, also gasped when they read about the stunt, and demanded compensation for the cost of replacing all sixty-five saddles.

'Fat Bottomed Girls' was a thigh-slapping hoedown with a great swinging guitar riff and what would now be considered a politically incorrect lyric. Where Brian came up with its sexually voracious nanny, 'Big Fat Fanny', remains a mystery. But it's difficult to imagine another band with the balls and bravado to release a song called 'Fat Bottomed Girls', or a vocalist other than Freddie Mercury who'd dare sing it.

On the flipside, 'Bicycle Race' was one of Freddie's most adventurous compositions, one that defied categorisation. In July 1978, the world-famous Tour de France had passed through Montreux. 'Fred was gazing [at the race] with absolute amazement and it triggered something in his imagination,' recalled Roger Taylor. Others claim Freddie's admiration went further and that he had spent the night with a young rider who had dropped out of the race with a hamstring injury.

Whatever the inspiration, it resulted in a song that exalted the joys of cycling compared with Peter Pan, John Wayne, Superman, *Jaws* and the just-released *Star Wars*. All this, over barbershop quartet-style vocals, needling heavy metal guitars and jingling bells. 'Every cycle shop in the [Montreux] area was scoured in order to build a collection of various tones and actions of bell,' said Peter Hince. 'Bicycle Race' delivered all this in just over three minutes. It was one of the oddest pop songs of the 1970s.

Jazz was full of examples of Freddie's ambitious songwriting, and Queen's ability to turn that ambition into reality. The opening song, 'Mustapha', began with something akin to a muezzin's call to prayer and had Freddie singing in English, Arabic and gibberish. You couldn't imagine another pop group attempting anything quite like it.

Freddie rarely revealed anything about his songs. For all his painstaking exactitude in the studio, he still described his work as 'disposable', like 'Bic razors' and 'used tissues'. As ever, it was a double bluff. Two of Freddie's songs on *Jazz* actually said much about his life.

'You have to have confidence in this business. It's useless saying you don't need it. If you start saying to yourself, "Maybe I'm not good enough, maybe I'd better settle for second place," it's no good. If you like the icing on the top, you've got to have confidence.'

FM, 1974

'*Most of my songs are love ballads and things to do with sadness and torture and pain. In terms of love, you're not in control and I hate that feeling. I seem to write a lot of sad songs because I'm a very tragic person. But there's always an element of humour at the end.*'

FM, 1974

On 'Let Me Entertain You' he presented himself as an old stager – 'a musical prostitute', as he called himself – willing to do anything and everything for his audience. It wasn't far off reality. Meanwhile, 'Don't Stop Me Now' was more revealing than those outside Queen's inner circle knew. The song has been used in many TV adverts and sung by countless TV talent-show hopefuls. 'But they don't know the darkness behind it,' said Roger Taylor.

Asked in 2013 whether 'Don't Stop Me Now' was, basically, about taking lots of drugs and having sex with lots of men, Roger replied: 'Your interpretation is spot on.' Roger loved the song. Brian May was less comfortable with the subject matter: 'Yes, it's a great party song. But it related to a detrimental time in Freddie's life, and we were all rather worried about him.'

Freddie had snuck in a mention of cocaine in the lyrics to 'Bicycle Race'. 'Don't Stop Me Now' was a love letter to the drug. Freddie wasn't the only member of Queen partaking, although Brian has always maintained he never took 'anything stronger than an aspirin'. But from 1977 onwards, cocaine and alcohol played increasingly prominent roles in Freddie's social life.

Booze and coke removed his inhibitions, and having split from Mary Austin, the now thirty-something Freddie threw himself into a journey of sexual discovery. After all that secrecy and soul searching, Freddie ditched David Minns for an American dancer, Dane Clark, who was soon on the payroll as Freddie's dresser. On Queen's 1977 US tour, he met a young chef named Joe Fanelli, who later moved to England with him. One-night or even half-a-night stands came and went in the blink of an eye, or the time it took for Freddie to drag himself from another anonymous hotel bed and call for a taxi.

For Brian May, Queen's 1977 tour was when he realised his friend's sexual preferences had changed. The guitarist noted Freddie now 'had boys following him into his hotel room instead of girls … I always had plenty of gay friends,' he added. 'I just didn't realise Freddie was one of them.'

One of Freddie's old friends once said, 'The three boys in Queen weren't scared [of Freddie's homosexuality]. Just apprehensive. They didn't know how to handle it.' Interviewed in 2008, Roger Taylor offered a succinct, 'We didn't give a shit.'

But it was still only ten years since homosexuality had been made legal in the UK and prejudice was still rife. Elton John and David Bowie had publicly declared their bisexuality. But Freddie wasn't ready to do the same. 'He wasn't like Bowie who used it as a way of gaining media attention,' said Mick Rock. 'With Freddie, it was something everybody knew about, but he didn't own up to it until the end of his life.'

Instead, Freddie preferred to double bluff the press when asked: 'I sleep with men, women, cats, you name it. I'll go to bed with anything.'

Left: Dane Clark, Freddie's ex-lover turned wardrobe assistant.
Opposite: Freddie with 'every freak and eccentric in New Orleans', *Jazz* launch party, Fairmont Hilton Hotel, 31 October 1978.

Freddie once described Queen as a 'four-headed gorgon', pulling in four different directions. *Jazz* would see the band living up to that description. Released in November 1978, it peaked at a respectable number two in the UK and number six in the US. But it wasn't the world-conquering hit Queen craved. At times, it sounded as if the hydra was in danger of pulling itself apart. Even Freddie, who rarely criticised his work publicly, described *Jazz* as 'a slight dip'.

Queen, as always, kept up appearances. *Jazz* was launched on Hallowe'en night, with a pre-release party that scaled new heights of decadence and in which all sexual preferences were catered for. After Queen's sold-out performance at New Orleans Municipal Auditorium, between three and four hundred guests arrived at the elegant Fairmont Hotel on the stroke of midnight.

Tables in the vast ballroom were piled high with ice buckets of champagne and pyramids of oysters, lobsters and stuffed crabs. Fifty skeletal dead trees had been scattered around the space to make it resemble a fairy-tale witch's forest. Queen's US publicist, meanwhile, had followed the band's strict instruction and rounded up 'every freak and eccentric in New Orleans' and brought them to the hotel. Wandering between the branches of the dead trees were dozens of snake-charmers, contortionists, jugglers, face-painted clowns, dancers, transvestites, transsexuals, prostitutes, groupies and strippers disguised as nuns.

'One of the reasons for the party was to scuff up the band's refined, standoffish image,' wrote *Los Angeles Times* music correspondent Robert Hilburn. 'The refined aspect was easily erased. There were so many strippers in the Fairmont Hotel's ballroom that one Bourbon Street club had to close for the night. The band had hired all its dancers.'

Legend has it that dwarves with cocaine on silver salvers strapped to their heads roamed the room while dispensing their wares. Roger Taylor said he 'almost wished that were true', but is sure it wasn't. 'There *was* a dwarf at the *Jazz* party in New Orleans,' confirmed Peter Hince. 'But he lay underneath piles of cold cuts and sliced meat – and quivered when people approached the table.'

Others claim there were rooms at the party in which guests could be orally pleasured by prostitutes of either sex, a naked woman writhing in a bath of uncooked liver and an overweight Samoan who 'smoked' a cigarette in her vagina. Or were there? 'I'm afraid to say a lot of stories from that night may have been exaggerated,' admitted Roger. Yet the $200,000 bill and Queen's collective hangover were very real.

By 3 a.m., Freddie had left the party and was roaming New Orleans's French Quarter with a couple of friends, admiring the passing trade. Freddie was looking for something, anything. And while he kept looking, he had no intention of slowing down.

'I'm a man of extremes. I have a soft side and a hard side with not a lot in between. If the right person finds me I can be very vulnerable, a real baby, which is invariably when I get trodden on. But sometimes, I'm hard, and when I'm strong no one can get to me.'

FM, 1974

A perfectionist at work: Freddie, Mountain Studios, Montreux, Switzerland, 1979.

MACHINE GUNS READY TO GO

'It's not Mozart, is it.'

FM DESCRIBING QUEEN'S MUSIC, 1981

Opposite: Bird of a feather.
Hot Space 'Rock 'n' America' tour, 1982.

'I'd like to see
Mick Jagger try
doing something like that
– or Rod Stewart.'

FM ON PERFORMING WITH
THE ROYAL BALLET, 1979

TIMELINE

With Brian May and film crew, Musicland Studios, Munich, October 1980.

1979

17 January–1 March: *Jazz* European tour.

13 April–6 May: *Jazz* tour of Japan.

22 June: Release of *Live Killers,* the band's first live album, recorded during the European *Jazz* tour.

June–July: Queen start recording *The Game* at Musicland Studios, Munich.

October: Queen buy Mountain Studios in Montreux.

7 October: Freddie dances and sings with the Royal Ballet at the London Coliseum, to orchestral arrangements of 'Bohemian Rhapsody' and 'Crazy Little Thing Called Love'.

1980

23 February: 'Crazy Little Thing Called Love' becomes Queen's first US #1 single, staying on top for four weeks.

February–March: Sessions for *Flash Gordon,* Queen's first soundtrack album, at Townhouse Studios, London.

February–May: Second series of sessions for *The Game,* again at Musicland Studios, Munich.

30 June: *The Game* is released, topping the charts in the UK, US, Holland and Canada.

30 June–30 September: *The Game* North American tour.

October–November: Second series of sessions for *Flash Gordon* at the Music Centre and Advision Studios, both in London.

4 October: 'Another One Bites the Dust' becomes the band's second US chart-topping single of the year, spending three weeks at #1.

8 December: *Flash Gordon* is released in the UK, peaking at #10 in the chart.

1981

February: *Flash Gordon* is released in the US.

28 February: Queen begin the South American leg of the long-running *Game* tour in Buenos Aires, Argentina, the first rock band to undertake a stadium tour of Latin America.

20–21 March: The band perform in front of 251,000 fans on two consecutive nights in São Paulo, Brazil.

June–July: Queen start recording *Hot Space* at Mountain Studios, Montreux.

26 October: *Greatest Hits* released. The multi-platinum compilation tops the UK albums chart and goes on to become the UK's best-selling album of all time.

21 November: 'Under Pressure', written and recorded with David Bowie for *Hot Space,* reaches #1 in the UK.

December–March 1982: Further sessions for *Hot Space,* at Musicland Studios, Munich.

1982

9 April–5 June: *Hot Space* European tour, which concludes with a major appearance at the huge open-air Milton Keynes Bowl.

21 May: Release of *Hot Space,* Queen's disco-oriented tenth studio album.

21 July–15 September: *Hot Space* North American tour. The final date, at the Forum in Los Angeles, is Freddie's last ever live performance in the US.

19 October–3 November: *Hot Space* Asian tour.

December: Freddie and the other members of Queen are named in the *Guinness Book of Records* as Britain's highest-paid executives.

'We could all write songs, but Freddie was born to it.'

ROGER TAYLOR, 2015

For Queen, the 1980s began early – in the bathtub of Freddie Mercury's suite at Munich's Bayerischer Hof Hotel in summer 1979.

The band was in Munich to record at Musicland Studios, a state-of-the-art facility previously used by the Rolling Stones, Led Zeppelin and ELO. Queen had hired the studio and its engineer Reinhold Mack (known as Mack) as an experiment. 'We weren't planning to make an album,' said Roger Taylor. 'There was no deadline. We just wanted to see what would happen.'

Freddie, who never flew unaccompanied as he liked having an unofficial bodyguard and somebody to talk to, arrived in Munich with the band's road manager, Peter Hince. No sooner had he checked in at his hotel and started running a bath than he was writing a song. 'Fred asked me to bring his acoustic guitar into the bathroom,' Hince recalled. 'I wasn't sure what was going on, but it seems Fred had an idea.' Freddie, wrapped in a towel, seized the guitar and immediately began picking out some simple rock 'n' roll chords.

Freddie's next question was, how quickly could they get to the studio? Roger Taylor and John Deacon were already at Musicland, but there was no sign of Brian May.

'Freddie said, "Quick, let's do this before Brian gets here,"' recalled Mack, who recorded the trio's first run-through of the song without telling them. The result was 'Crazy Little Thing Called Love', an unpretentious rock 'n' roll number

that took between four and five hours to complete – a new first for Queen.

Freddie had been concerned that Brian would over-think the track. 'There were two camps of songwriting [in Queen] – Freddie and Brian,' suggested Mack. 'Fred was easy. It took him fifteen to twenty minutes to come up with something absolutely brilliant. Brian would come up with a great idea, but get lost in insignificant details.'

Queen's plan to 'see what would happen' in the studio soon evolved into the making of *two* new albums – one in Munich, the other in London. And shortly before flying out to Munich, Freddie had committed to another, completely different project: dancing and singing with the Royal Ballet.

It was former EMI chairman Sir Joseph Lockwood who had suggested Freddie for the Royal Ballet's gala charity performance in London. 'I'm almost certain they asked Kate Bush first,' said EMI's Bob Mercer. They had, but when Kate turned them down Freddie was next on the list. 'After finding out what it involved, it really scared me,' Freddie admitted. Still, he agreed to carry on and submitted to weeks of punishing rehearsals in London.

Freddie performed with the Royal Ballet at the London Coliseum on 7 October 1979. The traditional ballet audience was joined for one night only by Roger Taylor. Freddie, in a leather jacket and silver catsuit, was carried aloft by a trio of male dancers and performed his moves while singing 'Crazy Little Thing Called Love' and 'Bohemian Rhapsody'.

Asked about the performance later, Roger offered a tactful, 'I thought he was very brave.' The dancers also admired his energy and commitment. There was some strange method in Freddie's madness. 'What was a funky rock 'n' roll audience going to say about this prancing

Freddie and 'Freddie', Musicland Studios, Munich, spring 1980.

ballerina?' he wondered. 'Because it's basically a form of outrage and shock.'

Shortly after Freddie's ballet debut, his bathtub composition returned Queen to the charts. 'Crazy Little Thing Called Love' reached number two in the UK, and, later, number one in the United States. It was their biggest hit since 'Bohemian Rhapsody', but it had none of that song's bombast. Instead, Freddie playfully rhymed 'hitch-hike' with 'motorbike' and offered an Elvis impersonation in which you could almost sense his top lip quivering.

Like 'Bohemian Rhapsody', though, Queen sold the song with a memorable video. The band members all wore black leather, with Freddie in the blackest leather of all while shimmying with a coterie of male and female dancers. According to rock critic Barney Hoskyns, 'His queerness, like the name of his band, was so in-your-face – yet no one even noticed it.'

Brian May's meticulous approach might not have suited 'Crazy Little Thing Called Love', but it proved to be invaluable when Queen agreed to record their first movie soundtrack. Dino De Laurentiis, the acclaimed Italian producer behind the 1960s hit *Barbarella*, enlisted them to write music for his latest project, the sci-fi comic strip adaptation *Flash Gordon*. But with sessions now booked for a new Queen studio album, the band spent a frantic four months in early 1980 dashing between Munich and London recording the two projects.

It was an intense period, but there was still time to relax. In Munich, the main distraction was the Sugar Shack, a nightclub referred to in the Queen song of the time 'Dragon Attack'. The club had an astonishing sound system, noted

for its volume and clarity, on which Queen tested their new songs after hours amid plentiful supplies of alcohol and other substances.

While Brian, Roger and John frequented the Sugar Shack, Freddie and his entourage headed to gay clubs such as Old Mrs Henderson and Ochsengarten. Here Freddie enjoyed a freedom denied him in London, where he always worried a reporter might be lurking. In Munich, nobody cared. On other nights, he joined his band mates at the Shack to consume more vodka, always his favourite tipple, and share tales of his latest misadventures.

These sessions often ended with a 6 a.m. champagne nightcap in one of the band members' hotel suites, before a few hours of fitful sleep and a late-afternoon breakfast. 'And we lived like that for a year,' recalled Peter Hince. 'It took its toll.' The days blurred into nights and back into days again. 'It was enormous fun,' Roger Taylor told me. 'But perhaps not so good in other ways.'

Hangovers aside, making the album proved to be a struggle. Queen wanted to try something different, but initially resisted some of Mack's suggestions. 'Queen were set in their ways, like pensioners,' he told me. 'Their credo was, "This is how we are used to doing things."' Mack encouraged them to think more simply. 'Never two notes played if one would do,' explained Brian May. They were also persuaded to break their self-imposed ban on synthesizers.

Above: Musicland Studios, Munich, spring 1980.
Opposite: Flying without wings. Royal Ballet rehearsals, London, October 1979.

'If people ask me if I'm gay, I tell them it's up to themselves to find out.'

FM, 1976

Indeed, the first sound heard on the resulting album, *The Game*, released on 30 June 1980, was the futuristic whoosh of an Oberheim polyphonic synthesizer. This, then, was a 'new' Queen. Two of Freddie's three contributions, 'Crazy Little Thing Called Love' and the less well known 'Don't Try Suicide', were positively spartan. But the other song, 'Play the Game', was closer to the 'old' Queen, a grand ballad written about Freddie's latest live-in partner, motorcycle courier Tony Bastin. 'Play the Game' became a UK top twenty hit. When Freddie later discovered Bastin had been unfaithful, he threw him out of the flat but insisted on keeping his pet tomcat Oscar.

Nothing on *The Game* followed Mack's 'one note, not two' policy as closely as John Deacon's 'Another One Bites the Dust'. To the casual fan, John was always 'the other one' in Queen. In reality, he kept a close eye on the money and the business, and also wrote the occasional huge hit. 'Another One Bites the Dust' was a prime example of what Mack called 'Deacy laying one of his golden eggs'.

At first, Brian and Roger were baffled when they heard the song's jagging bass line (borrowed from Chic's recent hit 'Good Times'). John insisted that Roger stuff his bass drum with blankets to deaden the noise until it matched the tight disco drum sound he required.

Freddie, however, loved the song right from the start. Like John, he was a fan of Michael Jackson's recent chart-topping disco album *Off the Wall*. John knew how he wanted the vocals to sound, but, lacking any singing ability, struggled to convey this to Freddie. But Freddie persevered.

'He wanted to make it special,' recalled Brian, who watched astonished as Freddie sang with such ferocity his throat eventually started bleeding.

'Another One Bites the Dust' would have sounded magnificent pumped through the sound system at the Sugar Shack at 4 a.m. But nobody in Queen imagined it as a single. It was too much of an anomaly. Their audience would surely never accept Queen 'going disco'.

Like most Queen albums, *The Game* attracted a mix of cautious praise and outright contempt. The British pop fortnightly *Smash Hits* called it 'utterly unoriginal corn'. The American rock magazine *Trouser Press* was more impressed: '[Queen] stay well above the dung heap of ultra-successful (and relatively talentless) hard rock bands.'

On the same day that *The Game* was released, Queen began the North American leg of an epic world tour with Freddie unveiling a new image. 'When I look back on all that black nail varnish, chiffon, satin, I think, "God! What was I doing?"' he said. Instead, with his new short haircut, matador's moustache and leather stage garb, he adopted the 'clone' look popular in American gay clubs. As ever, he was hiding his sexuality in plain sight.

Freddie first grew his moustache in Munich and asked Peter Hince to take a photograph so he could inspect it. 'He immediately stated, "Yes – I love it!"' recalled Hince. 'He was in the minority.'

'One man grows a moustache – not a big deal,' remarked Roger Taylor. 'But it obviously was in his case. It represented the gay scene at the time. It didn't bother us at all. Do what you want.'

Neither the critics nor Freddie's facial hair did anything to hinder sales. *The Game* was soon topping the album charts in the UK and the US. But the singles 'Save Me' and

Previous: Hair apparent. Road-testing the new moustache during the *Game* tour, 1980.
Opposite left: Raging bull. Joe Louis Arena, Detroit, 20 September 1980.
Opposite right: Mirror, mirror. Sports Arena, San Diego, 5 July 1980.

'Play the Game' did not fare so well. Then an influential New York urban radio station, WBLS, began playing 'Another One Bites the Dust', believing Queen to be a new black act. Nobody at Elektra, the band's American record label, felt inclined to put them straight.

The message was driven home when, in July, Michael Jackson visited Queen backstage after their show at the Los Angeles Forum and told them they had to release the track as a single. They took notice and Jackson was proved right. A month later, 'Another One Bites the Dust' was in the UK top ten and had reached number one in the US. 'It sold about four million copies in America,' Roger Taylor told me. 'How delightfully wrong can you be?'

Roger and Brian may have had reservations about Queen's new direction, but Freddie was in his element. This was his take on the dance music pumping out of gay clubs across New York. The video for 'Another One Bites the Dust' showed him pacing the stage of Detroit's Joe Louis Arena, wearing a baseball cap with cattle horns on it, looking like a priapic bull in search of a mate.

Queen's US tour ended at Madison Square Garden. Freddie was late arriving having enjoyed himself too much the night before. No sooner had he swanned on stage than he had doused the front rows with champagne and declared they were 'all cunts'. In London this would have been met with cheers and likeminded insults. But the New Yorkers were not impressed. Similarly, when Freddie asked audiences across the US what they thought of his moustache, he was frequently met with jeers and disposable razors thrown from the crowd. His response was always the same: grin delightedly, stroke his top lip and tell the audience to 'fuck off'. But over the next two years, Queen would discover to their cost just how different American and British audiences could be.

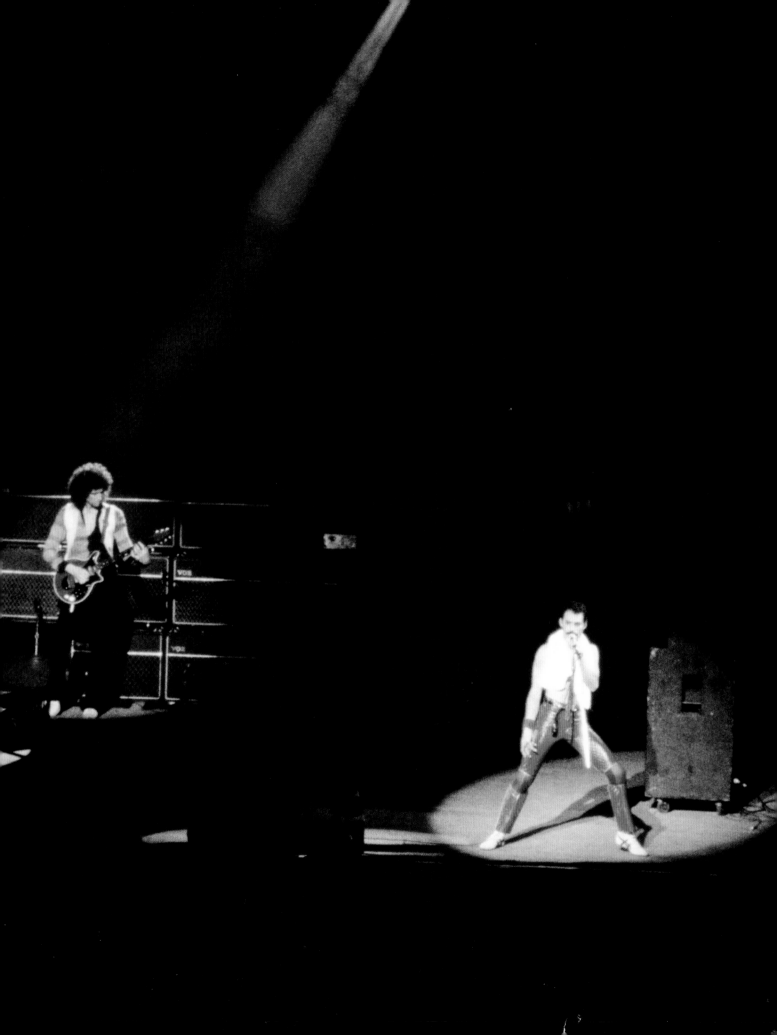

In the meantime, though, they were a band reborn. The *Flash Gordon* soundtrack arrived in December 1980 and yielded another UK top ten single, 'Flash's Theme' (known simply as 'Flash'). With the song's unique mix of music and dialogue, Queen had taken a revolutionary approach to a movie theme, for which they arguably deserve more credit. The single's unforgettably camp 'Flash! A-ah!' chorus would become as recognisable as the multiple 'Galileo, Figaros' in 'Bohemian Rhapsody'.

Like 'Another One Bites the Dust', 'Flash' brought Queen to a younger audience raised on pop music, TV and Hollywood blockbusters. There was something apt about Freddie appearing on stage during 'We Will Rock You' on the shoulders of a roadie dressed as Darth Vader (at least until *Star Wars* director George Lucas's lawyers served the band with a cease-and-desist order). Freddie was a technicolour pop star who could have pirouetted straight off the big screen.

Queen's power and global appeal was driven home when they played South America in spring 1981. They broke new ground by performing in Brazil and Argentina to audiences of over 250,000 a night and a further 30 million viewers on TV. It was a strange, disorientating experience. They were fêted by Argentinian football star Diego Maradona and Argentina's next president, General Roberto Viola, and accompanied everywhere by an armed guard.

At São Paolo's Estádio do Morumbi, 251,000 Brazilians bellowed the chorus of 'Another One Bites the Dust' as if it were their national anthem. Queen returned to Britain having grossed $3.5 million from the seven dates.

On stage, Freddie seemed invincible; offstage, less so. His companion in South America was a male model and London nightclub bouncer named Peter Morgan. When Freddie saw Morgan secretly meeting a handsome younger man in Rio, he had him booked on the first plane back to the UK. As payback, he kept Morgan's leather jacket and wore it at the next gig despite the stifling heat. 'Although Freddie might have allowed himself to be unfaithful, others were not allowed that privilege,' observed Peter Freestone, Freddie's personal assistant for the last twelve years of his life.

The downside to Freddie's fame was acutely obvious on that South American trip. Freestone and others in Freddie's entourage could walk the streets and beaches of Rio unhindered. The boss could not. Freddie spotted Peter Morgan with another man while on the balcony of his hotel suite, effectively imprisoned there and unable to go down to the street and confront him.

Previous: In the spotlight. CNE, Toronto, 30 August 1980.
Above: Queen with police escort before their show at Estadio José María Minella, Mar del Plata, Argentina, 4 March 1981.
Opposite: All the world's a stage. Soundchecking at Estádio do Morumbi, São Paulo, Brazil, 20 March 1981.

QUEEN & DAVID BOWIE
UNDER PRESSURE

'I really do love performing. I mean, it's totally natural for me. I'm a dandy, a show-off. I get very high on all the attention. I love it.'

FM, 1974

As his love life spiralled into chaos, Freddie consoled himself the best way he knew how: by spending money. Before long, he would acquire a three-bedroom apartment on New York's East Fifty-Eighth Street with panoramic views of the city. But also, back in London, he bought an eight-bedroom Georgian townhouse called Garden Lodge in Logan Place, Kensington, which his former girlfriend Mary Austin had found for him.

After extensive renovations lasting five years, Garden Lodge, with its mahogany and maplewood gallery, its mirrored dressing rooms and walled Japanese garden, would become Freddie's sanctuary. 'Whenever I watched Hollywood movies set in plush houses with lavish décor, I wanted that for myself,' he said. 'I achieved that dream with this wonderful house.'

Eager to capitalise on the success of *The Game*, Queen were back recording new music by summer 1981. The sessions for what was to become their most controversial album, *Hot Space*, were split between Munich's Musicland Studios and Montreux's Mountain Studios, with Mack again co-producing.

As they had for *The Game*, the band began with scraps of ideas rather than complete songs, and conflicting opinions about how the album should sound. Buoyed by 'Another One Bites the Dust', Freddie and John Deacon wrote 'Cool Cat', a dance track on which Freddie sang in a

shrill falsetto. The song was so far beyond Queen's comfort zone that Brian May and Roger Taylor didn't even play on it.

David Bowie lived near Montreux and was invited to sing backing vocals on the track. Queen were a bigger-selling act at the time, but Bowie had been a superstar for longer. He sang backup on 'Cool Cat' (though later insisted his vocal be erased from the mix). But the collaboration didn't end there. 'He kept popping into the studio,' said Freddie in 1985. 'And we were jamming to some of his songs and some of ours. We had a few bottles of wine and things, and we suddenly said, "Why don't we try something totally new?"'

The new song, provisionally called 'People on Streets', later retitled 'Under Pressure', was created during one long, lively night. Mack recalled a gold disc being removed from the studio wall and used as a 'chopping board' for a large pile of cocaine. Not everyone indulged, but the studio was soon full of incessant chatter – as Mack put it, 'so much verbal diarrhoea'.

Once Queen completed the backing track, Bowie suggested he and Freddie each sing whatever they thought the melody should be. He then proposed that they record their vocals 'blind', without one hearing what the other had done. Unknown to Freddie, Bowie eavesdropped while

Above: 'It took Freddie fifteen minutes to come up with something brilliant.' With Queen's producer Reinhold Mack.
Opposite: In transit. Waiting for a flight, 1982.

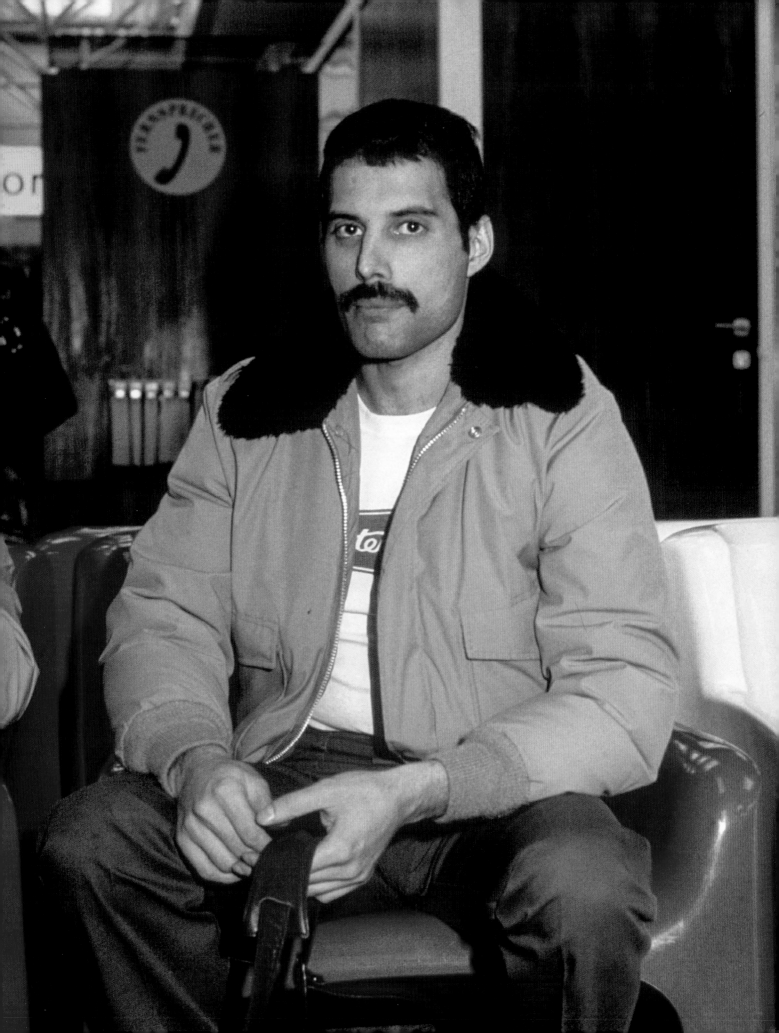

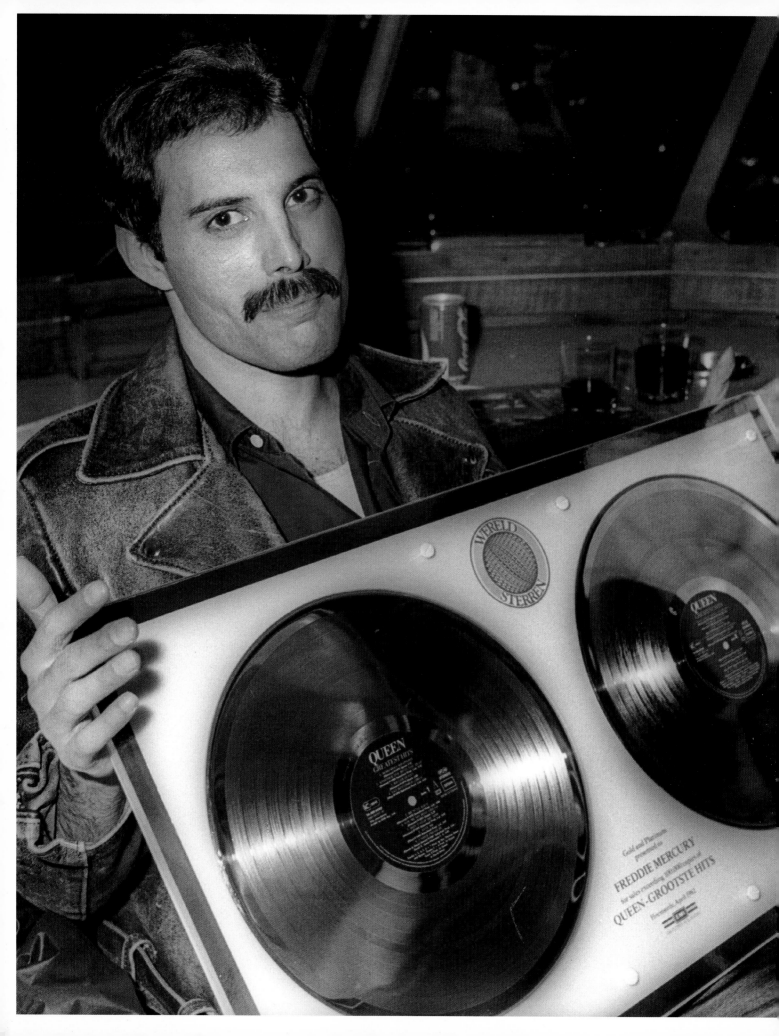

'It's a precarious life, but I think I like it that way. I like it a little risky. I'm quite well off, but money in the bank doesn't mean anything to me. I could be penniless tomorrow, but I wouldn't care that much. I have this survival instinct in me.'

FM, 1981

he was singing. When Bowie went in to record his vocal, Freddie was astonished at how perfectly Bowie's 'ad-libs' fitted with what he had been doing.

However, the experience of mixing the song was less harmonious. Eventually, Brian walked away, leaving Bowie, Freddie and Roger to finish it at New York's Power Plant studio. 'There was an ego clash there,' admitted Roger. 'But I got on well with Bowie – and so did Freddie. I could have imagined us doing more things together.'

Back in Munich, Queen succumbed to the usual temptations. In the studio, frayed nerves, hangovers and awkward phone calls from wives and girlfriends back home compounded the already fraught mood. The rows over Queen's new direction grew more heated. When John Deacon told Brian May he didn't like the way he played guitar on his new songs, Brian walked out of a session.

Although himself known for his tantrums, Freddie was often required to play the mediator. 'It might surprise people, but Fred was very good at that,' said Brian. 'He was very good at calming us down.' Like a musical referee, Freddie would separate his band mates, releasing the tension with one of his trademark 'Oh, for fuck's sake!'s or 'Now, come on, dear's. 'Fred was the glue that kept us together,' said Roger.

Their mood was not improved when they took a break from recording in September 1981 for a round of dates in Venezuela and Mexico. The visit to Argentina and Brazil earlier that year had been a triumph. But this return to

Latin America quickly became a logistical nightmare. It was blighted by widespread corruption, cancelled dates and the band's promoter being jailed (others say kidnapped) until they paid $25,000 bail money.

An air of intimidation and violence hung over the tour, which, according to Peter Hince, ending up losing 'a phenomenal seven-figure sum' – something that especially rankled with money man John Deacon. Not for nothing was the trip later nicknamed the 'Gluttons for Punishment' tour. Queen returned to Munich chastened by the whole affair. Then they received some welcome good news. 'Under Pressure' had just topped the charts in the UK, Netherlands and Argentina. A jigsaw puzzle of a song that fused Bowie's nervy art-rock with Queen's deft pop, it would become one of the band's most enduring hits. Its John Deacon bass line also reached a new audience when American rapper Vanilla Ice sampled it on his 1990 hit single 'Ice Ice Baby', and had to pay Queen and Bowie handsomely for the rights.

Queen's *Greatest Hits* album, complete with a band portrait taken by royal photographer Lord Lichfield, arrived at the end of October 1981. It would go on to sell more than 25 million copies worldwide. Clearly, none of the band members, now listed in the 1982 *Guinness Book of Records* as Britain's highest-paid company directors, would be 'people on streets' any time soon.

Hot Space, the product of all those long, vodka-soaked nights in Munich, was released in May 1982. The electro rhythms and blaring horns on its opening track, 'Staying Power', announced this as a very different Queen album. Apart from the John Lennon tribute 'Life Is Real (Song for Lennon)', Freddie's contributions were exclusively dance/disco songs. One track, 'Body Language', had a sleek, Michael Jackson-style groove and featured Freddie moaning and sighing in faux ecstasy.

Solid gold. Collecting a disc for Queen's *Greatest Hits*, the Netherlands, April 1982.

Freddie knew these songs wouldn't appeal to all of Queen's audience – they didn't even appeal to all of his band mates. But he didn't care. 'His music, first and foremost, was for himself,' explained Pete Freestone. 'It was his perfection he was seeking, not other people's.'

The songs also channelled Freddie's current listening habits. A night on the town with his friends was usually preceded by a blast of his new favourite album, *The Dude*, by Michael Jackson's producer Quincy Jones. The horns on 'Staying Power' were arranged by Arif Mardin, the venerable producer who had collaborated with many of the great names of soul and jazz, including one of Freddie's idols, Aretha Franklin.

Queen's meshing of funk and rock extended beyond Freddie's songs. Although Brian May's 'Dancer' and 'Put Out the Fire' included some mighty guitar solos, both songs were a long way from the pomp-rock of *Queen II* or *Sheer Heart Attack*.

Received wisdom has it that *Hot Space* was a commercial disaster. This is not entirely true. It did reach number four in the UK and hit the top ten in Japan and numerous European countries. However, by Queen's exacting standards it was a disappointment. In the tribal world of 1980s pop, consumers were confused by a 'white' rock band playing black dance music.

A further sign of Queen's new direction was the addition of a touring keyboard player, ex-Mott the Hoople member Morgan Fisher. In June, Queen, with Fisher in tow, finished

a short UK stadium tour with a show at the Milton Keynes Bowl. Freddie prefaced 'Staying Power' with a tetchy explanation – 'We're gonna do some songs in the black funk category … That doesn't mean we've lost our rock 'n' roll feel, OK?' – before throwing himself into the song as if trying to prove it was still Queen.

It was a fine performance disguising some emotional and physical pain. A day earlier Freddie's latest boyfriend, a volatile New Jerseyan named Bill Reid, had bitten his hand in a jealous rage, splattering blood over the floor of Freddie's flat, and leaving him in agony.

Six weeks later, Queen arrived in Montreal for the first date of what was being billed as the 'Rock 'n' America' tour. A week after that, they landed in New York to play two nights at Madison Square Garden. But there was a problem: *Hot Space* wasn't selling.

Dance workouts such as 'Body Language' and 'Staying Power' were too much for Queen's traditional American fan base. The ultimate seal of disapproval came when *Rolling Stone* described parts of the album as 'barely competent'.

Queen finished their two-night stand at Madison Square Garden with a party in which the drink flowed and female mud wrestlers writhed in an inflatable bath. But it had begun on the previous afternoon with a less glamorous engagement: a meet-and-greet at Crazy Eddie, an electrical goods and record store in Brooklyn.

The notion of Queen making an appearance in a British record shop would have been unthinkable. However, their

status in America was less exalted. Lined up behind a trestle table like judges at a garden fête, the band signed copies of *Hot Space* and smiled through gritted teeth. Freddie looked like he would rather be anywhere else and kept a bottle of Moët beside him as a reminder of his true standing.

Hot Space stalled at number twenty-two in the US and was soon freewheeling back down the charts. This was bad enough, but Queen's support act, Boston hard rocker Billy Squier, also had a new album, *Emotions in Motion*, which was heading in the opposite direction – straight into the top ten. Worse still, Freddie and Roger had sung on the Mack-produced album, which, in parts, wasn't so different from *Hot Space*.

The difference was that Billy Squier, with his pretty-boy looks and long hair, adhered to a safe image and played radio-friendly hard rock. Queen's 'black funk' music, compounded by Freddie's new image and its social implications, made some fans uneasy. 'The word "gay" was really very dodgy for a long time in the States,' said Brian May.

Publicly, Freddie remained defiant, telling one interviewer that Queen's new single 'Body Language' was 'just as good' as 'Bohemian Rhapsody' 'but in different ways'. Tellingly, the video featured Freddie surrounded by lots of straining leather and bare flesh. The rest of Queen didn't appear until two-and-a-half minutes into the film, with Brian, especially, looking extremely embarrassed.

Brian later confessed that he thought 'Body Language' was too much of a 'gay anthem' and worried that it might alienate Queen's heterosexual fan base. His misgivings extended to the whole album. 'I think *Hot Space* was a mistake,' he said in 2014. 'If only timing-wise. Disco was a dirty word by then.' He had a point. And yet six months after the album's release, Michael Jackson topped the charts worldwide with the similarly funk-, pop- and rock-inspired *Thriller*. 'I think [*Hot Space*] was way ahead of its time,' insisted Freddie.

Queen's US tour ended at the Los Angeles Forum on 15 September 1982. Their crown might have slipped, but their celebrity pulling power was undiminished. Mingling backstage were Donna Summer, Michael Jackson and Rod Stewart. Backs were slapped, champagne spilled and toasts made. Nobody knew it then, of course, but it was the end of another era. Freddie Mercury would never play a show in America again.

Above: Queen, Elland Road Football Stadium, Leeds, 29 May 1982.
Opposite: Save me. In-store signing at Crazy Eddie, New York, 27 July 1982.

GOD KNOWS!

'One of the world's best performers, singers, composers, lyricists and divas.'

GIORGIO MORODER, 2015

'Freddie Mercury is not someone to take along on a sea cruise, since he can't seem to resist going overboard.'

PEOPLE REVIEW OF *MR BAD GUY*, 1985

Over the top. On the set of the video for 'It's a Hard Life', 1984.

TIMELINE

1983

January: Freddie begins work on first solo album.

August–January 1984: Queen record their eleventh studio album, *The Works*, at the Record Plant, Los Angeles, and Musicland, Munich.

1984

23 January: Release of 'Radio Ga Ga', which tops the charts in eight European countries and hits #2 in the UK.

27 February: *The Works* released, hitting the #2 spot in the UK album chart.

24 August–15 May 1985: *The Works* world tour.

4–8 September: Record-breaking four nights at London's Wembley Arena during the *Works* tour of Europe.

10 September: Freddie releases first solo single, 'Love Kills'.

22 September: 'Love Kills' enters UK singles chart, peaking at #10.

5–20 October: Queen play nine dates at the Sun City Super Bowl in South Africa.

Autumn: Freddie begins relationship with hairdresser Jim Hutton, who will be his partner for the rest of his life.

1985

January: Freddie finishes recording solo album *Mr Bad Guy* at Musicland Studios, Munich.

29 April: *Mr Bad Guy* released.

11 May: *Mr Bad Guy* enters UK chart where it reaches #6.

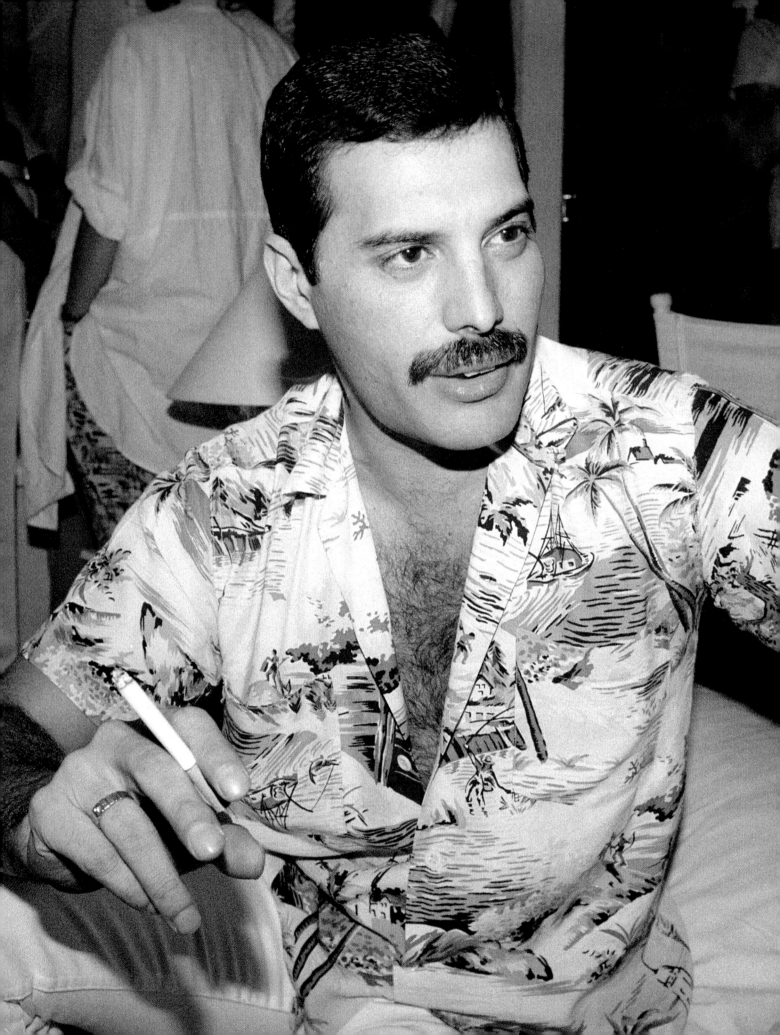

'I love nightlife and I love flamboyancy.'

FM, 1974

The *Hot Space* tour came to an end in the Seibu Lions Stadium, Tokorozawa, Japan in November 1982. The music stopped, the house lights came on, the fans filed out and everyone was ready to go home. 'We were getting on each other's nerves,' said Brian May, 'which happens from time to time.'

The band members agreed to a break during which they would work on their own projects. John Deacon returned to his family – his wife, Veronica, was expecting their third child – while Brian recorded a solo album in Los Angeles and Roger Taylor did the same in Montreux.

Freddie Mercury, meanwhile, wanted to make more music in the same vein as *Hot Space*, but without Queen. He signed a solo deal with Michael Jackson's record company, CBS, around the time Jackson's *Thriller* was averaging a million sales a week. The pair had stayed in touch after being introduced at a Queen show, and had talked about working together since 1980. There could be no better launchpad for Freddie's solo career than a duet with Michael Jackson.

In spring 1983, Jackson summoned Freddie to his heavily guarded mansion in Encino, California. The house was half pop star's hideaway, half children's playground. As well as a home cinema, which doubled as a chapel on Sundays, it included an ever-expanding menagerie and a room filled with amusement arcade games. Once inside, Freddie reverted to his shy self and hesitantly asked if he could smoke. He had begun smoking in his early thirties, partly because he liked the huskiness it gave his voice. Yet, according to friends, he never looked entirely convincing with a cigarette.

The duo worked on three songs, Jackson's 'Victory' and 'State of Shock' and Freddie's 'There Must Be More to Life Than This', over a six-hour session. But what happened that afternoon is clouded by conflicting memories and hearsay. Jim Beach, Queen's manager since 1978, claimed Freddie phoned him aghast at having to sing while Jackson's pet llama was in the room. Others say he was uneasy sharing a settee with Bubbles, Jackson's chimpanzee. In 1987, the *Sun* newspaper reported that Jackson had caught Freddie snorting cocaine through a $100 bill and asked him to leave.

Opposite: 'Olá!' Freddie backstage during the Rock in Rio festival, January 1985.
Right: Freddie's duet partner and king of pop Michael Jackson.
Far right: 'We were getting on each other's nerves.' Freddie on Queen's *Hot Space* 'Rock 'n' America' tour, Madison Square Garden, New York, 1982.

Freddie's personal assistant, Peter Freestone, who was there that day, insisted the biggest problem was Freddie's immaculate white boxer boots getting splattered with mud while he wandered around Jackson's home zoo.

Musically, the two sparked off each other and the session ended with a promise to finish the songs at a future date. But it never happened. A year later, new versions of 'Victory' and 'State of Shock' turned up on the Jackson 5's comeback album, also called *Victory*. To Freddie's fury, Michael had recorded a new version of 'State of Shock' with Mick Jagger, another new CBS signing.

Crowded schedules had made arranging another session difficult. But perhaps it was just that recording with Mick Jagger, arguably a bigger star than Freddie, was a better commercial move for the Jackson 5. 'Fred came out of it all a little upset,' recalled Brian May. 'He lost out.' A version of Freddie and Michael's duet 'There Must Be More to

Life Than This' would finally surface on the *Queen Forever* compilation released in 2014.

What brought Queen back together in summer 1983 was the offer of another movie soundtrack. Director Tony Richardson asked them to score his next project, *The Hotel New Hampshire*, a comedy drama based on a novel by John Irving and starring Jodie Foster and Rob Lowe. Freddie wrote a new song for the movie, a burnished soft-rock number called 'Keep Passing the Open Windows', but the commission was soon cancelled.

Having assembled in Los Angeles for the movie project, Queen now turned their attention to a new studio album. With co-producer Mack, they started recording at the Record Plant.

Freddie and his entourage took over a bright pink rented mansion in Beverly Hills whose previous inhabitants

ROGER TAYLOR, 2015

included Elizabeth Taylor. After hours, he launched himself into West Hollywood's lively gay scene, and found a new companion, a strapping biker known as 'Vince the Barman'. His band mates and road crew, meanwhile, discovered Osko's nightclub, where the entertainment included female mud wrestlers. When Rod Stewart and guitarist Jeff Beck called in on a Queen session, the party even came to the studio.

The Record Plant sessions were a success, but after Freddie celebrated his thirty-seventh birthday in September 1983 with a lavish party at the pink mansion, Queen returned to Munich and the same old distractions. The late nights at the Sugar Shack and the dawn nightcaps resumed. In the studio Mack often found himself working with each band member separately, and rarely all four at the same time.

'Everyone was also on a different schedule, which made it hard,' he told me. 'I'd come in and ask, "Where's John?" "Oh, he's gone to Bali …"' John's trip to the Pacific was unplanned and spontaneous, and it was Peter Hince, John's personal roadie, who had to tell the rest of the band where he'd gone. It seemed he just needed some time away from them all.

Despite the disjointed nature of its recording, Queen's eleventh studio album, *The Works*, was complete by January 1984. Unlike the radical *Hot Space*, it was an astute mix of old and new Queen. At one end of the scale was Brian's riff-heavy 'Tear It Up' and 'Hammer to Fall'; at the other, Roger's 'Radio Ga Ga' and John's 'I Want to Break Free' with their robotic beats and bleating synthesizers.

Queen were still crediting these songs to individual writers. But they were all contributing to each other's material, with Freddie particularly involved with Roger and

John's compositions. Roger wrote 'Radio Ga Ga', a salute to a lost golden age of radio, after watching America's new music channel MTV. 'It seemed to me there was far too much emphasis on a band's visual image and not enough on the music,' he complained.

The song's title came from his three-year-old half-French son Felix, who uttered the words 'radio ca ca' ('caca' meaning excrement in French). Queen changed it to 'ga ga' to keep their record company happy.

Like 'We Will Rock You' and 'We Are the Champions', 'Radio Ga Ga' had one of Queen's familiar rallying-cry choruses. But, initially, Freddie was more convinced it was going to be a hit than Roger, who gave him license to tinker. Queen's session keyboard player Fred Mandel also made a vital contribution with the song's memorable synthesizer fanfare.

John Deacon's 'I Want to Break Free' was another typical Queen anthem, given an eighties makeover. John didn't sing, so Freddie developed the vocal, with its melodramatic cries of 'God knows!' and other memorable flourishes.

'With Roger and John's songs I get in there at quite an early stage, and they don't mind me tearing things apart and piecing it back together again,' said Freddie. It was a magnanimous approach, as both songs outshone Freddie's credited contributions to *The Works*.

'Keep Passing the Open Windows' remained from the proposed *Hotel New Hampshire* soundtrack, and 'Man on the Prowl' revived the rockabilly flavour of 'Crazy Little Thing Called Love'. But neither would enjoy a long shelf life. Much better was 'It's a Hard Life', a ballad which Freddie based partly on the 'Vesti la giubba' aria from Ruggero Leoncavallo's opera *Pagliacci*.

In 'Vesti la giubba', meaning 'put on the costume', the heartbroken clown Pagliacci must get ready to perform on stage after discovering his wife's infidelity. This was Freddie back to his operatic old self. Dig deeper, though, and it was clearly a reference to his tortuous love life.

Above: Freddie performing on his thirty-eighth birthday with Queen's extra guitarist Spike Edney and Brian May, Wembley Arena, 5 September 1984.
Opposite: Two years later, he was able to celebrate his fortieth birthday at home, Garden Lodge, London, 5 September 1986.

In his memoir *Queen Unseen*, Peter Hince described an incident during the recording of *The Works*. Freddie arrived at the studio clearly upset about another romantic setback. Every attempt to cheer him up failed, until he finally turned on his band mates shouting, 'It's OK for all of you – you have your wives and families.' 'Apart from the initial shock,' said Hince, 'I thought it was a terribly sad thing to say.'

In Munich, Freddie had grown close to Mack and his family. The producer named his third child after the singer and described him as 'a caring, concerned and over-the-top godfather'. Yet the gulf between Freddie's lifestyle and that of his band mates was clearer now than it had been in the 1970s; even Roger Taylor, Queen's great playboy, now had a partner and a young son.

Freddie, meanwhile, was juggling two relationships. One was with local restaurateur Winnie Kirchberger, whose lack of English made communication difficult; the other with Barbara Valentin, an actress and model once described as Germany's answer to Britain's Diana Dors (who was herself often considered to be Britain's answer to Marilyn Monroe). Barbara, who died in 2002, was six years Freddie's senior, blonde and exuberant and able to match his outrageous behaviour.

The pair shared a cocaine habit and often a bed, though nobody is certain whether their relationship was consummated. But there was a deep friendship. 'Barbara and I have formed a bond that is stronger than anything I've had with a lover in the last six years,' said Freddie, who would live with both Kirchberger and Valentin, though separately, for a time in Munich.

The first single from *The Works* was 'Radio Ga Ga', released a month before the album, in January 1984. Director David Mallet's video showed Queen cruising Fritz Lang's *Metropolis* landscape in an airborne car, and conducting an army of Queen fan club members in synchronised salutes and handclaps. Suspicious critics compared the scene to Hitler presiding over his troops at the Nuremberg Rally. But the alcohol-avoiding Führer would probably not have hidden a bottle of vodka behind his podium, as Freddie did in the footwell of Queen's flying car.

Above: Blondes have more fun. With Barbara Valentin, Xenon nightclub, London, 1985.
Opposite: The band directs an army of fans during the video for 'Radio Ga Ga', Pinewood Studios, London, 1983.

'Queen come across as very serious. But we've always been humorous underneath.'

FM, 1984

'Radio Ga Ga' made the top five in countries across Europe, including the UK where it peaked at number two. It was Queen's biggest hit since 'Another One Bites the Dust'. But not in America. 'Radio Ga Ga' was Queen's first release on their new US label, the EMI affiliate Capitol Records. It had cost them $1 million to break from their previous US label, Elektra, whom Freddie blamed for the failure of *Hot Space*. Signing with Capitol in America cemented Queen's relationship with EMI worldwide.

Unfortunately, release of the single coincided with the publication of a US government report on payola, an illegal practice in which record promoters, known as 'pluggers', induced radio stations to play the records they were representing. To distance themselves from any accusations of bribery and corruption, Capitol at once severed ties with their independent promotions teams. 'Radio Ga Ga' reached number sixteen in the US, but when Capitol stopped paying the pluggers the single vanished into thin air. Similarly, when *The Works* was released at the end of February 1984 it reached number two in the UK and was a top ten hit in most major markets worldwide. Yet, despite *Rolling Stone* praising it as 'the *Led Zeppelin II* of the eighties', it missed the US top twenty.

However, there was more to Queen's troubled relationship with the US than problems with Capitol. At the head of Freddie's coterie of gofers and bag-carriers was his personal manager, Paul Prenter, whom Queen inherited from former manager John Reid in 1977. By 1984, he was regarded as a divisive figure by the rest of the group. 'None of the band cared for him, apart from Freddie,' said Peter Hince, who saw Freddie's favouring of Prenter as an act of 'misguided loyalty'.

Prenter always seemed to be by Freddie's side, bathing in the reflected glory and exerting a pernicious influence. According to Mack, he loathed rock music and was whispering in Freddie's ear throughout the *Hot Space* sessions. The other band members later discovered Prenter had refused all requests from US radio stations wanting to interview Freddie during their 1982 tour. 'This guy, in the course of one tour, told every record station to fuck off,' said Brian May. 'But not just "fuck off", but "Freddie says, 'fuck off'".'

Prenter's actions would be extremely damaging. But Queen's very British sense of humour further eroded the band's position in America. 'I Want to Break Free' was released as a single in April, with a David Mallet-directed video. Roger's girlfriend suggested Queen dress as women for the shoot.

The results were inspired and hilarious in equal measure. There was Brian May fussing around in a nightdress and fluffy rabbit slippers, John Deacon as a sullen-looking grandmother in a black dress and fox fur stole, and Roger Taylor as a worryingly convincing schoolgirl. And then, of course, there was Freddie, whose ensemble included a wig, high heels, PVC mini-skirt, fake breasts and a vacuum cleaner – a device he had little experience of using – which he shunted around the living room. Best of all, though, he kept his moustache.

'We had more fun making that video than any video ever,' said Roger. But as David Mallet recalled, while the rest of Queen couldn't wait to get into their frocks, 'Freddie was desperately shy. It was a hell of a job to get him out of the dressing room.'

In Britain, a nation raised on pantomime dames and kitchen-sink soap operas such as *Coronation Street*, 'I Want to Break Free' was a number three hit. Europe also understood the joke. But MTV and America did not. While promoting the single in the US, Brian May saw how 'visibly embarrassed' some DJs were by the video. A year earlier, Culture Club with androgynous lead singer Boy George had wowed America. But Culture Club were a *pop* group. It was a subtle, but significant difference.

Opposite: Queen played to a combined audience of around one million in their two shows at the first Rock in Rio festival, January 1985.
Right: Strange but true. Queen during the filming of the video for 'I Want to Break Free'.

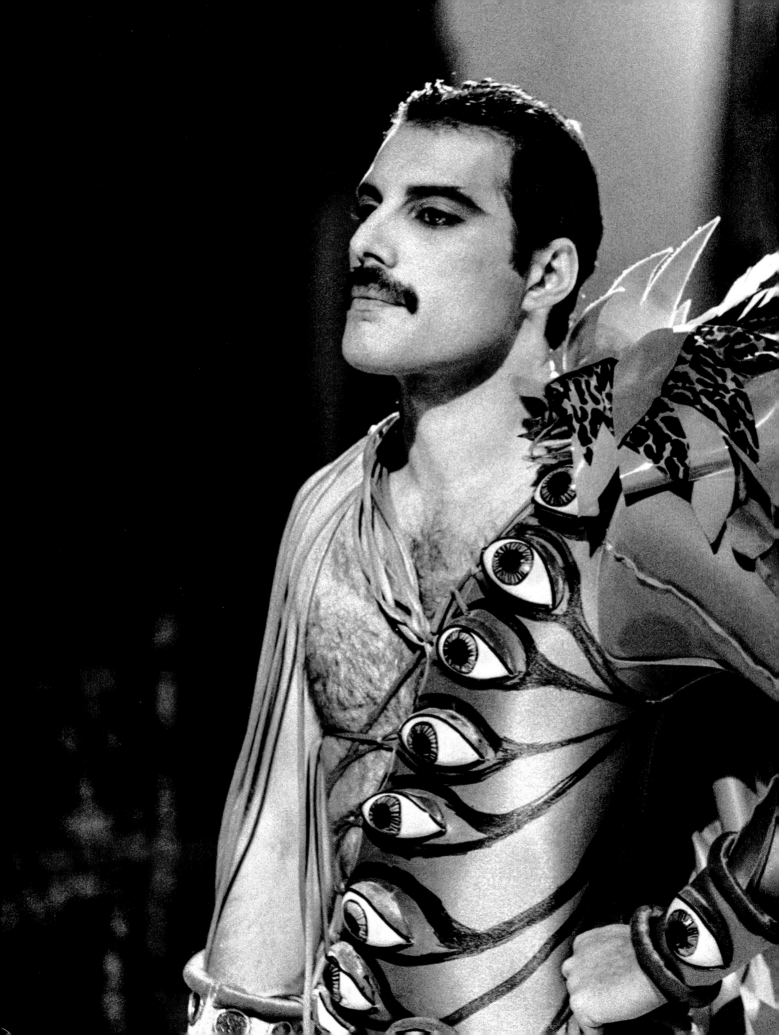

'In America they still regarded [Queen] as heavy rockers,' explained Freddie. 'They reacted with, "Why are my idols dressing in frocks?"' 'In those days on MTV, it was Whitesnake and fucking Whitesnake, and then another Whitesnake track,' protested Roger. 'They must've thought men dressing up in drag wasn't *rock* enough.'

As Brian later commented, 'Over here people got the joke, because we were spoofing *Coronation Street*, but they didn't get that in America. I remember being out on promotion and people being so shocked. I remember presenters going white and not wanting to be a part of that – how could rock stars do this?'

When MTV asked Queen to make a performance video of 'I Want to Break Free' as an alternative, the band refused. Queen dug their heels in, but America dug harder. The single failed to make even the top forty.

The video for Queen's next single, 'It's a Hard Life', was unlikely to repair the relationship. Again, it exemplified the struggle between Freddie the songwriter and Freddie the performer. Brian adored the song but not the video, in which Freddie, dressed like 'a giant Mediterranean prawn' in a feathered red jumpsuit, cavorted with a gang of fellow Munich partygoers. Brian had helped coax the song's very personal lyric out of Freddie, but thought its message was lost in the 'ironic, joke-within-a-joke video'.

The Works tour began in Brussels in August 1984 and reached Britain a week later. Freddie hobbled through several shows with a torn ligament (sustained during a riotous night out), but that did not stop him donning his black wig and false boobs for 'I Want to Break Free'.

However, North America was absent from the tour schedule. Demoralised by poor sales for *The Works*, Freddie couldn't bear the prospect of Queen playing smaller venues again. He wanted to wait until they had another US hit before touring there. But, as Queen learned in the 1970s, you had to tour to have the hit. Radio stations and music magazines also wanted to interview Freddie. But Freddie was refusing to speak to them.

'Fred had this weird relationship with the press,' explained Peter Hince. 'I know he had a fear of being misquoted. But the trouble with America is they forget you very quickly. With *The Works*, the arrogance took over – "We won't tour America. Fuck 'em!"' Queen would forever blame Capitol, Paul Prenter and Freddie's fake breasts for their failure in the States. But their refusal to compromise also played its part.

America may not have wanted them, but other countries did. In October 1984, Queen made the ill-judged decision to break a United Nations anti-apartheid cultural boycott and play the Sun City resort in Bophuthatswana, South Africa. The reason, said Jim Beach, was simple: 'an enormous sum of money'. The backlash from the Musicians' Union and the music press was also enormous, and again fuelled the image of Queen as elitist and out of touch. For the next thirty years Roger Taylor and Brian May would insist they did not support apartheid and had not played to a segregated audience. It was true. But in 2014 Roger glumly admitted their audience had been predominantly white and that, 'on balance [the South Africa trip] was a mistake'.

Freddie, despite having being born in Africa, never commented. Two of the Sun City shows were cancelled after he lost his voice. But when he was not on stage he was sequestered in his hotel suite with Winnie Kirchberger, isolated from the outside world in every possible way. As Peter Freestone explained, Freddie believed in 'leaving politics to the chaps who are paid to do the job, dear'.

Three months later, *The Works* tour reached South America. Queen played the opening and closing nights of the ten-day Rock in Rio festival, on a bill that included AC/DC, Rod Stewart and Roger Taylor's nemesis, Whitesnake. The audience at the purpose-built Cidade do Rock exceeded 250,000 with millions more watching on television, all of which made Freddie's faux pas during the opening night so spectacular.

'If I wanted children I could just go out and buy one. Buy two, you get a nanny thrown in.'

FM, 1984

Unknown to Queen, 'I Want to Break Free' had become a song of hope and empowerment to millions of Brazilians living under a military dictatorship. Seeing it performed by a man wearing plastic breasts left the audience angry and confused. Within seconds, the stage was littered with stones and bottles.

The adverse reaction was a forthright reminder that Queen's humour did not always translate. Freddie was contrite, telling the press he had not understood the situation and that he had thought there were 'lots of transvestites' in Rio. But on the closing night he left his wig and breasts in the dressing room.

The Works tour ended in Japan in May 1985, and Queen once again faced an uncertain future. They had conquered the world but lost America. There was now the possibility they might have lost Freddie Mercury as well.

In April 1985, Freddie finally released his debut solo album. *Mr Bad Guy* was recorded in Munich in fits and starts over a two-year period with Mack co-producing. In the press, Freddie insisted his solo project did not pose any threat to Queen. Instead, he joked with interviewers about needing to make his own album before he was too old and 'ended up in a wheelchair'. He was thirty-eight.

However, one aspect of Freddie's solo contract would rankle with his band mates. Jim Beach had negotiated the one-off album deal with CBS Records president Walter Yetnikoff. Freddie's advance was rumoured to be as much as $6 million. Whatever the exact figure, it was more than Queen received from EMI/Capitol for *The Works*.

Above: Queen Down Under. Press conference in Sydney during the *Works* tour, April 1985.
Right: Montreux Golden Rose Pop Festival, 12 May 1984.

'Of course we're all in it for the money, and I'm not afraid to say that ... I love the money.'

FM, 1984

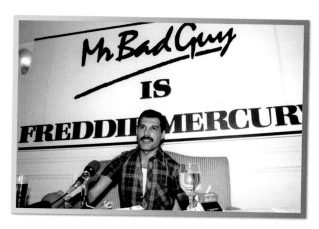

Yetnikoff, a former New York attorney, had helped steer the solo careers of Paul McCartney and Michael Jackson. He was not used to making mistakes. But having signed Queen's lead singer he had to wait for a solo album as Freddie recorded *The Works* and went on tour. When *Mr Bad Guy* eventually came out, its disappointing sales figures prompted Yetnikoff to describe the deal as 'the worst one I ever made'.

The early signs were not encouraging. Freddie's debut single, the Giorgio Moroder collaboration 'Love Kills', appeared in summer 1984, while Freddie was busy touring with Queen. It shared a pulsing electronic beat with Moroder's worldwide hit 'I Feel Love' by Donna Summer. But the comparison ended there. 'Love Kills' only just made the UK top ten and barely registered in America.

The greatest problem Freddie faced making *Mr Bad Guy* was the absence of Queen. He was used to their demands, as they were to his, and the band's rows and tantrums built a creative tension that enhanced the music. Without them, however, he was answerable to no one but himself. 'In some ways it *was* easier,' said Mack. 'Because it was one opinion, not four. He used to get pretty annoyed working with the others, because there was always Brian saying, "It needs to be more rock 'n' roll."

'But there was also a lot of hanging around when Freddie couldn't or didn't want to come up with anything. He had the studio booked, but we had nothing to do. So we'd have these designated days – an "office day" was where we didn't do music but just made phone calls. Then we'd have "game days", where we just played Scrabble ...'

Freddie plugged the gaps with session musicians, an orchestra, and, where possible, ad hoc contributions from his band mates. Roger and Brian also played on the original 'Love Kills'.

'I don't think Freddie really wanted to go solo,' said Roger. 'It's just that he got an awful lot of money from CBS. When it came down to actually doing a solo album, he did sort of miss us. He used to ring me up and I'd have to fly to Munich to do his backing vocals.'

Stylistically, *Mr Bad Guy* was *Hot Space* part two, but with even less guitar. Across its eleven songs, Freddie veered from macho hedonist to broken-hearted clown; either imploring his audience to get up, dance and have rampant sex, or crying on their shoulders. It didn't take a psychologist to unravel the meaning behind 'Living on My Own' or 'There Must Be More to Life Than This'.

In 'Living on My Own', Freddie dressed up a song about loneliness with a throbbing dance beat. It was released as a single in September 1985, with a video showing him peacocking around a nightclub filled with leather-clad boys, under-dressed girls, gurning drag queens and Brian May disguised as a witch. But the gender confusion and surfeit of naked bottoms made MTV uneasy, and the single failed to chart in the US.

A pattern was developing. Four singles were issued from *Mr Bad Guy* and none but the first, 'I Was Born to Love You', managed to break into the UK top fifty. The album itself was briefly a hit in Britain, but peaked at a disastrous number 159 in the States. 'Freddie liked the album but he was very disappointed that it didn't sell,' said Mack. *Mr Bad Guy's* sleeve notes contained the self-aware message: 'Thanks to ... Walter Yetnikoff and all at CBS for having the sheer nerve to take me on.'

Ultimately, Yetnikoff took a sanguine view of the affair. 'For an offshoot of Queen it was disappointing,' he conceded. 'But I'm glad I did it. The fact it didn't work? Fuck it!' It was a statement that could have come straight from Freddie. At this moment, Freddie Mercury was not destined to become a solo superstar.

Above: The Six Million Dollar Man. Facing the press at the launch of *Mr Bad Guy*, spring 1985.
Opposite: Living on my own. Freddie in Rio de Janeiro, January 1985.

HELLO WORLD!

'Queen smoked 'em all. They walked away being the greatest band you'd ever seen in your life.'

FOO FIGHTERS' DAVE GROHL
ON QUEEN AT LIVE AID, 2005

Opposite: His finest hour (or twenty minutes, to be precise).
Live Aid, Wembley Stadium, 13 July 1985.

'Freddie was unique – one of the biggest personalities in the whole of pop music. He was not only a singer but also a fantastic performer, a man of the theatre and someone who constantly transformed himself.'

LADY GAGA, 2011

Freddie hugs Wham's Andrew Ridgeley, Live Aid concert finale.

TIMELINE

1985

13 July: Queen make a sensational appearance at the Live Aid concert at Wembley Stadium, London, which attracts an estimated worldwide television audience of 1.5 billion.

September–April 1986: Recording sessions for A *Kind of Magic* at Musicland Studios, Munich, Mountain Studios, Montreux, and Townhouse Studios, London. It is Queen's first album to be recorded digitally.

November: Freddie 'marries' Jane Seymour at a charity fashion show at the Albert Hall, London.

1986

January–February: Freddie records three tracks for the album version of Dave Clark's stage musical *Time*.

7 March: The film *Highlander* is released in the US, using several songs from the upcoming *A Kind of Magic* on the soundtrack.

9 April: World premiere of Dave Clark's musical *Time* at the Dominion Theatre, London.

April: *Time* concept album is released.

6 May: Freddie's single 'Time' is released.

2 June: *A Kind of Magic* is released – a UK #1, selling 100,000 copies in its first week.

7 June–9 August: Queen's *Magic* tour of Europe, which would be the last by the band with Freddie.

9 August: Freddie's final live gig with Queen, at Knebworth Park, Stevenage, England, in front of an estimated crowd of up to 200,000.

29 August: *Highlander* is released in the UK.

1 December: Queen release *Live Magic,* recorded during the *Magic* tour.

'Thank God that's over.'

FM'S FIRST WORDS AFTER QUEEN PLAYED LIVE AID, 13 JULY 1985

There was a fleeting moment during Queen's performance at Live Aid when it seemed as if Freddie Mercury had exhausted his endless supply of stage moves. Queen had been playing for eleven minutes, and Freddie had done the lot. He had pumped his arms as if jogging on an invisible treadmill. He'd marched across the stage with that familiar loping gait – think Led Zeppelin's Robert Plant crossed with Liza Minnelli in *Cabaret*. And he'd wielded his microphone stand like an imaginary guitar, a makeshift sword and a substitute penis.

Finally, in the absence of anything else to do, Freddie turned round, bent down and briefly offered his denim-clad backside to the 72,000-strong audience. The crowd roared, Freddie grinned and he was off again …

Queen triumphed at Live Aid in 1985, but the previous year had ended on a flat note for the band. Their final release of 1984 had been the festive single 'Thank God It's Christmas'. But it didn't stand a chance as Bob Geldof, lead singer of the Boomtown Rats, and Ultravox vocalist Midge Ure had nagged, coaxed and bullied around forty pop stars including Phil Collins, Boy George, Sting, Bono, George Michael and various members of Duran Duran and Spandau Ballet into forming a charity 'supergroup'. Calling themselves Band Aid, they recorded the song 'Do They Know It's Christmas?' to raise money for Ethiopian famine relief. The single went straight to number one in the UK upon its release in December 1984.

Opposite: Queen in 'three days of intensive rehearsals' before Live Aid, Shaw Theatre, London, July 1985.

TV news reports had brought disturbing images of drought-stricken Ethiopia into the nation's living rooms. Band Aid was an opportunity, then, for Britain's pampered pop stars to raise money for those much less fortunate. Freddie, arguably the most pampered of the lot, joked that he had been excluded from Band Aid for being 'too old'. In reality, he was a little aggrieved not to have been asked. Others wondered whether Queen had been passed over because of their recent shows in segregated South Africa.

However, the famously persistent Geldof was not done yet; in spring 1985 he announced Live Aid, a charity concert to be held at London's Wembley Stadium. Geldof wanted Queen, but was initially told they would not be available: the *Works* tour was drawing to a close, and the group was planning at least six months off. 'We were all getting very despondent and we all wanted to do different things,' admitted Freddie. 'We were so jaded,' added Roger Taylor.

Eventually, Geldof cornered Brian May at an industry awards ceremony and browbeat him into submission. Brian agreed in principle to play the show but had to persuade the others, notably Freddie. 'Queen were not a political band and were not known for doing things for a good cause,' Peter Hince told me. 'It was all about, "Buy the record, see the show … Forget the rest." I think Freddie had to be talked into doing Live Aid.'

Once they had committed, though, Queen prepared rigorously. They booked the Shaw Theatre near Kings Cross for three days of intensive rehearsals. Each act at Live Aid was allotted twenty minutes. Several plastic clocks were placed in front of the rehearsal stage, so Queen could time their performance to the last second. They were due to perform in daylight without their usual lighting rig, PA and pyrotechnics. It had to be all about the songs.

Heated arguments ensued before Queen found a simple solution: play the hits.

In the run-up to Live Aid, the band made itself unusually available to the press. One BBC reporter asked the obvious question: was playing Live Aid about supporting a good cause or keeping Queen's profile high? 'Honestly,' replied Freddie, who knew that old rivals Elton John and David Bowie were appearing, 'it's a bit of both.' 'It wasn't a career move,' insisted Roger in 2013. 'But of course that's in the back of everybody's mind.'

Live Aid took place on 13 July 1985. The scale of the event was beyond anything Queen had envisaged when they signed up. Besides the concert at Wembley, a parallel show was staged at Philadelphia's JFK Stadium, featuring, among others, Bob Dylan, the Beach Boys and a reunited Led Zeppelin. Performances from both concerts would be beamed around the globe by satellite to a potential audience of 1.5 billion.

Queen were not due on stage until the early evening. In the meantime, the good, the bad and the indifferent of 1980s rock and pop, including Status Quo, the Style Council, Adam Ant, Sting, Phil Collins and U2, performed their allotted twenty minutes. There was enough goodwill in the stadium to ensure everyone went down well. But some still went down better than others. To keep everyone on schedule, a set of traffic lights at the side of the stage flashed from green to amber when each act's time was up, and from amber to red, as a final warning the power would be cut if they didn't get off.

Freddie arrived at Wembley an hour before Queen were due on. He was suffering from a virulent but unspecified throat condition and his doctor had advised him not to sing. Three weeks earlier, BBC Radio 1 DJ Simon Bates had interviewed Freddie, who had confessed he had been working – and playing – too hard, and insisted on showing the DJ his mottled and discoloured tongue. 'It was the unhealthiest sight I'd ever seen,' said Bates.

Freddie's ailments were forgotten, though, when he jogged onstage at 6.40 p.m. to give the most memorable performance of his life. A homemade banner reading 'Hello World!' fluttered in the crowd. It could have been made for Queen. The stars had aligned in the band's favour: there were, potentially, over a billion people watching around the globe and Queen's sound engineer had sneakily removed the limiters on the stadium PA. This ensured that Queen would be louder than everyone else.

The performance began with Freddie at the Steinway piano picking out the opening flourishes to 'Bohemian Rhapsody'. Then, just as the song was about to shift gear, it stopped short and segued into 'Radio Ga Ga'. Unlike other acts who had played their new single and a couple of hits, Queen had devised a medley of as many hits or parts of hits as they could jam into twenty minutes. Bob Geldof had billed Live Aid as 'a global jukebox' and Queen were fulfilling the brief to perfection.

Below: Freddie backstage at Wembley with his then new partner Jim Hutton (right).
Opposite: Will you do the fandango? Having fun with a BBC cameraman during 'Hammer to Fall' at Live Aid.

'I find even when people have let you down, you just want to go on stage. It's very gratifying to know that all sorts of people want you.'

FM, 1985

The band was aware the Live Aid audience was not exclusively their audience. But, to their amazement, thousands of pairs of hands began clapping in unison overhead during 'Radio Ga Ga', just like the choreographed army in the song's video. Perversely, a song about the superiority of radio to television had been turned into a hit by the power of a video seen on TV.

From that moment, Queen were on a victory lap. A gloriously messy 'Hammer to Fall' saw Freddie teasing a BBC cameraman and grinning into his lens, before 'Crazy Little Thing Called Love' prompted the audience to break into an a cappella singalong. The crowd hardly had time to catch their collective breath before 'We Will Rock You' led into 'We Are the Champions' and Freddie was standing at the edge of the stage blowing them all goodnight kisses. Queen's mantra when it came to playing live was: 'blind 'em and deafen 'em'. It never failed.

Three hours later, Brian and Freddie returned to the stage to perform 'Is This the World We Created …?', a gentle ballad from *The Works* about poverty and man's inhumanity to man. It was a well-intentioned gesture, but it couldn't compete with what they had achieved earlier.

'Queen were absolutely the best band on the day,' said Bob Geldof. 'And it was the perfect stage for Freddie. He could ponce about in front of the whole world.' According to some, Elton John cornered Queen after they had come offstage and screamed, 'You bastards! You stole the show!' They had. Not only from Elton, Bowie, the Who and Paul McCartney, all of whom had to follow them, but also from Bob Dylan and Led Zeppelin whose shambolic performances in Philadelphia were among the day's 'misses'.

That night, Freddie left the Live Aid after-show party early and went home with friends to watch a video of the Wembley concert. Comfortably numb after consuming a river of his favourite tipple, Stolichnaya vodka, he caught up on the performances he had missed earlier; joking and bitching about his rivals, he was quietly proud that Queen had outdone them all.

Freddie's guests that night included the British actor John Hurt, who had been at Live Aid and had followed the party to Garden Lodge, and an Irish hairdresser named Jim Hutton. Freddie had met Hutton a few months earlier in a Kensington gay club. His opening gambit was to ask Jim about the size of his penis. Hutton didn't know who Freddie was, ignored the question and told him to stop talking in a fake American accent. It was an amusing if inauspicious start to a relationship that would last until Freddie's death.

Hutton had never been to a rock concert before Live Aid and had never knowingly listened to a Queen record. But before long, he was spending his weekends at Garden Lodge or in Munich. Wherever he had been, he would leave Freddie's world behind every Monday morning to catch a bus to the Savoy Hotel where he worked as a barber. The relationship was the first sign of Freddie slowing down his manic private life. After Live Aid, though, the notion of Queen slowing down seemed ridiculous.

Left: Performing 'Is This the World We Created …?' with Brian May at Live Aid.
Opposite: Pop royalty. Freddie with George Michael, Paul McCartney, Bono, Bob Geldof and others, Live Aid finale.

Queen's planned six-month break shrank to six weeks. By September they were back in Munich recording a new single and celebrating Freddie's thirty-ninth birthday. He hired his favourite club, Old Mrs Henderson, had it redecorated and then paid for two hundred guests to fly in from London. As he had said many times before, 'Fuck the cost! Let us live a little.'

The new single, 'One Vision', was inspired by a combination of the late civil rights leader Martin Luther King, Jr. and the band's experience at Live Aid. A showboating hard rock song with an immediate chorus, its message was one of communal peace and love. 'One Vision' gave Queen another top ten hit in the UK and across Europe. 'I got a sort of new-found force,' admitted Freddie. 'Suddenly, there was more left in Queen.'

As before with *The Works*, it was a movie project that was the catalyst for Queen's next album. Australian film director Russell Mulcahy built his reputation shooting videos for Elton John and Duran Duran, before taking on the fantasy drama *Highlander*, a tale of time-travelling immortals starring Sean Connery and Christopher Lambert. Mulcahy needed a dramatic soundtrack. 'I thought about one band – Queen,' he said. 'They write strong, anthemic songs and this movie needs their energy.'

Queen split into two camps to work on the soundtrack. Freddie and John were paired with Mack in Munich, while Brian and Roger worked with the Mountain Studios resident engineer David Richards in Montreux. But midway through the sessions Queen decided their new album shouldn't be a film soundtrack after all.

Instead, the finished album, *A Kind of Magic*, contained alternative versions of songs used in *Highlander* as well as tracks that had nothing to do with the film. The standout was Brian's reflective 'Who Wants to Live Forever', one of the *Highlander* songs. But the album's schizophrenic nature was obvious in the void between Brian's gothic heavy metal song 'Gimme the Prize (Kurgan's Theme)', which also featured in the movie, and Freddie and John's 'Pain Is So Close to Pleasure', which did not, and which sounded like a Motown tribute.

'We had to try to bring two projects together,' admitted Freddie at the time. 'We were fighting as to who liked which songs. So we couldn't agree at all.' Freddie and Mack spent days painstakingly recording the brawny hard rocker 'Princes of the Universe'. But the song was released as a single only in North America, where it barely registered.

In the UK, Queen released the title track instead. 'A Kind of Magic' was a Roger Taylor composition. With his blessing,

'I like to write songs for fun, for modern consumption. People can discard them like a used tissue afterwards. You listen to it, like it, discard it, then on to the next.'

FM, 1981

Freddie reworked the song and added a dance beat to it while Roger was away on holiday. 'He said [to Roger], "You bugger off, while I make it a hit,"' recalled Brian. Sure enough, when 'A Kind of Magic' came out in March 1986 it reached number three.

The album of the same name arrived three months later. Queen may have triumphed at Live Aid, but not everyone was on side. According to *The Times*, their new release was 'as chic as a set of flying ducks on the wall'. But *A Kind of Magic* sold 100,000 copies in its first week and gave Queen their first number one album in the UK since *The Game* six years earlier.

The album delivered two further UK hits – 'Who Wants to Live Forever' and 'Friends Will Be Friends'. Meanwhile, *Highlander* mimicked Queen's mid-1980s career trajectory: a box-office hit in Europe but rather a flop in America.

It's hard not to wonder whether *A Kind of Magic*'s success was down to the ripple effects of Live Aid as much as the music itself. 'I don't know what Queen stand for,' admitted Freddie at the time. 'It's four different writers who write very different songs.' But whatever doubts each of the band members might have been harbouring, it would have been foolish for Queen to split up now.

Queen's *A Kind of Magic* had been preceded in May by another Freddie Mercury solo single, 'Time'. It was taken from the cast album of the sci-fi rock musical *Time*, produced by Freddie's friend Dave Clark, former leader of the Dave Clark Five who had achieved major success in the 1960s.

Time had its premiere at London's Dominion Theatre (later home to the Queen tribute musical *We Will Rock You*) in April 1986. Clark had offered Freddie the lead role, but he had declined, and Cliff Richard took the part instead. Freddie, however, attended the premiere. In the interval he commandeered an ice cream seller's cart and distributed

its contents free of charge. Audience members stared at the moustachioed man throwing tubs of ice cream into the stalls and wondered whether it was *really* Freddie Mercury.

The single 'Time' was a typically grand Freddie Mercury ballad, but failed to break into the top thirty. Nevertheless, it introduced Freddie to songwriter, producer and musician Mike Moran, who would play a significant part in his next non-Queen venture. Moran had been scoring music for films and TV since the early 1970s, and had overseen the rest of the *Time* album, to which Freddie contributed 'In My Defence' as well as the title track.

Dave Clark persuaded Freddie to record with Moran, promising him that if he didn't like what they did he could rerecord the songs with Mack in Munich. The day before the session Mike was involved in a car accident. Determined not to cancel, he arrived at London's Abbey Road Studios with sprained wrists and four broken ribs, and was heavily dosed up on morphine.

Moran insisted that Freddie not be told about his condition. But as it approached midnight and Freddie demanded yet another take of 'In My Defence', Moran's painkillers were wearing off and Dave Clark spoke up.

'Freddie replied, "Oh, really, you should have said something, dear,"' recalled Moran. Freddie then turned to his personal assistant, Peter Freestone. 'Freddie said, "Give her a line [of cocaine] and a large Stolly, she'll be fine."' It was Mike Moran's initiation into Freddie Mercury's world. The two left the session promising to work together again.

However, Freddie's solo plans were held back while Queen prepared for more live shows. What no one could have imagined then was that the *Magic* tour would be Queen's last with Freddie Mercury. The dates began in June 1986 in Sweden before moving on to other European countries including France, West Germany, Ireland, Spain and the UK. Once again, the US, where *A Kind of Magic* had only just managed to scrape into the top fifty, was excluded from the itinerary.

The tour lived up to Freddie's old aphorism, 'the bigger, the better in everything, dear'. Queen were booked to play several stadiums and had commissioned a purpose-built 160-feet wide stage which included two large ramps on which Freddie could pose, preen and generally 'be Freddie'.

Getting high on the set of the 'Friends Will Be Friends' video shoot, JVC studios, Wembley, May 1986. As with the video for 'Radio Ga Ga', the audience is made up of invited fan club members.

As if to prove this, Freddie had acquired a new outfit for the show's finale: a jewel-encrusted crown and a velvet, silk and ermine gown, modelled on Napoleon's 1804 coronation robe, and created by his friend the costume designer Diana Moseley. Freddie debuted his majestic ensemble at the Paris Hippodrome show in June, arriving on stage wearing it at the end of 'We Are the Champions'.

If the humour was slightly lost in a republic that had executed its royal family in the eighteenth century and has mixed feelings about Napoleon, then it went over better at home. Queen had sold all 150,000 tickets for their two nights at Wembley Stadium in July. But their gargantuan stage set was too big for the venue.

In a scene reminiscent of the 1984 satirical rock movie *This Is Spinal Tap*, the road crew discovered that Queen's 20-feet by 30-feet video screen would not fit in the gap between the top of the stage and the stadium roof. According to some, a small part of the world-famous venue was surreptitiously removed (that is to say, sawn off) to make room for the screen.

Offstage, Queen maintained their reputation as rock's greatest party band by throwing an after-show bash at a brothel in Cologne, and another in London where guests were served by waiters and waitresses who wore nothing but body paint. 'But we were utterly in control when we had the responsibility of playing to people,' Brian May told me. 'We played hard, yes, but we were completely in control on stage.'

Freddie was still fuelling himself with drugs and alcohol, but his other recreations included lengthy games of Scrabble, a reliable way to kill time as the *Magic* tour crossed Europe. 'Freddie and I loved Scrabble,' said Roger Taylor. 'We all played, but it got a bit too serious so the others dropped out. Freddie was brilliant because he could score more with fewer tiles.' One of his favourite Scrabble words, 'innuendo', would give Queen a title for their final album released during Freddie's lifetime.

The demand for tickets on the UK leg of the tour was so great Queen could have played further nights in Newcastle, Manchester and Wembley. Instead a final show was arranged for 9 August at Knebworth Park, the stately home in Hertfordshire where Led Zeppelin had played their last UK dates seven years earlier. It would be Freddie's final Queen show.

The official attendance figure for Knebworth was 120,000, but in reality the audience was closer to 200,000. Queen's support acts included old stagers Status Quo and brighter, younger things Big Country and Belouis Some.

After battering the senses with lights, dry ice and 'One Vision', Queen hardly let up with 'Tie Your Mother Down', 'Seven Seas of Rhye' and 'Under Pressure', before throwing in a medley of covers including Little Richard's 'Tutti Frutti' and Shirley Bassey's 'Big Spender'. But the set list mostly adhered to the band's own hits – old and new. During 'A Kind of Magic' helium-filled inflatables of the cartoon band members as seen on the album cover bobbed over the audience. At Wembley, the blow-up Freddie broke its moorings, sailed out of the stadium and later crash-landed in a garden in Chelmsford, more than 40 miles away.

Everything about the *Magic* tour was larger than life, including Freddie, who seemed to grow as a performer as if filling Queen's new stage. With his moustache and gym vest (now augmented by a canary yellow bolero jacket), he looked much like he did at Live Aid, adding to the impression that these shows were Queen at Live Aid *again*, just with a longer set list.

At a time when so many rock musicians were taking themselves so seriously, it was amusing to see a singer having fun while delivering a performance that left his rivals in the dust. 'Freddie's sense of humour *was* underestimated,' insisted Brian May. 'I don't think the press realised how willing he was to take the piss out of himself.'

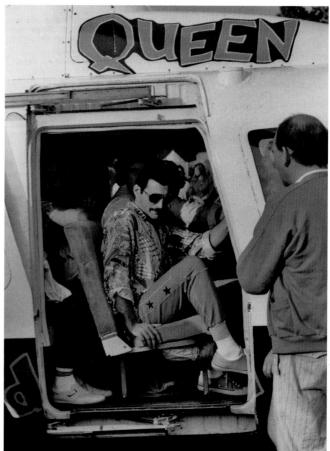

The audience's euphoric reaction when the headliners arrived on site by helicopter made it clear to the other artists that this was very much Queen's show.

That euphoria lasted from the opening bars of 'One Vision' to the final strains of 'God Save the Queen' and the spectacle of Freddie parading in his custom-made crown and ermine. Some fans, however, spotted John Deacon smashing his bass against his amp at the end of the show, and wondered if all was well. 'Goodnight and sweet dreams,' declared Freddie, the last words he would ever speak on stage during a Queen concert.

Peter Hince had left Queen's entourage a year earlier to begin a new career as a photographer. But he returned temporarily for the *Magic* tour: 'At Knebworth, I somehow felt it was going to be the last for all of us. I had no idea as to Fred's health condition. I just saw it as being the last show for me and them.'

'Freddie said something like, "Oh, I can't fucking do this anymore, my whole body's wracked with pain!"' recalled Brian May. 'But he normally said things like that at the end of a tour, so I don't think we took it seriously.' However, a week before Knebworth at a show in Spain, Freddie had been arguing with John Deacon backstage. 'He said, "I'm not going to be doing this forever. This is probably the last time,"' said Brian, who recalled the band being troubled by his outburst.

However assured Freddie appeared on stage, privately he was concerned that he was becoming too old to play the rock star. He was approaching forty, his hair was thinning slightly and a *Daily Mirror* article had recently teased him about the beginnings of a beer-and-vodka belly ('Flabulous Freddie!' screamed the headline). His four-octave voice was still impeccable, but there were times when you noticed a rasp that had not been there before.

Encroaching old age was one factor, but there was more to it than that. Freddie was also very worried about his health. Nothing was said. But privately his band mates shared his concerns. It would be a few months yet before Freddie would discover the truth.

Previous: King of the castle. Surveying his subjects at Slane Castle, Dublin, 5 July 1986.
Above left: The happy couple. Escorting actress Jane Seymour at the Fashion Aid charity show, London, 6 November 1985.
Above right: Freddie arriving by helicopter for his final Queen show, Knebworth Park, Hertfordshire, 9 August 1986.
Opposite: A kind of magic. In the famous yellow bolero jacket, Forest National, Brussels, 16 June 1986.
Overleaf: Champion of the world. Freddie Mercury, Wembley Stadium, 12 July 1986.

'All the costumes and everything, a lot of people took it so seriously. I didn't give a damn. I thought: "My God, they've read far too much into it."'

FM, 1987

YOU CAN'T TURN BACK THE TIDE

'I have lived a full life, and if I'm dead tomorrow, I don't give a damn. I really have done it all.'

FM, 1987

'He was still spending money and buying things at auction right up to the point that he died, which I thought was hilarious.'

ELTON JOHN ON FM, 2012

TIMELINE

Gone but not forgotten: Floral tributes and messages outside Freddie Mercury's house, Garden Lodge, London.

1987

January: Freddie begins recording sessions at Townhouse Studios for the album *Barcelona*, a collaboration with the world-famous opera singer Montserrat Caballé.

January–February: Freddie records a solo version of the Platters' 1955 hit 'The Great Pretender'.

23 February: 'The Great Pretender' released, making the #4 spot in the UK singles chart.

c. April: Freddie is diagnosed with AIDS.

29 May: First public performance of 'Barcelona' with Montserrat Caballé at the Ku club, Ibiza.

26 October: 'Barcelona' single released, peaking at #8 in the UK chart.

1988

January: Recording begins on Queen's thirteenth studio album, *The Miracle*.

14 April: Freddie appears at a special gala performance of *Time* at the Dominion Theatre, London.

June: Final sessions for *Barcelona*, at Mountain Studios in Montreux.

8 October: Freddie's final live performance, singing three songs with Montserrat Caballé at a Barcelona music festival called La Nit held to celebrate the arrival of the Olympic flag from the Seoul games.

10 October: *Barcelona* album released.

22 October: *Barcelona* enters the UK chart where it spends eight weeks and reaches #15.

1989

January: Final recording sessions for Queen album *The Miracle*.

22 May: *The Miracle* released, topping the album chart in the UK, Austria, Germany, Holland and Switzerland.

4 December: Release of *At the Beeb*, a collection of BBC sessions recorded in 1973.

1990

18 February: Freddie joins the rest of Queen at London's Dominion Theatre to collect the Brit Award for Outstanding Contribution to Music, his last onstage appearance with the band.

March–November: Queen record tracks for their next album, *Innuendo*, at Metropolis Studios, London, and Mountain Studios, Montreux.

November: Queen sign a new US record deal with Hollywood Records.

1991

26 January: 'Innuendo' tops the UK singles chart.

January–May: At Queen's Mountain Studios in Montreux, Freddie records a number of songs, including 'A Winter's Tale', 'Mother Love' and 'You Don't Fool Me', all of which will be included on the posthumous Queen album *Made in Heaven*.

5 February: *Innuendo* released, topping five European charts including the UK.

30 May: Freddie films what will be his final video for Queen, 'These Are the Days of Our Lives'.

Summer: Increasingly ill, Freddie retires to Garden Lodge, his home in Kensington, London.

14 October: Single 'The Show Must Go On' released.

28 October: The *Greatest Hits II* compilation is the last Queen album to be released during Freddie's lifetime.

22 November: Having not made it public previously, Freddie announces he is terminally ill with AIDS.

24 November: Freddie Mercury dies peacefully at his London home, from bronchopneumonia brought on by AIDS.

'Most of the stuff I do is pretending, it's like acting, you know, so you go on stage and I pretend to be a macho man and all that.'

FM, 1987

In 1956, when Farrokh Bulsara was just a schoolboy in India, the American vocal group the Platters topped the US charts with 'The Great Pretender'. A song about loneliness and heartbreak, putting on a brave face and trying to convince the world you're doing fine, it could almost have been written for the future Freddie Mercury.

The song had been covered by many performers, including Gene Pitney and Roy Orbison, before Freddie enlisted Mike Moran in January 1987 to help him record his defining version of the Platters' hit. Ignoring the muted reaction to *Mr Bad Guy*, he was planning on making another solo record. 'Freddie said, "I'm taking a year off from Queen and I want to do something crazy,"' Moran told me. 'He thought "The Great Pretender" would be a bit of light relief – "And if it's a hit, then that's marvellous, dear."'

Recording the song at Moran's home studio in Hertfordshire, Freddie might have perceived it as 'light relief', but he threw himself into the work. 'There was one rule with

Freddie – and that was that nothing was ever a rehearsal,' said Moran. 'He would give everything one hundred per cent, whatever he was doing.'

Once Freddie stepped into the recording booth, Moran was amazed by how his friend transformed into 'Freddie Mercury'. 'He turned into this monster of a man. Like Arnold Schwarzenegger, but with a great voice. He gave every take an incredible amount of passion and determination.'

'The Great Pretender' appeared as a single in February 1987 and reached the UK top five. David Mallet directed a highly theatrical video in which Freddie, flanked by life-size cutouts of himself, hammed it up alongside Peter Straker and Roger Taylor as suspiciously masculine 'female' backing singers. The film also showed clips of Freddie through the years in all his guises, raising the question: which one was the real Freddie Mercury?

Freddie had already booked London's Townhouse Studios, and he and Moran pushed on with material for a second solo album. But then came an unexpected turn of events. When Queen were in Madrid on the *Magic* tour, a TV reporter asked Freddie to name his favourite Spanish singer. He chose the great opera star Montserrat Caballé. It wasn't a pre-rehearsed answer. Freddie was a genuine fan.

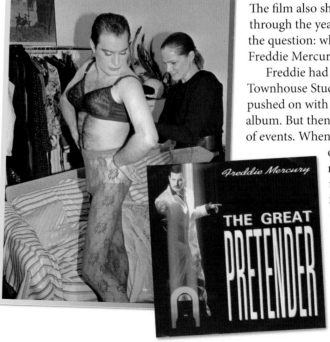

Opposite: Pretty in pink. Filming the video for 'The Great Pretender' in 1987.
Right: Freddie in bra and stockings on the set of 'The Great Pretender'.

169

Montserrat turned out to be wonderful company with, according to Mike Moran, a 'very wicked sense of humour'. 'She jokes and she swears and she doesn't take herself too seriously,' as Freddie put it. After lunch and buoyed by several glasses of champagne, Freddie told the singer that he had brought her a gift: a cassette recording of 'me pretending to be you'.

The recording, 'Exercises in Free Love', was a piano instrumental over which Freddie sang what Moran called 'various oohs and aahs' in a falsetto voice. It had been recorded quickly in the small hours of the morning, when the pair suddenly realised they needed to come up with a B-side for 'The Great Pretender'.

Caballé, however, presumed Freddie had written the song specifically for her to record. No one wanted to correct her. After listening intently, she announced she would perform 'Exercises in Free Love' at her recital in Covent Garden in three weeks' time – and that Mike Moran would be her accompanist.

'It was nerve-wracking,' said Moran. 'But it worked. She performed "Exercises in Free Love" as her third encore, and I played piano.' After the show 'Montsy', as Freddie and Mike called her, joined them at Freddie's home, Garden Lodge, for dinner, more champagne, and singing around the piano. It was then that she suggested they record a song together, and soon.

It was a daunting proposition. 'There was a lot of, "Oh God! What do we do now?"' admitted Moran. 'The problem was there was no template for this sort of thing.' This was three years before José Carreras, Placido Domingo and Luciano Pavarotti topped the UK charts with the first of their 'Three Tenors' concert albums and more than a decade before Andrea Bocelli began having classical crossover hits in the UK and US.

'She has that same kind of emotion as Aretha Franklin,' he said later. But he thought no more of it. Then the band's Spanish promoter contacted Caballé's management and told them about her famous fan.

'And then suddenly Freddie gets a phone call from Montserrat asking him to come to Barcelona for a lunch meeting,' said Mike Moran. Freddie agreed but insisted on taking Mike for moral support. The pair were waiting in the restaurant of the Ritz Hotel (since renamed El Palace) when Caballé swept in 'like the Queen of Sheba', to be greeted by an attentive maître d'hôtel and a line of bowing waiters. For once, Freddie Mercury was not the most important person in the room.

But Freddie and Moran went back to the piano at Garden Lodge and composed what would become 'Barcelona'. Their only stipulations were that Freddie should not try to sing opera, and Montserrat should not try to sing rock 'n' roll. It was, claimed Moran, 'a mammoth exercise'. Recordings were made in which Freddie sang both his and Montserrat's vocal parts, and the tapes were sent by courier to Spain for Montserrat's approval.

The piece underwent countless refinements before being recorded at the Townhouse. Prior to Caballé's arrival at the studio, Freddie insisted the women's lavatory be redecorated and filled with flowers: 'It was like we were having a visit from the Queen,' said Moran.

'Barcelona', a song about the first meeting between future lovers, somehow bridged the divide between opera and pop, having all the pomp and ceremony of the former and the immediacy of the latter. Freddie did not use his trademark falsetto; he sang in his natural baritone to complement Montserrat's swooping soprano. He never tried to out-sing her; it would have been impossible. But instead he bluffed his way through with great nerve and boundless enthusiasm. 'His technique was astonishing,' said Caballé. 'He was able to find the right colouring or expressive nuance for each word.'

The duo performed 'Barcelona' for the first time at the Ibiza Festival in San Antonio's Ku club in May 1987. Although backed by a small orchestra rather than Brian May and dressed in a black tuxedo rather than jeans and

a tight vest, Freddie still looked as if he was struggling to stop himself promenading across the stage like he did with Queen. At the end the pair received a standing ovation.

Backstage, though, Freddie had been in great distress. A large red mark had appeared on his cheek and it was disguised only with an extra layer of make-up. It had been diagnosed as Kaposi's sarcoma, a cancerous skin lesion that often afflicted those infected with HIV (Human Immunodeficiency Virus). By the mid-1980s, HIV and the disease into which it developed, AIDS (Acquired Immune Deficiency Syndrome), were having a profound and devastating effect, particularly, but not exclusively, on the gay community. Although the virus can now be managed with medication, at the time an HIV-positive diagnosis was terminal.

Anyone who asked after Freddie's health that evening received vague if well-rehearsed answers: he had been drinking too much, he had a liver complaint, "there was nothing to worry about, dear …"

However, in the UK the tabloid press was already circling. Just after Queen played Knebworth, in August 1986, the *News of the World* ran a story claiming Freddie had been tested for HIV at a Harley Street clinic. Freddie denied it, but he knew it was only a matter of time before the truth was discovered.

Above: 'She has a very wicked sense of humour.' Freddie and Montserrat at the piano, 1987.
Opposite: Cool cat. September 1987.

'I was extremely promiscuous, but I've stopped all of that. I'm an old bird now, dear.'

FM, 1987

Since meeting Jim Hutton in 1984, Freddie had been spending less time in the clubs in Munich and New York. 'He tried to be faithful,' said Peter Freestone, 'because it upset Jim when he wasn't.' Then, in November 1986, Freddie's ex-lover Tony Bastin, the inspiration for 'Play the Game', died of AIDS. It is understood that Freddie had taken the test in spring 1987. Some claim he was diagnosed HIV positive; others that he was told by his doctor that he had already contracted AIDS.

Freddie told Jim Hutton and fellow Garden Lodge residents Peter Freestone and Joe Fanelli. Everyone was sworn to secrecy. He also informed Jim Beach, but with one proviso: Beach was forbidden to tell the rest of Queen. At a time when AIDS was still reported in the press as 'a gay plague', Freddie, besides protecting his privacy, wanted to shield his band mates from the stigma and prejudice. In doing so, he placed the rest of Queen in an extraordinarily difficult position.

In May, the *Sun* newspaper claimed Freddie had told his now ex-personal manager Paul Prenter that he was terrified of dying of AIDS. Over the next few days, the *Sun* ran stories in which Prenter discussed Freddie's drug use and sex life and named Jim Hutton as his current boyfriend. This last detail alone caused embarrassment. Jim had now moved into Garden Lodge. But when Freddie's parents visited, their son pretended Jim was his gardener. His sexuality might have been an open secret in the music business, but it would compromise the Bulsaras' Parsee faith.

Prenter's betrayal was especially hard to take. Queen had fired him in 1985, but Freddie put him on his payroll, and, when the work ended, let him live rent-free flat in his old flat. Their friendship eventually soured when Prenter threw a party in which the flat's furnishings were either damaged or destroyed. But the *Sun* exposé undermined Freddie's plan to keep his condition secret from the rest of the band.

Despite knowing that he probably did not have long to live, Freddie took a pragmatic view of the situation. 'He never, ever spent time talking to me, wondering where he got it, which country, which city,' said Peter Freestone. 'It was a fact, it was happening. He knew he was going to die, so why waste time regretting?'

With cruelly bad timing, Freddie's diagnosis coincided with his biggest solo

hits. 'The Great Pretender' was followed by another UK top ten single, 'Barcelona', in October 1987. The city had been awarded the 1992 Olympic Games, and 'Barcelona' was one of the contenders for the Olympic theme song. A collaborative album with 'Montsy' now superseded plans for a more conventional solo project. 'Freddie said, "This has come at the perfect time in my life – to be able to do something different,"' said Mike Moran.

Sessions for the album, also called *Barcelona*, had to accommodate Caballé's hectic performing schedule, which meant it took over a year to record. Compositions such as 'Ensueño' and 'The Fallen Priest' were lushly romantic, orchestrated pieces constructed around what Freddie jokingly called Mike Moran's 'flashy piano things'. This was quite unlike the music he had made with Queen, but, like dancing with the Royal Ballet, it was another challenge, another adventure.

Barcelona, the album, was released in October 1988 and became a UK top twenty hit. But it was about more than sales. 'Freddie's attitude was, "What the hell?"' said Mike Moran. 'It was worth a year of our lives, and it was something he was very proud of.'

On 8 October, two days before the album's release, Freddie made his last ever live appearance, at an outdoor concert in Barcelona to welcome the Olympic flag from the recently concluded Seoul games. Again he performed with Caballé, and it was another grand spectacle. But, as before at the Ku club, they mimed rather than sang live.

The following day, Freddie granted a brief interview to the UK music magazine *Q*. He looked tired and distracted and chain-smoked cigarettes. Freddie insisted the songs were too complex to sing live without adequate rehearsal time, hence the miming. When the interviewer teasingly asked if it was wise for an opera singer to risk his voice by smoking, Freddie grinned, puffed a plume of smoke and offered a good-natured "Oh, *do* fuck off!"

Opposite: 'This has come at the perfect time in my life.' The pop diva and the opera star, 1988.
Overleaf: Freddie's final live performance, La Nit, at the Barcelona Music Festival, 8 October 1988.

While Freddie was busy with Montserrat Caballé, the rest of Queen had attended to their own solo projects, which in Brian May's case included a relationship with actress Anita Dobson, star of the British TV soap *EastEnders*. Brian, who was still married, now found himself a target for the tabloid press.

He channelled his anger at this episode into a new song called 'Scandal' for Queen's next album, *The Miracle*. Its story of a private life turned into a public freak show was, of course, also applicable to Freddie. Yet, having all been raised with that very British respect for discretion, none of the band members – including Freddie – would discuss his situation directly when Queen returned to the studio in January 1988.

The Miracle would take just under a year to record in London and Montreux with co-producer David Richards. In April, Freddie appeared at a gala performance of *Time* staged to raise funds for the HIV/AIDS charity the Terrence Higgins Trust. His band mates speculated about his

health, but as Roger Taylor explained, 'We knew he was ill. But we kept hoping it might be something else.'

Before the sessions began, Queen passed a new edict: every song would be credited to the four of them, regardless of whose idea it was. 'We made a decision we should have made fifteen years ago,' admitted Brian May. This eased some of the tension that came from having, as Brian put it, 'four artists trying to paint on the same canvas'.

But it was often obvious who brought what to the studio. Only Freddie could have conceived 'Khashoggi's Ship', a song inspired by the billionaire arms dealer Adnan Khashoggi's $100 million yacht. Freddie's looming mortality had not negated his love of the high life. This was the man who had once asked an interviewer, "What's a mortgage, darling?"

Above: Soap opera. With *EastEnders* actress and Brian May's partner Anita Dobson, Ibiza, September 1987.
Opposite: Freddie and Mary Austin at the Ivor Novello Awards, London, 15 April 1987. Queen won a special award for outstanding contribution to British music.

'*From now on dressing up crazily on stage is out. I don't think a forty-two-year-old man should be running around in his leotard any more.*'

FM, 1987

Other songs on *The Miracle* were more reflective. The title track was a trite ballad in which Freddie marvelled at the wonders of Mother Nature and prayed for an end to all wars. On 'Was It All Worth It', he questioned the wisdom of spending one's life making music and the sacrifices such a choice entailed.

It had been two years since Freddie had recorded with Queen, during which he had made an album with one of the world's biggest opera stars. So there was an inevitable period of readjustment. 'It was OK, but we had our various fisticuffs,' he said diplomatically.

Upon its release in June 1989, *The Miracle* reached number one in the UK and twenty-four in the US. 'Somewhere out there, there's a cruel prankster circulating a rumour that *The Miracle* is Queen's official return to hard rock,' complained *Rolling Stone*. 'Well, off with his head …'

Promoting the album led to awkward questions. In a BBC Radio 1 interview, Freddie revealed that the rest of Queen wanted to tour but he did not. He wouldn't say why. Later, the others offered vague excuses, including that Freddie considered himself too old to be leaping around on stage – unlike, say, the forty-six-year-old Mick Jagger, who was leading the Rolling Stones on a comeback tour at the time.

In Germany, a reporter asked Roger Taylor outright whether Freddie had AIDS. Roger dismissed it as 'a stupid rumour'. But the rumours were rife. Mick Rock had not seen Freddie since the early 1980s when he had accompanied him on a night out to New York's most famous gay club, the Anvil, but he, too, heard the singer was ill. 'Two ladies who knew Freddie came up to me in Ronnie Wood's club in New York,' he recalled. 'They said to me, "You know Freddie's not very well …" Without them laying it right out there, it was obvious what was wrong.'

The Miracle would yield four singles, with Brian May's crowing hard rocker 'I Want It All' charting

the highest. Those seeking clues to Freddie's health would have to look closely at the videos. He had grown a beard to disguise the marks on his cheeks, but in the promo for 'Breakthru' still managed to pout, shimmy and play mic-stand guitar on top of a moving steam train.

There would be no tour. But there *would* be more music. *The Miracle* had just reached the shops when Freddie asked to go back into the studio. The others were surprised, but agreed. 'I think right up to the end the studio was his greatest escape,' said Brian.

The sessions for *Innuendo*, the last Queen studio album released during Freddie's lifetime, again took place in London and Montreux. The band worked for three weeks at a stretch followed by two-week breaks. The routine suited Freddie who had now bought a penthouse apartment overlooking Lake Geneva.

There was a time when Freddie couldn't wait to leave squeaky-clean Montreux for the clubs and bars in Munich. Not any more. Since his diagnosis Freddie had avoided his German drug/party buddies including Barbara Valentin. That era was over.

At some point during the *Innuendo* sessions, Freddie finally confirmed his band mates' worst fears and told them he was dying. He could not hide his condition any longer: he had lost a great deal of weight and was suffering with two painful lesions, one on his leg, the other on the ball of his foot, which would soon make walking difficult.

'He said, "I'm going to talk about this only once. I'm going to tell you what's happening, and after this, I don't want to talk about it any more,"' recalled Brian. 'He only asked two things,' said Roger. 'The first was, let's keep working. The other was when he was really sick, just come and visit me.'

But, again, Freddie swore the rest of Queen to secrecy. Having denied

rumours he had AIDS without knowing the truth, they now did know the truth but still had to deny it to the press and even to their families. 'We lied through our teeth to protect his privacy,' admitted Brian.

On 18 February 1990, Freddie made his last public appearance with Queen to collect an Outstanding Contribution to Music Award at the Brit Awards. He looked painfully thin in his duck-egg blue suit and, after Brian's acceptance speech, offered only a hastily whispered 'thank you, goodnight'.

Back in the studio, Freddie refused to be pitied or treated differently. Mindful of his depleted immune system and the risk of infection, he gave up cigarettes and indeed banned anyone else from smoking in his presence. But he still kept a bottle of Stolichnaya on ice from which he would swig between takes.

Above: On the right track. Shooting the 'Breakthru' video with model and Roger Taylor's future partner Debbie Leng, 1989.
Opposite: 'Thank you, goodnight.' Freddie's final TV appearance, the Brit Awards, 1990.

Reassuringly, Queen bickered about their new music, just as they had always done. Freddie's song 'Delilah' was a twee tribute to his favourite cat. Roger loathed it. While recording 'All God's People', Freddie mocked Brian's attempts at a solo until he delivered the perfect take, while Freddie grinned knowingly from behind the studio glass.

Inevitably, there was a valedictory feel to *Innuendo*. Roger Taylor's 'These Are the Days of Our Lives' suggested a man pondering a life well lived. 'The Show Must Go On' was the ultimate curtain call, with Freddie cast as a rock 'n' roll Judy Garland. Brian May, who wrote most of the song, was convinced its title was too predictable and offered to change it. Freddie refused.

When it was time to record the track, Freddie could barely stand. 'I said, "Fred, I don't know if this is going to be possible to sing,"' Brian told *Rolling Stone*. 'And he went, "I'll fucking do it, darling" – vodka down – and went in and killed it.'

Freddie would not talk about his illness, but he was putting it out there in the music. 'Songs like "The Show Must Go On", in my case, or "These Are the Days of Our Lives",

in Roger's case, were things that we gave to Freddie as a way of him working through stuff with us,' said Brian. 'The Show Must Go On' did not stint on the drama or the directness of its message. Other bands in a similar situation might have taken a more tangential approach. That was not the Queen way. They had made their name with unambiguous lyrics like 'We Will Rock You' and 'We Are the Champions', so why change now?

Meanwhile, Jim Beach brokered a new US record deal. Hollywood Records paid $10 million to buy the band out of their Capitol contract. With great foresight, Queen had acquired their back catalogue from Capitol and Hollywood planned to reissue Queen's old albums on CD.

Hollywood Records was part-owned by the Walt Disney Company, whose chief executive, Michael Eisner, opposed the deal on the grounds that Queen had not achieved a US top twenty album hit since *Hot Space* in 1982 and would not tour to support any new release.

'He never seemed to let his illness get him down.
He was always full of humour and enthusiasm.
He would make jokes about it.'

BRIAN MAY, 2015

However, Hollywood's label president, Peter Paterno, saw the value of the Queen catalogue and was desperate to sign them. Then Eisner heard the rumour that Freddie had AIDS. 'He thought we should put a clause in the contract regarding what would happen if Freddie died,' said Paterno. 'I said, "If he does, as morbid as that sounds, that sells records, too."' Paterno was right. Hollywood Records recouped their $10 million within three years of Freddie's death and went on to make much more.

The first taster of Queen's final album with Freddie Mercury was the title track, 'Innuendo', which was released as a single in January 1991. Lasting over six minutes and blending dinosaur-footed heavy rock with choral harmonies and flamenco guitars, the song broke every rule of modern pop music, just like 'Bohemian Rhapsody' had done over fifteen years earlier. And like that song, it went straight to number one in the UK.

The album had been scheduled for release in December of the previous year, but Freddie was too ill to complete it in time. *Innuendo* finally arrived in February 1991. 'What is astounding is that in twenty years Queen have lost none of their appetite for music of the most grandiose banality,' marvelled *The Times*, ensuring an unbroken run of hilariously negative reviews. *Innuendo* gave Queen their third UK number one album in a row. In the US, Hollywood Records' new signings had to make do with number thirty.

By now, though, Freddie's health was deteriorating rapidly. It is tempting, then, to question the wisdom of Queen making videos in which the world could monitor their singer's decline. But, again, it was Freddie who insisted Queen maintain the façade.

In March came the single 'I'm Going Slightly Mad'. The song's cheery lyrics were interpreted through a video in which Freddie disguised his frailness with wigs, geisha-like make-up and a baggy suit. But he had to pad himself out with another layer of clothes under the suit, and needed a

bed on set so he could rest between takes. Fans and critics gawped at his hollow cheeks and wondered how much longer he had.

The tipping point came in May. Just as before, Freddie wanted to keep recording after Queen finished *Innuendo*. His instructions were simple and unsentimental: he would keep recording for as long as he could, and his band mates could finish the songs when he was no longer around. 'He kept saying, "Look, I could pop off at any moment,"' recalled Roger.

Despite the circumstances, the mood during these final sessions in Montreux was upbeat, even joyful. On 22 May, Freddie recorded his final vocal, for the ballad 'Mother Love', a song in which he yearned for the simplicity of childhood. Not wanting to waste a second, Freddie urged Brian to scribble the lyrics on scraps of paper so he could keep singing. But, despite Brian's protests, he kept pushing himself with one take after another, determined to improve on what he had already done.

Fortified by another hit of vodka, Freddie eventually gave an extraordinary performance. 'The middle eight of "Mother Love" soars to incredible heights,' said Brian. 'And this is a man who can't really stand any more without incredible pain, and is very weak, and has no flesh on his bones, and you can hear the power, the will that's he's got.' 'Mother Love' would remain unfinished. Freddie knew this was the end. But that didn't stop his black humour. 'He said, "Oh, Brian, I can't do any more. I'm dying here,"' Brian told *Q* magazine.

A week later, Freddie was in Limehouse Studios in London to film a video for the single 'These Are the Days of Our Lives', knowing there was every chance he would not be alive when it came out. Queen had also commissioned an animated film should Freddie be too sick to appear in the video. Discovering this had convinced him to take part.

'Seeing the end result, I sometimes think it should have never been made,' wrote Peter Freestone in 1998. 'You can see how frail and ill he looks.' In the black-and-white performance video, Freddie didn't bother masking his gaunt appearance with wigs, costumes or heavy make-up. It was too late for that. He clenched his fists, cocked his head and stared into the camera before delivering the song's payoff line, 'I still love you …' with a coy smile and a brief pout.

'We lied through our teeth to protect his privacy.' Brian May on Freddie, shown here in 1989.

In the British press, speculation about Freddie's health intensified. Brian May admitted he was ill but denied that he had AIDS. Undeterred, reporters and photographers camped outside Garden Lodge, waiting for their prey to break cover.

Instead, Freddie closed the door and stayed home. On 5 September he celebrated his forty-fifth and final birthday with a small dinner party. Many of his oldest friends, including the rest of Queen, were absent. But Mike Moran was among those invited. 'Freddie was at the stage where he really wasn't well at all and had become quite reclusive,' he said. 'I don't think he wanted people to see him like that. He wanted them to remember him as he was. So my wife and I felt privileged to be there.'

Where Freddie's dinner parties once carried on long into the night, he excused himself early from this one. 'He said, "I'm a bit tired now," and he went off to bed. It had been a lovely evening, but I had a feeling that would be the last time we'd see him.'

It was not long after that when Freddie announced to his friends at Garden Lodge that he would no longer be taking his medication. He could no longer perform or record music, was too weak to walk and was losing his sight. 'The disease killed the showman, and without the showman, the person was unable to continue,' commented Peter Freestone.

Inevitably, Queen's latest single, 'The Show Must Go On', with its dramatic tale of strength through adversity, invited more ghoulish speculation. This time Freddie appeared in the video only in a montage of old clips.

Mary Austin joined the others at Garden Lodge in helping to care for Freddie during the final weeks of his life. Brian and Roger visited. Freddie was confined to his bedroom, but when his eyesight allowed it, he could still see the garden he loved from the window. When his sight failed,

The show must go on? Promoting the *Innuendo* album, 1990.

Brian described the scene for him. 'The word "goodbye" didn't happen, but we reached a very peaceful place,' said Brian of his final visit.

During a final meeting with Jim Beach, whom Freddie had nominated as an executor of his will, Freddie agreed to release a public statement, at midnight on Friday 22 November. It read: 'Following the enormous conjecture in the press over the last two weeks, I wish to confirm that I have been tested HIV positive and have AIDS. I felt it correct to keep this information private to date in order to protect the privacy of those around me. However, the time has now come for my friends and fans around the world to know the truth and I hope everyone will join with me, my doctors and all those worldwide in the fight against this terrible disease.'

Some close to Freddie expressed surprise that he had agreed to make the news public. Queen and their management insisted it was Freddie's attempt to regain control and prevent the press from exposing the truth after his death. 'It was absolutely the right thing to do,' said Roger.

The following day Freddie drifted in and out of consciousness. Mary Austin and Dave Clark took it in turns with Jim Hutton, Joe Fanelli and Peter Freestone to sit by his bedside. On Sunday 24 November, Freddie's doctor visited and told them it would be a matter of days. In fact, it was a matter of hours.

Roger was on Kensington High Street on his way to Garden Lodge when he received the call. It was Peter Freestone: 'I was about 300 yards up the street when Peter rang me and said, "Don't come, he's just gone."' Freddie had died at 6.48 p.m.

'He lived life to the full. He devoured life. He celebrated every minute. And, like a great comet, he left a luminous trail which will sparkle for many a generation to come.'

BRIAN MAY, 2011

THE SHOW MUST GO ON

*'I don't expect to make old bones.
What's more, I don't really care.'*

FM, 1987

Opposite: Mercury rising. Freddie's statue by Irene Sedlecká,
Montreux, Switzerland.

'I'm trying to remind people how amazing Freddie was, without trying to imitate him.'

ADAM LAMBERT, 2015

TIMELINE

1991

27 November: Freddie is cremated in a Zoroastrian ceremony conducted by Parsee priests at the West London Crematorium, Kensal Green.

21 December: Double A-side 'Bohemian Rhapsody' / 'These Are the Days of Our Lives' becomes Queen's fourth UK #1 single.

1992

12 February: Freddie is posthumously given a Brit Award for Outstanding Contribution to British Music.

20 April: 'Freddie Mercury Tribute Concert for AIDS Awareness' is held at London's Wembley Stadium.

25 July: Video of Freddie and Montserrat Caballé performing in 1988 is used at the opening of the Summer Olympics in Barcelona.

16 November: Compilation *The Freddie Mercury Album* is released in the UK, making #4 in the chart.

24 November: A slightly amended version of *The Freddie Mercury Album* is released in the US as *The Great Pretender*.

Mother Mercury: Roger Taylor and Brian May with Jer Bulsara, Rock and Roll Hall of Fame induction, New York, 19 March 2001.

1995

6 November: *Made in Heaven*, the final Queen studio album, is released, topping the chart in nine countries including the UK.

1996

25 November: Statue of Freddie Mercury by Czech sculptor Irene Sedlecká is unveiled in Montreux.

1997

October: John Deacon plays with Queen for the last time, on 'No-One But You (Only the Good Die Young)', the final song recorded under the name Queen.

2001

19 March: Freddie is inducted into the Rock and Roll Hall of Fame as a member of Queen.

2002

14 May: *We Will Rock You*, a musical based on the songs of Queen, opens at London's Dominion Theatre, where it will run for twelve years.

August: Freddie is placed at #58 in a BBC poll of the 100 Greatest Britons.

2003

12 June: Freddie is inducted into the Songwriters Hall of Fame as a member of Queen.

2004

11 November: Inducted into the UK Music Hall of Fame as a member of Queen.

2005

19 March: First public performance by Queen + Paul Rodgers, at an AIDS charity concert in George, South Africa.

2008

15 September: Release of *The Cosmos Rocks*, the only Queen + Paul Rodgers studio album.

November: Freddie is placed at #18 in *Rolling Stone*'s list of the '100 Greatest Singers of All Time'.

2009

May: Queen + Paul Rodgers announce the end of their collaboration.

2010

September: Announcement of plans for a film based on the life of Freddie Mercury.

2012

30 June: First full concert performance by Queen + Adam Lambert, a joint show with Elton John in Kiev's Independence Square to raise funds for an AIDS charity.

12 August: Freddie interacts with the crowd at the London Olympics closing ceremony by means of footage of one of his 'Dee-Oh' vocal improvisations from a 1986 Wembley show.

2014

10 November: Release of *Queen Forever*, a compilation including previously unreleased material from throughout the band's career.

2015

November: Fortieth anniversary of the release of 'Bohemian Rhapsody' is commemorated with a month of celebrations.

'I lost somebody who I thought was my eternal love ... When he died I felt we'd had a marriage. We'd done it for better for worse, for richer for poorer, in sickness and in health.'

MARY AUSTIN, 2000

Freddie Mercury's death was formally announced at midnight on Sunday 24 November 1991. In those vital few hours between his passing and the news breaking, a police roadblock held back the press while the undertaker removed his body from Garden Lodge.

The cause of death was 'bronchopneumonia brought on by AIDS', and the name on the death certificate 'Frederick Mercury, otherwise Frederick Bulsara'. Peter Freestone had provided the name. Neither he nor anyone else at Garden Lodge knew who Farrokh Bulsara was. 'It was almost as though he never had a childhood,' said Freestone later. 'He never referred to early life other than as a late teenager in London.'

'Freddie is dead' announced the *Sun*'s Monday morning headline above a picture of Freddie with arms outstretched wearing the Union Flag as a cape, like a patriotic comic-book superhero. Roger Taylor had complained bitterly about the photographers camped outside Freddie's house; he punched one and reversed his car over another's foot. But Queen's management were soon making deals with the newspapers.

The funeral service was arranged for Wednesday 27 November at the West London Crematorium in Kensal Green. On the day before, the *Daily Mirror* printed an interview with Dave Clark ('Freddie: The Last Moments, by pop legend at his bedside'). Mary Austin was photographed and interviewed in the same edition. Neither article referenced Jim Hutton or the others who had nursed the singer day and night.

At a time when AIDS was a disease shrouded in fear, misunderstanding and paranoia, Freddie's female soul mate and a 1960s pop star were perhaps deemed more acceptable to newspaper readers than the gay men with whom Freddie shared his home. Such selective press coverage might be interpreted as damage limitation. When the funeral cars arrived at the crematorium, Austin and Clark emerged from the first vehicle; Jim Hutton travelled in another car some way behind.

Around forty guests, including Freddie's family, his band mates, Jim Beach and Elton John attended a twenty-minute ceremony conducted by two Parsee priests. Freddie had not practised Zoroastrianism since childhood, but it was he who had requested the service. He had also never told his parents he had AIDS. 'He protected us by never discussing these matters,' said his mother Jer in 2012. 'Back then it would have been very hard for him to tell us and we respected his feelings. He didn't have to say anything, I knew he was very ill.'

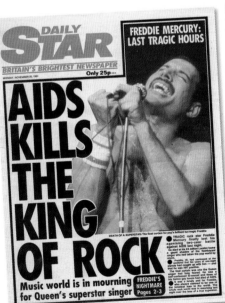

Opposite: Roger Taylor and Mary Austin with 1960s pop star Dave Clark at Freddie's funeral, 27 November 1991.
Overleaf: Floral tributes, including Elton John's rose heart, West London Crematorium.

In contrast, George Michael came close to matching the original with a bravura rendition of 'Somebody to Love'. Behind each guest, Brian, Roger and John looked rather dazed as they performed these songs for the first time without their inimitable front man.

Overwhelming applause was heard whenever Freddie's image flashed up on the video screens flanking the stage. There were also moments of farce and black comedy, of which, no doubt, Freddie would have approved. Without warning, David Bowie sank to one knee and recited the Lord's Prayer. ('I thought, "What the fuck is he doing?"' said Brian). Later Liza Minnelli out-camped even Freddie while leading an ensemble finale of 'We Are the Champions'.

Queen had usually managed to avoid comment on political and social causes, but in the weeks after Freddie's death, Roger Taylor and Brian May suddenly became unwitting spokesmen for AIDS awareness. In February 1992, they announced that the 'Freddie Mercury Tribute Concert for AIDS Awareness' would take place at Wembley Stadium on 20 April, and would be simultaneously broadcast to seventy-six countries around the globe. The concert would open with short sets by some of the world's biggest contemporary rock acts, including Metallica, then Queen's surviving members would perform alongside a revolving line-up of guests, including Elton John, David Bowie, George Michael and Liza Minnelli.

The show highlighted Freddie Mercury's catholic appeal. In one corner were his early heroes and rivals, including Elton, Bowie, Led Zeppelin's Robert Plant and the Who's Roger Daltrey. In another were Def Leppard, Extreme and Guns N' Roses, hard rock groups weaned on the monochrome satin-clad Freddie of *Queen II* and *Sheer Heart Attack*. And finally, Lisa Stansfield, George Michael and Paul Young, pop stars whose arrival coincided with Queen's mid-1980s renaissance.

Before the show, Robert Plant, one of Freddie's great idols, summed up the challenge ahead: 'Freddie Mercury sang all these songs originally, and he sang them better than we're going to sing them. He sang them in the correct keys, and he sang them with confidence, and he sang them well … and his personality and his whole projection is something we can't capture.'

He was not wrong. Plant struggled with 'Innuendo', as did Paul Young with 'Radio Ga Ga'.

However good some of these performances may have been, each of them underlined that Freddie was irreplaceable. 'Freddie could wring every last drop out of a song, he exhausted it,' explained Mike Moran, who played piano at the concert. 'And he brought the same attitude to being a performer. I don't think anyone else has come close.'

The show's important remit of raising AIDS awareness was not lost amid the musical celebration. Seventy-two thousand tickets were sold and the profits were used to launch the AIDS charity Mercury Phoenix Trust, which, to date, has funded over seven hundred AIDS-related projects around the world.

Freddie had told Brian May he believed the next generation would find a cure for the disease. Brian maintains that if Freddie had contracted the virus twelve months later, he might have benefited from the discovery of anti-retroviral therapies that have gone on to revolutionise HIV/AIDS treatment. But these medical developments came too late for him and some of his friends, including Joe Fanelli, who died of AIDS in 1992. Jim Hutton, who was diagnosed as HIV positive in 1990, was able to manage his condition, but died from lung cancer in 2010.

Above: A man down – John Deacon, Brian May and Roger Taylor, Freddie Mercury Tribute Concert, 1992.
Left: George Michael giving a 'bravura rendition' of 'Somebody to Love'.
Opposite: Annie Lennox and David Bowie get close while singing 'Under Pressure'.

Knowing that 'death sells', Freddie once predicted that he would have to die before Queen had another US hit. They did indeed enjoy a dramatic revival in the US shortly after his death, although the circumstances were not as he had envisaged. Shortly before Freddie died, the Canadian comedian and actor Mike Myers asked for permission to use 'Bohemian Rhapsody' in his movie *Wayne's World*. The teen comedy featured a scene in which Myers's character, Wayne, a lovably gormless adolescent rock fan, and his likeminded friends drive through their Illinois hometown singing along to the Queen hit. Although very ill, Freddie watched an early print of the scene and loved it. Following its release in February 1992, *Wayne's World* grossed over $120 million at the box office and a rereleased 'Bohemian Rhapsody' reached number two in the US charts.

But the surviving band members did not capitalise on this unexpected success. Queen was over. Brian May fell into what he described as 'a serious depression'. 'I didn't want to talk about Queen,' he said. 'I didn't want to be Queen. I went out and did my own tours and if people asked me about Queen I resisted talking because I thought, "No, it's over," and I wanted my life back.'

'There was an empty period,' concurred Roger Taylor. 'It was, "What do we do now? … Well, let's give up … Yeah, let's give up …"'

Slowly, the depression lifted and the mood changed. In early 1994, Roger and John listened to Queen's final recordings with Freddie, and began piecing some songs together. Before long, Brian – convinced they were doing everything wrong – had taken the tapes off them and was making his contribution. The old tensions soon resurfaced as the trio worked together on what would become a 'new' Queen album. Without Freddie there to mediate and offer advice, it proved to be a laborious process.

The album, *Made in Heaven*, was finally released on 6 November 1995. 'It was a long journey and a much bigger job than any of us realised,' understated Brian. The material covered an eleven-year period, from 'It's a Beautiful Day', which came from a 1980 session for *The Game*, to 'Mother Love' from Freddie's final recording session in May 1991. The project had needed a team of producers and some technological sleight of hand. 'Sometimes there was a complete first-take vocal,' explained Brian. 'While other times there was no more than three or four lines.'

Ultimately, though, *Made in Heaven* sounds very much like Freddie Mercury delivering his own eulogy: 'I'm just pieces of the man I used to be,' he sang on 'Too Much Love Will Kill You'. Yet it gave the band another number one in nine countries, and even some favourable reviews. 'A more-than-worthy epitaph to the great entertainer,' concluded the *Sunday Times*.

The album's arrival coincided with a 'new' Beatles single, 'Free as a Bird', featuring the late John Lennon. Both invited questions about whether groups should rework unfinished material featuring the ghost voices of dead band members. But *Made in Heaven* was only the start of Freddie Mercury's lucrative afterlife.

In November 1996, a 10-feet tall bronze statue of Freddie Mercury was erected in Montreux. Created by the Czech sculptor Irene Sedlecká, it portrayed Freddie in that familiar pose with his right hand reaching for the sky and his left clasping his sawn-off mic stand. Montserrat Caballé and Brian May spoke at the inauguration ceremony. But he had mixed feelings about the event. 'It's a lovely tribute and the ceremony was very moving, but I suddenly became overcome by anger,' Brian told *Q* magazine. 'I thought, "This is all that's left of my friend, and everybody's thinking it's normal and fabulous …"'

As the years passed, Freddie remained an inescapable presence for both his former band mates and his audience. A steady flow of compilations, live albums and box sets ensured his memory stayed strong. Over time, Queen's surviving members adjusted to the situation in different ways. Brian May and Roger Taylor settled into their shared role as Queen's gatekeepers, and John Deacon disappeared.

'John just decided he couldn't handle people,' Roger told me. 'Not just Queen, he didn't want to be around people. He was quiet even in Queen and not as mentally rugged as we were. I also think that period of knowing about Freddie's illness had a more damaging effect on him than on the rest of us.'

By 2000, Brian and Roger had released seven solo albums between them. But there was a nagging sense that they both wished they were still in Queen. A year later, they recorded a wretched new version of 'We Are the Champions' with ex-Take That member Robbie Williams, for the movie *A Knight's Tale*. It prompted John to break his silence: 'I don't wish to be nasty, but let's just say Robbie Williams is no Freddie Mercury. Freddie can never be replaced and certainly not by him.'

Instead, Queen found new ways to keep their music in the public consciousness. In May 2002, *We Will Rock You*, the musical, opened at London's Dominion Theatre. Written by comedian and scriptwriter Ben Elton, it was a futuristic fantasy in which rebel musicians, led by one Galileo Figaro, strike out against a worldwide corporation force-feeding manufactured pop to the masses. It featured more than twenty Queen songs. 'The story is slightly crass,' conceded Roger Taylor in 2013. 'But I think it has its good points.'

We Will Rock You was widely panned by the critics. But it ran in the West End for twelve years, with further productions staged worldwide, including in the US, Australia and Japan. Furthermore, for those twelve years a replica of Irene Sedlecká's statue of Freddie Mercury dominated the entrance to the Dominion Theatre and became a landmark for thousands of tourists. It was just the sort of absurd accolade Freddie would have enjoyed.

Some of the most dedicated Queen fans might have been dismayed by the notion of a watered-down musical, but *We Will Rock You* introduced a new audience to Freddie Mercury's music, many of whom were too young to have been able to see him perform live. 'People who think Freddie would be turning in his grave about the musical just don't get him,' insisted Roger Taylor. 'He would have loved it.' Though Roger did anticipate one problem: 'He'd have thought his statue wasn't big enough.'

Above left: Choreographer Arlene Phillips (left), writer Ben Elton (right) and backer Robert De Niro (centre) with Roger Taylor and Brian May at the press conference to launch *We Will Rock You*, March 2002.
Above right: Big enough? Freddie outside London's Dominion Theatre, where *We Will Rock You* ran for twelve years.
Opposite: Made in heaven. Freddie overlooking Lake Geneva. A man who always delivered, Freddie was also the subject of a 1999 Royal Mail commemorative stamp (inset).

Despite John Deacon's belief that Freddie could never be replaced, in 2004 Brian and Roger announced a tour with former Free and Bad Company vocalist Paul Rodgers. The shows were carefully billed as Queen + Paul Rodgers and included songs by all three groups.

Rodgers was a fine blues singer, and was the archetypal red-blooded 1970s rock star. Freddie had been a fan. But although he could do justice to full-throttle rock songs like 'Tie Your Mother Down' and 'Hammer to Fall', the more idiosyncratic entries in the Queen catalogue including 'I Want to Break Free' proved a challenge. Unavoidably, whenever Freddie appeared on the overhead screen playing the intro to 'Bohemian Rhapsody' it only served to highlight what was missing.

A Queen + Paul Rodgers album of new material, *The Cosmos Rocks*, came and went in 2008, and the trio disbanded a year later. 'We had fun,' said Roger. 'But I'm sure Paul must have got fed up of being asked about Freddie Mercury in every interview.'

Yet, in 2012, Queen took another leap into the unknown by playing shows with thirty-year-old American singer Adam Lambert, a runner-up in the 2009 edition of TV talent show *American Idol*. Queen would have struggled to find a better understudy. A flamboyant performer with a three-octave voice, Lambert was as comfortable with songs from Queen's 1970s pomp as he was with the 1980s hits.

'There's never going to be another Freddie,' he explained, 'and I'm not trying to replace him. I'm trying to keep the memory alive. I'm trying to share with the audience how much he inspired me.'

'Adam is the first person we've encountered who can do all the Queen catalogue without blinking,' said Brian May. 'He has that range and that affinity for things on the edge of camp that Freddie had.' As an openly gay man, Lambert was also a reminder of how attitudes towards homosexuality within the music business and society had changed for the better since Freddie Mercury's time.

Roger Taylor once said that seeing teenagers in the audience at *We Will Rock You* convinced him that Queen were right to endorse the musical: 'It meant we'd reached a new audience, we'd done our job.' Queen + Adam Lambert was an extension of that: it was almost as if Queen were becoming their own covers band or even a 'brand', a touring jukebox musical for those who had never seen the real thing. The collaboration continues in 2016.

This extension of what Roger himself has called 'the brand' led, in 2010, to the announcement of a biopic about Queen and Freddie Mercury, endorsed by the band. The British playwright and screenwriter Peter Morgan, known for his modern historical dramas such as the Academy Award-nominated *Frost/Nixon*, was hired to write a script. To date, though, finding someone to play Freddie has been as tortuous a process as the recording of any Queen album.

Initially, the British comic actor Sacha Baron Cohen signed up for the role. But the band later feared that Baron Cohen's comedy background would be a distraction. 'We felt Sacha probably wasn't right in the end,' said Roger in 2013.

Above: Tear it up. Queen with former guest singer Paul Rodgers, April 2005.
Left: *American Idol* contestant and Queen's guest singer Adam Lambert.
Opposite: 'He can do all the Queen catalogue without blinking.' Adam Lambert and Queen, Hammersmith Apollo, July 2012.

'Until you buggers stop buying our records, we'll still be here.'

FM, 1984

'We didn't want it to be a joke. We want people to be moved.' The next name mooted was that of the British stage and film actor Ben Whishaw. However, at the time of writing he was yet to confirm his involvement. 'We *will* get there,' insisted Roger. 'But it's been hard.'

A further reminder of how hard it is to replace the irreplaceable came during the closing ceremony of the London 2012 Olympic Games. During a segment of the show billed as 'A Symphony of British music', Freddie, as filmed at Wembley in 1986, appeared on four huge video screens in the middle of the Olympic stadium. He then led the audience in his famous vocal gymnastic call-and-response ('Dee-oh-dee-oh-dey-Op! …'). The fact that he was not there in the flesh did nothing to dampen the audience's excitement. Eventually, Brian, Roger and the chart-topping British R&B singer Jessie J appeared in real life and launched into 'We Will Rock You'. But Jessie did not stand a chance against the pre-recorded voice and image of the late Freddie Mercury, even after he had disappeared from view.

According to Jim Beach, Queen's manager and Freddie's executor, one of the singer's final requests was: 'You can do what you want with my music, but don't make me boring.' Beach took Freddie at his word and his songs have been used in ways no one could ever have imagined.

Confronted by dwindling physical sales and widespread piracy, musicians and record companies have had to find new sources of income. In 2014 in the UK alone, revenue generated from music licensed to TV shows, films, adverts and computer games was £20 million. The act that licensed the most music for commercial use that year was Queen.

Freddie Mercury's gospel ballad 'Somebody to Love' advertised a UK furniture chain and a dogs' home; his rockabilly throwback 'Crazy Little Thing Called Love' promoted a major supermarket; 'Bohemian Rhapsody' publicised a holiday tour operator; and 'Don't Stop Me Now', his celebration of cocaine and gay sex, helped sell a contactless credit card.

'There are two ways of looking at this,' said Roger Taylor. 'You can be very precious about your music and say, "No, we are not using it to advertise chocolate," or you can say, "OK." I don't want Queen's music to just be on some piece of vinyl from the 1970s. I want our music to be on the radio and to be everywhere.'

Freddie was once asked if he thought his songs would stand the test of time. His reply was typically glib and, one suspects, disingenuous: 'I don't give a fuck. I won't be around to worry about it. Are you mad?' The reality is that Queen and Freddie Mercury's music still soundtracks our lives, and Freddie, in death, has become a universally recognised icon.

His admirers span musical genres and generations. 'A man who could hold an audience in the palm of his hand', according to David Bowie. 'I never had a bigger teacher in all my life,' claimed Guns N' Roses' Axl Rose. 'The greatest front man of all time', declared the Foo Fighters' Dave Grohl. Even Grohl's ex-band mate in Nirvana the late Kurt Cobain told of how as a boy he would hide in a van when he should have been working and listen obsessively to a tape of Queen's *News of the World*. In his suicide note, Cobain wrote of how much he admired the way Freddie relished the 'love and adoration' of a crowd. Meanwhile, Lady Gaga, the US pop star who took her stage name from Queen's 1984 hit, has described Freddie as 'in short, a genius'.

But nobody, perhaps, can explain Freddie Mercury's enduring appeal better than the rest of Queen. 'I didn't really realise just what we had and how special he was,' admitted Roger Taylor. 'I miss his wickedness, that glint in his eye, his sense of humour,' said Brian May. 'But most of all I just miss him being here in the world. I often wake up from some strange dream that he's in, and in a very matter-of-fact way I think, "Yeah, of course, Fred's still here."'

Previous: Now I'm here. Freddie at the London Olympics closing ceremony, 12 August 2012.
Left: Queen with Jessie J performing 'We Will Rock You', London Olympics closing ceremony.
Opposite: Let me entertain you. Queen, Madison Square Garden, New York, July 1982.
Overleaf: Queen, Rainbow Theatre, London, March 1974.
© Mick Rock 1974, 2016

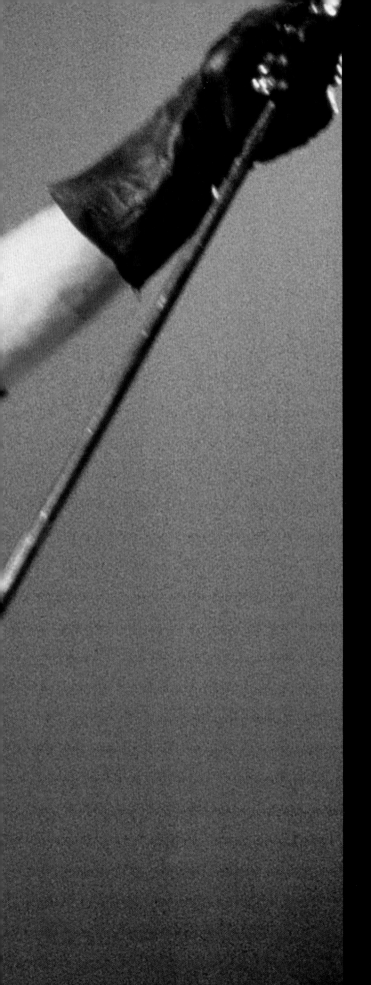

'Freddie was fully focused, never allowing anything or anyone to get in the way of his vision for the future. He was truly a free spirit. There are not many of these in the world. To achieve this, you have to be, like Freddie, fearless – unafraid of upsetting anyone's apple cart.'

BRIAN MAY, 2011

DISCOGRAPHY

QUEEN

STUDIO ALBUMS

QUEEN 1973

Recorded at De Lane Lea Studios, London; Trident Studios, London
Produced by Queen, John Anthony, Roy Thomas Baker

Personnel

Freddie Mercury: vocals, piano, Hammond organ
John Deacon: bass guitar
Brian May: guitars, backing vocals
Roger Taylor: drums, percussion, vocals

Additional credits

John Anthony: backing vocals

Cover art

Design: Brian May, Freddie Mercury, Douglas Puddifoot

Tracks

'Keep Yourself Alive' (May)
'Doing All Right' (May, Staffell)
'Great King Rat' (Mercury)
'My Fairy King' (Mercury)
'Liar' (Mercury)
'The Night Comes Down' (May)
'Modern Times Rock 'n' Roll' (Taylor)
'Son and Daughter' (May)
'Jesus' (Mercury)
'Seven Seas of Rhye' (Mercury)

Release date

13 July 1973

Highest chart position on release

UK 24, US 83

QUEEN II 1974

Recorded at Trident Studios, London
Produced by Queen, Roy Thomas Baker, Robin Cable

Personnel

Freddie Mercury: vocals, piano, harpsichord, string piano
John Deacon: bass guitar, acoustic guitar
Brian May: guitars, bells
Roger Taylor: drums, percussion

Additional credits

Roy Thomas Baker: castanets, stylophone
Robin Cable: piano effects

Cover art

Design: Queen, Mick Rock
Photography: Mick Rock

Tracks

'Procession' (May)
'Father to Son' (May)
'White Queen (As It Began)' (May)
'Some Day One Day' (May)
'The Loser in the End' (Taylor)
'Ogre Battle' (Mercury)
'The Fairy Feller's Master-Stroke' (Mercury)
'Nevermore' (Mercury)
'The March of the Black Queen' (Mercury)
'Funny How Love Is' (Mercury)
'Seven Seas of Rhye' (Mercury)

Release date

8 March 1974

Highest chart position on release

UK 5, US 49

SHEER HEART ATTACK 1974

Recorded at AIR Studios, London; Rockfield Studios, Monmouth, Wales; Trident Studios, London; Wessex Studios, London
Produced by Queen, Roy Thomas Baker

Personnel

Freddie Mercury: vocals, piano, jangle piano
John Deacon: bass guitar, guitars, double bass
Brian May: guitars, backing vocals
Roger Taylor: drums, percussion, vocals

Cover art

Design: Queen, Mick Rock
Photography: Mick Rock

Tracks

'Brighton Rock' (May)
'Killer Queen' (Mercury)
'Tenement Funster' (Taylor)
'Flick of the Wrist' (Mercury)
'Lily of the Valley' (Mercury)
'Now I'm Here' (May)
'In the Lap of the Gods' (Mercury)
'Stone Cold Crazy' (Mercury, May, Taylor, Deacon)
'Dear Friends' (May)
'Misfire' (Deacon)
'Bring Back That Leroy Brown' (Mercury)
'She Makes Me (Stormtrooper in Stilettos)' (May)
'In the Lap of the Gods … Revisited' (Mercury)

Release date

8 November 1974

Highest chart position on release

UK 2, US 12

A NIGHT AT THE OPERA 1975

Recorded at Sarm Studios, London; Roundhouse Studios, London; Olympic Studios, London; Rockfield Studios, Monmouth, Wales
Produced by Queen, Roy Thomas Baker

Personnel

Freddie Mercury: vocals, piano, jangle piano, woodwind vocalisation
John Deacon: bass guitar, double bass, electric piano
Brian May: guitars, ukulele, harp, toy koto,
Roger Taylor: drums, percussion, brass vocalisation

Cover art
Design: Freddie Mercury, Queen

Tracks
'Death on Two Legs (Dedicated to …)'
   (Mercury)
'Lazing on a Sunday Afternoon'
   (Mercury)
'I'm in Love with My Car' (Taylor)
'You're My Best Friend' (Deacon)
''39' (May)
'Sweet Lady' (May)
'Seaside Rendezvous' (Mercury)
'The Prophet's Song' (May)
'Love of My Life' (Mercury)
'Good Company' (May)
'Bohemian Rhapsody' (Mercury)
'God Save the Queen' (Traditional,
   arr. May)

Release date
21 November 1975

Highest chart position on release
UK 1, US 4

A DAY AT THE RACES 1976
Recorded at the Manor Studio,
   Oxfordshire; Sarm East Studios,
   London; Wessex Studios, London
Produced by Queen

Personnel
Freddie Mercury: vocals, piano
John Deacon: bass guitar,
   acoustic guitar
Brian May: guitars, vocals, harmonium
Roger Taylor: drums, percussion, guitar

Additional credits
Mike Stone: vocals

Cover art
Design: Freddie Mercury, Queen

Tracks
'Tie Your Mother Down' (May)
'You Take My Breath Away' (Mercury)
'Long Away' (May)
'The Millionaire Waltz' (Mercury)
'You and I' (Deacon)
'Somebody to Love' (Mercury)
'White Man' (May)
'Good Old-Fashioned Lover Boy'
   (Mercury)

'Drowse' (Taylor)
'Teo Torriatte (Let Us Cling Together)'
   (May)

Release date
10 December 1976

Highest chart position on release
UK 1, US 5

NEWS OF THE WORLD 1977
Recorded at Sarm West Studios,
   London; Wessex Studios, London
Produced by Queen, Mike Stone

Personnel
Freddie Mercury: vocals, piano,
   cowbell
John Deacon: bass guitar, acoustic
   guitar, backing vocals
Brian May: guitars, vocals, maracas
Roger Taylor: drums, percussion,
   guitar, bass guitar, vocals

Cover art
Design: Frank Kelly Freas, Queen

Tracks
'We Will Rock You' (May)
'We Are the Champions' (Mercury)
'Sheer Heart Attack' (Taylor)
'All Dead, All Dead' (May)
'Spread Your Wings' (Deacon)
'Fight from the Inside' (Taylor)
'Get Down, Make Love' (Mercury)
'Sleeping on the Sidewalk' (May)
'Who Needs You' (Deacon)
'It's Late' (May)
'My Melancholy Blues' (Mercury)

Release date
28 October 1977

Highest chart position on release
UK 4, US 3

JAZZ 1978
Recorded at Mountain Studios,
   Montreux, Switzerland; Super Bear
   Studios, Berre-les-Alpes, France
Produced by Queen, Roy Thomas
   Baker

Personnel
Freddie Mercury: vocals, piano,
   bicycle bells
John Deacon: bass guitar, electric and
   acoustic guitar, bicycle bells
Brian May: guitars, vocals, bicycle bells
Roger Taylor: drums, percussion,
   guitar, bass guitar, bicycle bells

Cover art
Design: Roger Taylor, Queen

Tracks
'Mustapha' (Mercury)
'Fat Bottomed Girls' (May)
'Jealousy' (Mercury)
'Bicycle Race' (Mercury)
'If You Can't Beat Them' (Deacon)
'Let Me Entertain You' (Mercury)
'Dead On Time' (May)
'In Only Seven Days' (Deacon)
'Dreamer's Ball' (May)
'Fun It' (Taylor)
'Leaving Home Ain't Easy' (May)
'Don't Stop Me Now' (Mercury)
'More of That Jazz' (Taylor)

Release date
10 November 1978

Highest chart position on release
UK 2, US 6

THE GAME 1980
Recorded at Musicland Studios,
   Munich
Produced by Queen, Reinhold Mack

Personnel
Freddie Mercury: vocals, piano,
   keyboards
John Deacon: bass guitar, electric
   guitar, acoustic guitar, piano
Brian May: guitars, vocals, piano,
   keyboards
Roger Taylor: drums, electronic drums,
   vocals, guitar, keyboards

Additional credit
Reinhold Mack: keyboards

Cover art
Concept: Queen
Design: Cream
Photography: Peter Hince

Tracks
'Play the Game' (Mercury)
'Dragon Attack' (May)
'Another One Bites the Dust' (Deacon)
'Need Your Loving Tonight' (Deacon)
'Crazy Little Thing Called Love'
  (Mercury)
'Rock It (Prime Jive)' (Taylor)
'Don't Try Suicide' (Mercury)
'Sail Away Sweet Sister' (May)
'Coming Soon' (Taylor)
'Save Me' (May)

Release date
30 June 1980

Highest chart position on release
UK 1, US 1

FLASH GORDON 1980
Recorded at Townhouse Studios,
  London; Music Centre, London;
  Advision Studios, London; Utopia
  Studios, London
Produced by Brian May, Reinhold Mack

Personnel
Freddie Mercury: vocals, piano,
  keyboards, synthesizer
John Deacon: bass guitar, rhythm
  guitar, synthesizer
Brian May: guitars, vocals, synthesizer
Roger Taylor: drums, timpani, vocals,
  guitar, synthesizer

Additional credit
Howard Blake: orchestral arrangements

Cover art
Design: Freddie Mercury, Queen

Tracks
'Flash's Theme' (May)
'In the Space Capsule (The Love
  Theme)' (May)
'Ming's Theme (In the Court of Ming
  the Merciless)' (Mercury)
'The Ring (Hypnotic Seduction of
  Dale)' (Mercury)
'Football Fight' (Mercury)
'In the Death Cell (Love Theme
  Reprise)' (Taylor)
'Execution of Flash' (Deacon)
'The Kiss (Aura Resurrects Flash)'
  (Mercury, Blake)

'Arboria (Planet of the Tree Men)'
  (Deacon)
'Escape from the Swamp' (Taylor)
'Vultan's Theme (Attack of the Hawk
  Men)' (Mercury)
'Battle Theme' (May)
'The Wedding March' (R. Wagner,
  arr. May)
'Marriage of Dale and Ming (And Flash
  Approaching)' (May, Taylor)
'Crash Dive on Mingo City' (May)
'Flash's Theme Reprise (Victory
  Celebrations)' (May)
'The Hero' (May, Blake)

Release date
8 December 1980

Highest chart position on release
UK 10, US 23

HOT SPACE 1982
Recorded at Mountain Studios,
  Montreux, Switzerland; Musicland
  Studios, Munich Produced by
  Queen, Arif Mardin, Reinhold Mack,
  David Bowie

Personnel
Freddie Mercury: vocals,
  piano, synthesizer, synth bass,
  Hammond organ
John Deacon: bass guitar, rhythm
  guitar, keyboards, drums
Brian May: guitars, vocals, keyboards
Roger Taylor: drums, vocals, guitar,
  keyboards

Additional credit
David Bowie: vocals, percussion,
  keyboards

Cover art
Design: Freddie Mercury, Queen

Tracks
'Staying Power' (Mercury)
'Dancer' (May)
'Back Chat' (Deacon)
'Body Language' (Mercury)
'Action This Day' (Taylor)
'Put Out the Fire' (May)
'Life Is Real (Song for Lennon)'
  (Mercury)
'Calling All Girls' (Taylor)

'Las Palabras de Amor (The Words of
  Love)' (May)
'Cool Cat' (Deacon, Mercury)
'Under Pressure' (Queen, Bowie)

Release date
21 May 1982

Highest chart position on release
UK 4, US 22

THE WORKS 1984
Recorded at the Record Plant, Los
  Angeles; Musicland Studios, Munich
Produced by Queen, Reinhold Mack

Personnel
Freddie Mercury: vocals, piano,
  keyboards, sampler
John Deacon: bass guitar, rhythm
  guitar, keyboards
Brian May: guitars, vocals, keyboards
Roger Taylor: drums, electronic drums,
  vocals, keyboards, Vocoder, sampler

Additional credits
Fred Mandel: keyboards, piano,
  sampler
Reinhold Mack: Fairlight CMI
  programming

Cover art
Design: Bill Smith
Photography: George Hurrell

Tracks
'Radio Ga Ga' (Taylor)
'Tear It Up' (May)
'It's a Hard Life' (Mercury)
'Man on the Prowl' (Mercury)
'Machines (Or "Back to Humans")'
  (May, Taylor)
'I Want to Break Free' (Deacon)
'Keep Passing the Open Windows'
  (Mercury)
'Hammer to Fall' (May)
'Is This the World We Created …?'
  (Mercury, May)

Release date
27 February 1984

Highest chart position on release
UK 2, US 23

A KIND OF MAGIC 1986
Recorded at Musicland Studios,
  Munich; Townhouse Studios, London
Produced by Queen, Reinhold Mack,
  David Richards

Personnel
Freddie Mercury: vocals, piano,
  synthesizer, sampler
John Deacon: bass guitar, electric
  guitar, keyboards, sampler
Brian May: guitars, vocals, keyboards
Roger Taylor: drums, electronic drums,
  vocals, keyboards

Additional credits
Joan Armatrading: vocals
Spike Edney: keyboards
Steve Gregory: alto saxophone
Lynton Naiff: string arrangement
  ('One Year of Love')
National Philharmonic Orchestra ('Who
  Wants to Live Forever') arranged
  by Michael Kamen and Brian May,
  conducted by Michael Kamen

Cover art
Design: Roger Chiasson

Tracks
'One Vision' (Queen, Taylor)
'A Kind of Magic' (Taylor)
'One Year of Love' (Deacon)
'Pain Is So Close to Pleasure'
  (Deacon, Mercury)
'Friends Will Be Friends' (Deacon,
  Mercury)
'Who Wants to Live Forever' (May)
'Gimme the Prize (Kurgan's Theme)'
  (May)
'Don't Lose Your Head' (Taylor)
'Princes of the Universe' (Mercury)

Release date
2 June 1986

Highest chart position on release
UK 1, US 46

THE MIRACLE 1989
Recorded at Olympic Studios, London;
  Townhouse Studios, London;
  Mountain Studios, Montreux,
  Switzerland
Produced by Queen, David Richards

Personnel
Freddie Mercury: vocals, piano,
  keyboards, synthesizers
John Deacon: bass guitar, electric
  guitar, keyboards
Brian May: guitars, vocals, keyboards
Roger Taylor: drums, electronic drums,
  keyboards, guitar, vocals

Additional credit
David Richards: keyboards, sampler

Cover art
Design: Richard Gray
Photography: Simon Fowler

Tracks
'Party' (Deacon, May, Mercury)
'Khashoggi's Ship' (Queen)
'The Miracle' (Mercury, Deacon)
'I Want It All' (May)
'The Invisible Man' (Taylor)
'Breakthru' (Mercury, Taylor)
'Rain Must Fall' (Deacon, Mercury)
'Scandal' (May)
'My Baby Does Me' (Mercury, Deacon)
'Was It All Worth It' (Mercury)

Release date
22 May 1989

Highest chart position on release
UK 1, US 24

INNUENDO 1991
Recorded at Metropolis Studios,
  London; Mountain Studios,
  Montreux, Switzerland
Produced by Queen, David Richards

Personnel
Freddie Mercury: vocals, piano,
  keyboards
John Deacon: bass guitar
Brian May: guitars, vocals, piano,
  keyboards
Roger Taylor: drums, percussion,
  vocals, keyboards

Additional credits
Steve Howe: classical guitar
Michel Moran: piano, keyboards

Cover art
Design: Richard Gray

Illustrations: Grandville, Angela Lumley
Photography: Simon Fowler

Tracks
'Innuendo' (Mercury, Taylor)
'I'm Going Slightly Mad' (Mercury,
  Straker)
'Headlong' (May)
'I Can't Live with You' (May)
'Ride the Wild Wind' (Taylor)
'All God's People' (Mercury, Moran)
'These Are the Days of Our Lives'
  (Taylor)
'Delilah' (Mercury)
'Don't Try So Hard' (Mercury)
'The Hitman' (Mercury, May, Deacon)
'Bijou' (May, Mercury)
'The Show Must Go On' (May)

Release date
5 February 1991

Highest chart position on release
UK 1, US 30

MADE IN HEAVEN 1995
Recorded at Mountain Studios,
  Montreux, Switzerland; Allerton Hill
  Studios, Surrey, England (Brian May's
  home studio); Cosford Mill Studios,
  Surrey, England (Roger Taylor's home
  studio); Metropolis Studios, London
Produced by Queen

Personnel
Freddie Mercury: vocals, piano,
  keyboards
John Deacon: bass guitar, guitar,
  keyboards
Brian May: guitars, vocals, piano,
  keyboards
Roger Taylor: drums, percussion,
  vocals, keyboards

Additional credits
Rebecca Leigh-White: backing vocals
Gary Martin: backing vocals
Catherine Porter: backing vocals
David Richards: keyboards
Miriam Stockley: backing vocals

Cover art
Design: Queen, Richard Gray
Photography: Richard Gray

Tracks
'It's a Beautiful Day' (Queen, Mercury)
'Made in Heaven' (Mercury)
'Let Me Live' (Queen)
'Mother Love' (May, Mercury)
'My Life Has Been Saved'
  (Queen, Deacon)
'I Was Born to Love You' (Mercury)
'Heaven for Everyone' (Taylor)
'Too Much Love Will Kill You'
  (May, Musker, Lamers)
'You Don't Fool Me' (Queen)
'A Winter's Tale' (Queen, Mercury)
'It's a Beautiful Day (Reprise)'
  (Queen, Mercury)
'Yeah' (Queen, Mercury)

Release date
6 November 1995

Highest chart position on release
UK 1, US 58

LIVE ALBUMS

LIVE KILLERS 1979
Recorded at various dates on the
  European *Jazz* tour between
  January and March 1979, including
  Stadthalle, Bremen, Germany,
  Sporthalle, Cologne, Germany, Rudi-
  Sedlmayer-Halle, Munich, Germany,
  and Festhalle, Frankfurt, Germany
Produced by Queen

Personnel
Freddie Mercury: vocals, piano
John Deacon: bass guitar, vocals
Brian May: guitars, vocals, keyboards
Roger Taylor: drums, timpani,
  tambourine, vocals

Cover art
Design: Queen
Photography: Koh Hasebe

Tracks
'We Will Rock You' (May)
'Let Me Entertain You' (Mercury)
'Death on Two Legs (Dedicated to …)'
  (Mercury)
'Killer Queen' (Mercury)
'Bicycle Race' (Mercury)
'I'm in Love with My Car' (Taylor)
'Get Down, Make Love' (Mercury)

'You're My Best Friend' (Deacon)
'Now I'm Here' (May)
'Dreamer's Ball' (May)
'Love of My Life' (Mercury)
''39' (May)
'Keep Yourself Alive' (May)
'Don't Stop Me Now' (Mercury)
'Spread Your Wings' (Deacon)
'Brighton Rock' (May)
'Bohemian Rhapsody' (Mercury)
'Tie Your Mother Down' (May)
'Sheer Heart Attack' (Taylor)
'We Will Rock You' (May)
'We Are the Champions' (Mercury)
'God Save the Queen' (Traditional,
  arr. May)

Release date
22 June 1979

Highest chart position on release
UK 3, US 16

LIVE MAGIC 1986
Recorded during the *Magic* tour at
  Knebworth Park, Stevenage, England,
  Népstadion, Budapest, Hungary, and
  Wembley Stadium, London, between
  July and August 1986
Produced by Queen, Trip Khalaf

Personnel
Freddie Mercury: vocals, piano
John Deacon: bass guitar, vocals
Brian May: guitars, vocals
Roger Taylor: drums, vocals

Additional credit
Spike Edney: keyboards, piano,
  guitar, vocals

Cover art
Design: Queen

Tracks
'One Vision' (Queen, Taylor)
'Tie Your Mother Down' (May)
'Seven Seas of Rhye' (Mercury)
'A Kind of Magic' (Taylor)
'Under Pressure' (Queen, Bowie)
'Another One Bites the Dust' (Deacon)
'I Want to Break Free' (Deacon)
'Is This the World We Created …?'
  (Mercury, May)
'Bohemian Rhapsody' (Mercury)

'Hammer to Fall' (May)
'Radio Ga Ga' (Taylor)
'We Will Rock You' (May)
'Friends Will Be Friends' (Mercury,
  Deacon)
'We Are the Champions' (Mercury)
'God Save the Queen' (Traditional,
  arr. May)

Release date
1 December 1986

Highest chart position on release
UK 3, US did not chart (DNC)

AT THE BEEB 1989
Recorded at BBC Langham 1 Studio,
  London, on 5 February and
  3 December 1973
Produced by Bernie Andrews

Personnel
Freddie Mercury: vocals, piano
John Deacon: bass guitar
Brian May: guitars, piano, vocals
Roger Taylor: drums, percussion,
  vocals

Cover art
Design: Richard Gray
Photography: Douglas Puddifoot

Tracks
'My Fairy King' (Mercury)
'Keep Yourself Alive' (May)
'Doing All Right' (May, Staffell)
'Liar' (Mercury)
'Ogre Battle' (Mercury)
'Great White Rat' (Mercury)
'Modern Times Rock 'n' Roll' (Taylor)
'Son and Daughter' (May)

Release date
4 December 1989

Highest chart position on release
UK 67, US DNC

LIVE AT WEMBLEY '86 1992
Recorded at Wembley Stadium,
  London, 12 July 1986
Produced by Queen

Personnel
Freddie Mercury: vocals, piano, guitar
John Deacon: bass guitar, vocals
Brian May: guitars, keyboards, vocals
Roger Taylor: drums, tambourine,
  vocals

Additional credit
Spike Edney: keyboards, piano,
  guitar, vocals

Cover art
Design: Richard Gray
Photography: Denis O'Regan

Tracks
'One Vision' (Queen, Taylor)
'Tie Your Mother Down' (May)
'In the Lap of the Gods … Revisited'
  (Mercury)
'Seven Seas of Rhye' (Mercury)
'Tear It Up' (May)
'A Kind of Magic' (Taylor)
'Under Pressure (Queen, Bowie)
'Another One Bites the Dust' (Deacon)
'Who Wants to Live Forever' (May)
'I Want to Break Free' (Deacon)
'Impromptu' (Queen)
'Brighton Rock Solo' (May)
'Now I'm Here' (May)
'Love of My Life' (Mercury)
'Is This the World We Created …?'
  (Mercury, May)
'(You're So Square) Baby I Don't Care'
  (Leiber, Stoller)
'Hello Mary Lou (Goodbye Heart)'
  (Pitney)
'Tutti Frutti' (Penniman, LaBostrie)
'Gimme Some Lovin'' (Winwood,
  Davis, Winwood)
'Bohemian Rhapsody' (Mercury)
'Hammer to Fall' (May)
'Crazy Little Thing Called Love'
  (Mercury)
'Big Spender' (Fields, Coleman)
'Radio Ga Ga' (Taylor)
'We Will Rock You' (May)
'Friends Will Be Friends' (Mercury,
  Deacon)
'We Are the Champions' (Mercury)
'God Save the Queen' (Traditional,
  arr. May)

Release date
26 May 1992

Highest chart position on release
UK 2, US 53

QUEEN ON FIRE – LIVE AT THE BOWL 2004
Recorded at Milton Keynes Bowl,
  Buckinghamshire, England,
  5 June 1982
Produced by Brian May, Roger Taylor,
  Justin Shirley-Smith

Personnel
Freddie Mercury: vocals, piano, guitar
John Deacon: bass guitar, rhythm
  guitar, vocals
Brian May: guitars, piano, vocals
Roger Taylor: drums, percussion,
  vocals

Additional credit
Morgan Fisher: keyboards, piano

Cover art
Design: Richard Gray
Photography: Denis O'Regan

Tracks
'Flash' (May)
'The Hero' (May)
'We Will Rock You' (May)
'Action This Day' (Taylor)
'Play the Game' (Mercury)
'Staying Power' (Mercury)
'Somebody to Love' (Mercury)
'Now I'm Here' (May)
'Dragon Attack' (May)
'Now I'm Here (Reprise)' (May)
'Love of My Life' (Mercury)
'Save Me' (May)
'Back Chat' (Deacon)
'Get Down, Make Love' (Mercury)
'Guitar Solo' (May)
'Under Pressure' (Queen, Bowie)
'Fat Bottomed Girls' (May)
'Crazy Little Thing Called Love'
  (Mercury)
'Bohemian Rhapsody' (Mercury)
'Tie Your Mother Down' (May)
'Another One Bites the Dust' (Deacon)
'Sheer Heart Attack' (Taylor)
'We Will Rock You' (May)
'We Are the Champions' (Mercury)
'God Save the Queen' (Traditional,
  arr. May)

Release date
25 October 2004

Highest chart position on release
UK 20, US DNC

QUEEN ROCK MONTREAL 2007
Recorded at the Montreal Forum,
  Montreal, 24–25 November 1981
Produced by Justin Shirley-Smith,
  Kris Fredriksson, Josh Macrae

Personnel
Freddie Mercury: vocals, piano,
  guitar, tambourine
John Deacon: bass guitar, vocals
Brian May: guitars, piano, vocals,
  synthesizer
Roger Taylor: drums, percussion,
  vocals, synthesizer

Cover art
Design: Richard Gray

Tracks
'Intro' (Queen)
'We Will Rock You (Fast)' (May)
'Let Me Entertain You' (Mercury)
'Play the Game' (Mercury)
'Somebody to Love' (Mercury)
'Killer Queen' (Mercury)
'I'm in Love with My Car' (Taylor)
'Get Down, Make Love' (Mercury)
'Save Me' (May)
'Now I'm Here' (May)
'Dragon Attack' (May)
'Now I'm Here (Reprise)' (May)
'Love of My Life' (Mercury)
'Under Pressure' (Queen, Bowie)
'Keep Yourself Alive' (May)
'Drum and Tympani Solo' (Taylor)
'Guitar Solo' (May)
'Flash' (May)
'The Hero' (May)
'Crazy Little Thing Called Love'
  (Mercury)
'Jailhouse Rock' (Leiber, Stoller)
'Bohemian Rhapsody' (Mercury)
'Tie Your Mother Down' (May)
'Another One Bites the Dust' (Deacon)
'Sheer Heart Attack' (Taylor)
'We Will Rock You' (May)
'We Are the Champions' (Mercury)
'God Save the Queen' (Trad., arr. May)

Release date
29 October 2007

Highest chart position on release
UK 20, US DNC

LIVE AT THE RAINBOW '74 2014
Recorded at the Rainbow Theatre, London, 31 March and 19–20 November 1974
Produced by Justin Shirley-Smith, Kris Fredriksson, Josh Macrae

Personnel
Freddie Mercury: vocals, piano, janglebox
John Deacon: bass guitar, vocals, triangle
Brian May: guitars, vocals, ukulele
Roger Taylor: drums, percussion, vocals

Cover art
Design: Richard Gray
Photography: Douglas Puddifoot

Tracks
Double CD/quadruple vinyl edition

Disc one (Queen II tour)
'Procession' (May)
'Father to Son' (May)
'Ogre Battle' (Mercury)
'Son and Daughter' (May)
'Guitar Solo' (May)
'Son and Daughter (Reprise)' (May)
'White Queen (As It Began)' (May)
'Great King Rat' (Mercury)
'The Fairy Feller's Master-Stroke' (Mercury)
'Keep Yourself Alive' (May)
'Drum Solo' (Taylor)
'Keep Yourself Alive (Reprise)' (May)
'Seven Seas of Rhye' (Mercury)
'Modern Times Rock 'n' Roll' (Taylor)
'Jailhouse Rock' (Leiber, Stoller)
'Stupid Cupid' (Greenfield, Sedaka)
'Be-Bop-A-Lula' (Vincent, Graves, Davis)
'Liar' (Mercury)
'See What a Fool I've Been' (May)

Disc two (Sheer Heart Attack tour)
'Procession' (May)

'Now I'm Here' (May)
'Ogre Battle' (Mercury)
'Father to Son' (May)
'White Queen (As It Began)' (May)
'Flick of the Wrist' (Mercury)
'In the Lap of the Gods' (Mercury)
'Killer Queen' (Mercury)
'The March of the Black Queen' (Mercury)
'Bring Back That Leroy Brown' (Mercury)
'Son and Daughter' (May)
'Guitar Solo' (May)
'Son and Daughter (Reprise)' (May)
'Keep Yourself Alive' (May)
'Drum Solo' (Taylor)
'Keep Yourself Alive (Reprise)' (May)
'Seven Seas of Rhye' (Mercury)
'Stone Cold Crazy' (Mercury, May, Taylor, Deacon)
'Liar' (Mercury)
'In the Lap of the Gods … Revisited' (Mercury)
'Big Spender' (Fields, Coleman)
'Modern Times Rock 'n' Roll' (Taylor)
'Jailhouse Rock' (Leiber, Stoller)
'God Save the Queen' (Traditional, arr. May)

Release date
8 September 2014

Highest chart position on release
UK 11, US 66

A NIGHT AT THE ODEON – HAMMERSMITH 1975 2015
Recorded at the Hammersmith Odeon, London, 24 December 1975
Produced by Justin Shirley-Smith, Kris Fredriksson, Josh Macrae

Personnel
Freddie Mercury: vocals, piano
John Deacon: bass guitar, vocals, triangle
Brian May: guitars, vocals, ukulele
Roger Taylor: drums, percussion, vocals

Cover art
Design: Marmalade London

Tracks
'Now I'm Here' (May)

'Ogre Battle' (Mercury)
'White Queen (As It Began)' (May)
'Bohemian Rhapsody' (Mercury)
'Killer Queen' (Mercury)
'The March of the Black Queen' (Mercury)
'Bohemian Rhapsody (Reprise)' (Mercury)
'Bring Back That Leroy Brown' (Mercury)
'Brighton Rock' (May)
'Guitar Solo' (May)
'Son and Daughter' (May)
'Keep Yourself Alive' (May)
'Liar' (Mercury)
'In the Lap of the Gods … Revisited' (Mercury)
'Big Spender' (Fields, Coleman)
'Jailhouse Rock (Medley)' (Leiber, Stoller)
'Seven Seas of Rhye' (Mercury)
'See What a Fool I've Been' (May)
'God Save the Queen' (Traditional, arr. May)

Release date
20 November 2015

Highest chart position on release
UK 40, US –

COMPILATIONS

GREATEST HITS 1981
Cover art
Photography: Snowden

Tracks
'Bohemian Rhapsody' (Mercury)
'Another One Bites the Dust' (Deacon)
'Killer Queen' (Mercury)
'Fat Bottomed Girls' (May)
'Bicycle Race' (Mercury)
'You're My Best Friend' (Deacon)
'Don't Stop Me Now' (Mercury)
'Save Me' (May)
'Crazy Little Thing Called Love' (Mercury)
'Somebody to Love' (Mercury)
'Now I'm Here' (May)
'Good Old-Fashioned Lover Boy' (Mercury)
'Play the Game' (Mercury)
'Flash' (May)
'Seven Seas of Rhye' (Mercury)

'We Will Rock You' (May)
'We Are the Champions' (Mercury)

Release date
26 October 1981

Highest chart position on release
UK 1, US 14

GREATEST HITS II 1991
Cover art
Design: Queen

Tracks
'A Kind of Magic' (Taylor)
'Under Pressure' (Queen, Bowie)
'Radio Ga Ga' (Taylor)
'I Want It All' (Queen, May)
'I Want to Break Free' (Deacon)
'Innuendo' (Mercury, Taylor)
'It's a Hard Life' (Mercury)
'Breakthru' (Mercury, Taylor)
'Who Wants to Live Forever'
   (May)

Release date
28 October 1991

Highest chart position on release
UK 1, US –

CLASSIC QUEEN 1992
Cover art
Design: Queen

Tracks
'A Kind of Magic' (Taylor)
'Bohemian Rhapsody' (Mercury)
'Under Pressure' (Queen, Bowie)
'Hammer to Fall' (May)
'Stone Cold Crazy' (Deacon, May,
   Mercury, Taylor)
'One Year of Love' (Deacon)
'Radio Ga Ga' (Taylor)
'I'm Going Slightly Mad' (Deacon, May,
   Mercury, Straker, Taylor)
'I Want It All' (May)
'Tie Your Mother Down' (May)
'The Miracle' (edited for CD) (Deacon,
   May, Mercury, Taylor)
'These Are the Days of Our Lives'
   (Deacon, May, Mercury, Taylor)
'One Vision' (Queen, Taylor)
'Keep Yourself Alive' (May)

'Headlong' (Deacon, May, Mercury,
   Taylor)
'Who Wants to Live Forever' (May)
'The Show Must Go On' (Deacon, May,
   Mercury, Taylor)

Release date
3 March 1992

Highest chart position on release
UK –, US 4

THE 12" COLLECTION 1992
Cover art
Design: Queen

Tracks
'Bohemian Rhapsody' (Mercury)
'Radio Ga Ga' (extended) (Taylor)
'Machines (Or "Back to Humans")'
   (12" instrumental) (Taylor, May)
'I Want to Break Free' (extended)
   (Deacon)
'It's a Hard Life' (12" extended)
   (Mercury)
'Hammer to Fall' (Headbanger's mix)
   (May)
'Man on the Prowl' (extended)
   (Mercury)
'A Kind of Magic' (extended)
   (Taylor)
'Pain Is So Close to Pleasure'
   (12" version) (Mercury, Deacon)
'Breakthru' (extended) (Queen)
'The Invisible Man' (12" version)
   (Queen)
'The Show Must Go On' (Queen)

Release date
May 1992

Highest chart position on release
UK DNC, US DNC

QUEEN ROCKS 1997
Cover art
Design: Richard Gray, Queen
Illustration: Damien Rochford

Tracks
'We Will Rock You' (May)
'Tie Your Mother Down' (May)
'I Want It All' (May)
'Seven Seas of Rhye' (Mercury)

'I Can't Live Without You'
   (Queen, May)
'Hammer to Fall' (May)
'Stone Cold Crazy' (Deacon, May,
   Mercury, Taylor)
'Now I'm Here' (May)
'Fat Bottomed Girls' (May)
'Keep Yourself Alive' (May)
'Tear It Up' (May)
'One Vision' (Queen, Taylor)
'Sheer Heart Attack' (Taylor)
'I'm in Love with My Car' (Taylor)
'Put Out the Fire' (May)
'Headlong' (Queen, May)
'It's Late' (May)
'No-One but You (Only the Good Die
   Young)' (May)

Release date
3 November 1997

Highest chart position on release
UK 7, US DNC

GREATEST HITS III 1999
Cover art
Design: Peacock, Queen,
   Richard Gray
Crest: Angela Lumley

Tracks
'The Show Must Go On' (live with
   Elton John, 1997) (Queen)
'Under Pressure (Rah mix)' (Queen,
   Bowie)
'Barcelona' (with Montserrat Caballé)
   (Mercury, Moran)
'Too Much Love Will Kill You' (May,
   Musker, Lamers)
'Somebody to Love' (live with George
   Michael, 1992) (Mercury)
'You Don't Fool Me' (Queen)
'Heaven for Everyone' (Taylor)
'Las Palabras de Amor (The Words of
   Love)' (May)
'Driven by You' (May)
'Living on My Own' (Julian Raymond
   album mix) (Mercury)
'Let Me Live' (Queen)
'The Great Pretender' (Ram)
'Princes of the Universe' (Mercury)
'Another One Bites the Dust'
   (Wyclef Jean remix) (Deacon)
'No-One but You (Only the Good Die
   Young)' (May)

'These Are the Days of Our Lives'
(Queen)
'Thanks God It's Christmas'
(May, Taylor)

Release date
8 November 1999

Highest chart position on release
UK 5, US –

STONE COLD CLASSICS 2006
Cover art
Design: Queen

Tracks
'Stone Cold Crazy' (Mercury, May,
Taylor, Deacon)
'Tie Your Mother Down' (May)
'Fat Bottomed Girls' (May)
'Another One Bites the Dust' (Deacon)
'Crazy Little Thing Called Love' (Mercury)
'We Will Rock You' (May)
'We Are the Champions' (Mercury)
'Radio Ga Ga' (Taylor)
'Bohemian Rhapsody' (Mercury)
'The Show Must Go On' (May)
'These Are the Days of Our Lives'
(Taylor)
'I Want It All' (Queen, May)
'All Right Now' (live with Paul Rodgers,
2005) (Fraser, Rodgers)
'Feel Like Makin' Love' (live with Paul
Rodgers, 2005) (Rodgers, Ralphs)

Release date
11 April 2006

Highest chart position on release
UK –, US DNC

THE A–Z OF QUEEN, VOLUME 1 2007
Tracks
'A Kind of Magic' (Taylor)
'Another One Bites the Dust' (Deacon)
'Bohemian Rhapsody' (Mercury)
'Bicycle Race' (Mercury)
'I Want It All' (Queen, May)
'Crazy Little Thing Called Love'
(Mercury)
'Don't Stop Me Now' (Mercury)
'Fat Bottomed Girls' (May)
'Flash' (May)

'Innuendo' (Queen)
'Good Old-Fashioned Lover Boy'
(Mercury)

Release date
10 July 2007

Highest chart position on release
UK –, US DNC

ABSOLUTE GREATEST 2009
Cover art
Design: Richard Gray
Photography: Johnny Dewe Mathews

Tracks
'We Will Rock You' (May)
'We Are the Champions' (Mercury)
'Radio Ga Ga' (Taylor)
'Another One Bites the Dust' (Deacon)
'I Want It All' (Queen, May)
'Crazy Little Thing Called Love'
(Mercury)
'A Kind of Magic' (Taylor)
'Under Pressure' (Queen, Bowie)
'One Vision' (Queen, Taylor)
'You're My Best Friend' (Deacon)
'Don't Stop Me Now' (Mercury)
'Killer Queen' (Mercury)
'These Are the Days of Our Lives'
(Taylor)
'Who Wants to Live Forever' (May)
'Seven Seas of Rhye' (Mercury)
'Heaven for Everyone' (Taylor)
'Somebody to Love' (Mercury)
'I Want to Break Free' (Mercury)
'The Show Must Go On' (Queen, May)
'Bohemian Rhapsody' (Mercury)

Release date
11 November 2009

Highest chart position on release
UK 3, US DNC

DEEP CUTS VOLUME 1 2011
Cover art
Design: Queen

Tracks
'Ogre Battle' (Mercury)
'Stone Cold Crazy' (Mercury, May,
Taylor, Deacon)
'My Fairy King' (Mercury)

'I'm in Love with My Car' (Taylor)
'Keep Yourself Alive' (May)
'Long Away' (May)
'The Millionaire Waltz' (Mercury)
''39' (May)
'Tenement Funster' (Taylor)
'Flick of the Wrist' (Mercury)
'Lily of the Valley' (Mercury)
'Good Company' (May)
'The March of the Black Queen'
(Mercury)
'In the Lap of the Gods … Revisited'
(Mercury)

Release date
14 March 2011

Highest chart position on release
UK 92, US –

DEEP CUTS VOLUME 2 2011
Cover art
Design: Queen

Tracks
'Mustapha' (Mercury)
'Sheer Heart Attack' (Taylor)
'Spread Your Wings' (Deacon)
'Sleeping on the Sidewalk' (May)
'It's Late' (May)
'Rock It (Prime Jive)' (Taylor)
'Dead On Time' (May)
'Sail Away Sweet Sister' (May)
'Dragon Attack' (May)
'Action This Day' (Taylor)
'Put Out the Fire' (May)
'Staying Power' (Mercury)
'Jealousy' (Mercury)
'Battle Theme' (May)

Release date
6 June 2011

Highest chart position on release
UK DNC, US –

DEEP CUTS VOLUME 3 2011
Cover art
Design: Queen

Tracks
'Made in Heaven' (Mercury)
'Machines (Or "Back to Humans")'
(May, Taylor)

'Don't Try So Hard' (Mercury)
'Tear It Up' (May)
'I Was Born to Love You' (Mercury)
'A Winter's Tale' (Queen, Mercury)
'Ride the Wild Wind' (Taylor)
'Bijou' (May, Mercury)
'Was It All Worth It' (Mercury)
'One Year of Love' (Deacon)
'Khashoggi's Ship' (Queen)
'Is This the World We Created …?'
    (Mercury, May)
'The Hitman' (Mercury, May, Deacon)
'It's a Beautiful Day' (Queen, Mercury)
'Mother Love' (May, Mercury)

Release date
5 September 2011

Highest chart position on release
UK DNC, US –

ICON 2013
US/Canada limited edition

Cover art
Design: Queen

Tracks
'Stone Cold Crazy' (Mercury, May,
    Taylor, Deacon)
'Tie Your Mother Down' (May)
'Fat Bottomed Girls' (May)
'Another One Bites the Dust' (Deacon)
'We Will Rock You' (May)
'We Are the Champions' (Mercury)
'Radio Ga Ga' (Taylor)
'Bohemian Rhapsody' (Mercury)
'I'm in Love with My Car' (Taylor)
'I Want It All' (May)
'The Show Must Go On' (May)

Release date
11 June 2013

Highest chart position on release
UK –, US DNC

QUEEN FOREVER 2014
Cover art
Design: Queen

Tracks
'Let Me in Your Heart Again' (May)
'Love Kills' (Mercury, Moroder)

'There Must Be More to Life Than This'
    (Mercury)
'It's a Hard Life' (Mercury)
'You're My Best Friend' (Deacon)
'Love of My Life' (Mercury)
'Drowse' (Taylor)
'Long Away' (May)
'Lily of the Valley' (Mercury)
'Don't Try So Hard' (Mercury)
'Bijou' (May, Mercury)
'These Are the Days of Our Lives'
    (Taylor)
'Las Palabras de Amor (The Words of
    Love)' (May)
'Who Wants to Live Forever' (May)
'A Winter's Tale' (Queen, Mercury)
'Play the Game' (Mercury)
'Save Me' (May)
'Somebody to Love' (Mercury)
'Too Much Love Will Kill You' (May,
    Musker, Lamers)
'Crazy Little Thing Called Love'
    (Mercury)
'I Was Born to Love You' (Mercury)

Release date
10 November 2014

Highest chart position on release
UK 5, US 38

BOX SETS

THE COMPLETE WORKS 1985
Comprises all studio and live albums
released from 1973 to 1984, as well
as a bonus disc called *Complete
Vision*, containing the following
tracks: 'See What a Fool I've Been',
'A Human Body', 'Soul Brother', 'I Go
Crazy', 'Thank God It's Christmas',
'One Vision', 'Blurred Vision'

BOX OF TRIX 1992
Comprises *The 12" Collection*
compilation album, plus a video
of *Queen – Live at the Rainbow*
(recorded in November 1974), an
album and single covers poster, sew-
on cloth Queen patch, metal Queen
pin, 32-page photo book, and a
Queen T-shirt

ULTIMATE QUEEN 1995
All the albums released from 1973
to 1995 (excluding *Greatest Hits*,
Greatest Hits II, *Greatest Hits III* and
Queen at the Beeb) repackaged as
20 litho-printed picture CDs

THE CROWN JEWELS 1998
Comprises the first eight studio albums
(*Queen* to *The Game*)

THE PLATINUM COLLECTION: GREATEST HITS I, II, AND III 2000
Comprises the three *Greatest Hits*
albums

THE SINGLES COLLECTION VOLUME I 2008
Limited edition comprising remastered
versions of the first thirteen
worldwide charting singles, including
B-sides – from 'Keep Yourself Alive' /
'Son and Daughter' to 'Don't Stop
Me Now' / 'In Only Seven Days'

THE SINGLES COLLECTION VOLUME II 2009
Limited edition comprising remastered
versions of the next thirteen
worldwide charting singles, including
B-sides – from 'Love of My Life' (live)
/ 'Now I'm Here' (live) to 'I Want to
Break Free' / 'Machines (Or "Back to
Humans")'

THE SINGLES COLLECTION VOLUME III 2010
Limited edition comprising remastered
versions of the next thirteen
worldwide charting singles, including
B-sides – from 'It's a Hard Life' /
'Is This the World We Created …?' to
'Scandal' / 'My Life Has Been Saved'

THE SINGLES COLLECTION VOLUME IV 2010
Limited edition comprising remastered
versions of Queen's next thirteen
worldwide charting singles, including
B-sides – from 'The Miracle' /
'Stone Cold Crazy' (live) to 'Under
Pressure' (Rah mix) / 'Under Pressure'
(Mike Spencer remix) / 'Under
Pressure' (live)

SINGLES

'Keep Yourself Alive' / 'Son and Daughter' *(6 Jul 1973, DNC)*

'Seven Seas of Rhye' / 'See What a Fool I've Been' *(23 Feb 1974, UK 10)*

'Killer Queen' / 'Flick of the Wrist' *(11 Oct 1974, UK 2, US 12)*

'Now I'm Here' / 'Lily of the Valley' *(17 Jan 1975, UK 11)*

'Bohemian Rhapsody' / 'I'm in Love with My Car' *(31 Oct 1975, UK 1, US 9)*

'You're My Best Friend' / ''39' *(18 May 1975, UK 7, US 16)*

'Somebody to Love' / 'White Man' *(12 Nov 1976, UK 2, US 13)*

'Tie Your Mother Down' / 'You and I' *(4 Mar 1977, UK 31, US 49)*

'We Are the Champions' / 'We Will Rock You' *(7 Oct 1977, UK 2, US 4)*

'Spread Your Wings' / 'Sheer Heart Attack' *(10 Feb 1978, UK 34)*

'Bicycle Race' / 'Fat Bottomed Girls' *(28 Oct 1978, UK 11, US 24)*

'Don't Stop Me Now' / 'In Only Seven Days' *(10 Feb 1979, UK 9, US 76)*

'Love of My Life' (live) / 'Now I'm Here' (live) *(29 Jun 1979, UK 63)*

'Crazy Little Thing Called Love' / 'We Will Rock You' (live) *(5 Oct 1979, UK 2, US 1)*

'Save Me' / 'Let Me Entertain You' (live) *(25 Jan 1980, UK 11)*

'Play the Game' / 'A Human Body' *(30 May 1980, UK 14, US 42)*

'Another One Bites the Dust' / 'Dragon Attack' *(22 Aug 1980, UK 7, US 1)*

'Flash' / 'Football Fight' *(24 Nov 1980, UK 10, US 42)*

'Future Management' / 'Laugh or Cry' *(30 Mar 1981, DNC)*

'Under Pressure' (with David Bowie) / 'Soul Brother' *(26 Oct 1981, UK 1, US 29)*

'Body Language' / 'Life Is Real' *(19 April 1982, UK 25, US 11)*

'Las Palabras de Amor (The Words of Love)' / 'Cool Cat' *(1 Jun 1982, UK 17)*

'Backchat' / 'Staying Power' *(9 Aug 1982, UK 40)*

'Radio Ga Ga' / 'I Go Crazy' *(23 Jan 1984, UK 2, US 16)*

'I Want to Break Free' / 'Machines (Or "Back to Humans")' *(2 Apr 1984, UK 3, US 45)*

'It's a Hard Life' / 'Is This the World We Created …?' *(16 Jul 1984, UK 6, US 72)*

'Hammer to Fall' / 'Tear It Up' *(10 Sep 1984, UK 13)*

'Thank God It's Christmas' / 'Man on the Prowl' / 'Keep Passing the Open Windows' *(26 Nov 1984, UK 21)*

'One Vision' / 'Blurred Vision' *(4 Nov 1985, UK 7, US 61)*

'A Kind of Magic' / 'A Dozen Red Roses for My Darling' *(17 Mar 1986, UK 3, US 42)*

'Friends Will Be Friends' / 'Seven Seas of Rhye' *(9 Jun 1986, UK 14)*

'Who Wants to Live Forever' / 'Killer Queen' *(15 Sep 1986, UK 24)*

'I Want It All' / 'Hang on in There' *(2 May 1989, UK 3, US 50)*

'Breakthru' / 'Stealin'' *(19 Jun 1989, UK 7)*

'The Invisible Man' / 'Hijack My Heart' *(7 Aug 1989, UK 12)*

'Scandal' / 'My Life Has Been Saved' *(9 Oct 1989, UK 25)*

'The Miracle' / 'Stone Cold Crazy' (live) *(27 Nov 1989, UK 21)*

'Innuendo' / 'Bijou' *(14 Jan 1991, UK 1)*

'I'm Going Slightly Mad' / 'The Hitman' *(4 Mar 1991, UK 22)*

'Headlong' / 'All God's People' *(13 May 1991, UK 14)*

'The Show Must Go On' / 'Keep Yourself Alive' *(14 Oct 1991, UK 16)*

FREDDIE MERCURY

STUDIO ALBUMS

MR BAD GUY 1985

Recorded at Musicland Studios, Munich
Produced by Reinhold Mack, Freddie Mercury

Personnel

Freddie Mercury: vocals, piano, synthesizer
Jo Burt: fretless bass
Curt Cress: drums
Fred Mandel: piano, synthesizer, guitar
Paul Vincent: guitar
Stephen Wissnet: bass guitar, Fairlight CMI, drum programming

Additional credit

Reinhold Mack: Fairlight CMI, drum programming

Cover art

Design: The Artful Dodger
Photography: A. Sawa

Tracks

'Let's Turn It On' (Mercury)
'Made in Heaven' (Mercury)
'I Was Born to Love You' (Mercury)
'Foolin' Around' (Mercury)
'Your Kind of Love' (Mercury)
'Mr Bad Guy' (Mercury)
'Man Made Paradise' (Mercury)
'There Must Be More to Life Than This' (Mercury)
'Living on My Own' (Mercury)
'My Love Is Dangerous' (Mercury)
'Love Me Like There's No Tomorrow' (Mercury)

Release date

29 April 1985

Highest chart position on release

UK 6, US 159

BARCELONA 1988

Recorded at Townhouse Studios, London; Mountain Studios, Montreux, Switzerland
Produced by Freddie Mercury, Mike Moran, David Richards

Personnel

Freddie Mercury: vocals, piano
Montserrat Caballé: vocals
John Deacon: bass guitar
Mike Moran: keyboards

Additional credits

Barry Castle: horn
Deborah Ann Johnston: cello
Homi Kanga: violin
Laurie Lewis: violin
Pamela Quinlan: piano, backing vocals
Frank Ricotti: percussion
Madeline Bell: backing vocals
Dennis Bishop: backing vocals
Lance Ellington: backing vocals
Miriam Stockley: backing vocals
Peter Straker: backing vocals

Mark Williamson: backing vocals
Carol Woods: backing vocals

Cover art
Design: Richard Gray
Photography: Peter Hince

Tracks
'Barcelona' (Mercury, Moran)
'La Japonaise' (Mercury, Moran)
'The Fallen Priest' (Mercury,
  Moran, Rice)
'Ensueño' (Mercury, Moran, Caballé)
'The Golden Boy' (Mercury,
  Moran, Rice)
'Guide Me Home' (Mercury, Moran)
'How Can I Go On' (Mercury, Moran)
'Overture Piccante' (Mercury, Moran)

Release date
10 October 1988

Highest chart position on release
UK 25, US DNC

COMPILATIONS

THE FREDDIE MERCURY ALBUM 1992
Issued in the US as *The Great Pretender* with 'Barcelona' omitted and 'My Love Is Dangerous' and Living on My Own' added

Cover art
Design: Richard Gray
Photography: Peter Hince

Tracks
'The Great Pretender' (Ram)
'Foolin' Around' (Mercury)
'Time' (Clark, Christie)
'Your Kind of Lover' (Mercury)
'Exercises in Free Love' (Mercury,
  Moran)
'In My Defence' (Clark, Daniels,
  Soames)
'Mr Bad Guy' (Mercury)
'Let's Turn It On' (Mercury)
'Love Kills' (Mercury, Moroder)
'Barcelona' (Mercury, Moran)

Release date
16 November 1992

Highest chart position on release
UK 4, US DNC

REMIXES 1993
Cover art
Design: Richard Gray
Photography: Peter Hince,
  Simon Fowler

Tracks
'Living on My Own' (1993 No More
  Brothers extended mix) (Mercury)
'Time' (1992 Nile Rodgers remix)
  (Clark, Christie)
'Love Kills' (1992 Richard Wolf Euro
  mix) (Mercury, Moroder)
'The Great Pretender' (1992 Brian
  Malouf remix) (Ram)
'My Love Is Dangerous' (1992 Jeff
  Lord-Alge remix) (Mercury)
'Living on My Own' (1993 Roger S
  remix) (Mercury)

Release date
21 October 1993

Highest chart position on release
UK 5

SOLO 2000
Freddie's two original studio albums,
  plus a bonus disc of selected tracks
  from *The Solo Collection* box set

Tracks

Disc one
Mr Bad Guy (1985)

Disc two
Barcelona (1988)

Disc three
'I Can Hear Music' (Larry Lurex, 1973
  single) (Barry, Greenwich, Spector)
'Love Kills' (original 1984 single
  version) (Mercury, Moroder)
'The Great Pretender' (original 1987
  single version) (Ram)
'Living on My Own' (1993 radio mix)
  (Mercury)
'In My Defence' (2000 remix) (Clark,
  Daniels, Soames)
'Time' (2000 remix) (Clark, Christie)

'Love Kills' (rock mix) (Mercury,
  Moroder)

Release date
7 November 2000

Highest chart position on release
UK 13

LOVER OF LIFE, SINGER OF SONGS – THE VERY BEST OF FREDDIE MERCURY SOLO 2006
Included an accompanying two-disc DVD, containing *The Untold Story* documentary on disc one and various music videos on disc two

Cover art
Design: Outside Line
Image: Based on photograph by
  Neal Preston

Tracks

Disc one
'In My Defence' (2000 remix) (Clark,
  Daniels, Soames)
'The Great Pretender' (original 1987
  single version) (Ram)
'Living on My Own' (1993 radio mix)
  (Mercury)
'Made in Heaven' (Mercury)
'Love Kills' (original 1984 single
  version) (Mercury, Moroder)
'There Must Be More to Life Than This'
  (Mercury)
'Guide Me Home' (Mercury, Moran)
'How Can I Go On' (Mercury, Moran)
'Foolin' Around' (Steve Brown remix)
  (Mercury)
'Time' (Clark, Christie)
'Barcelona' (Mercury, Moran)
'Love Me Like There's No Tomorrow'
  (Mercury)
'I Was Born to Love You' (Mercury)
'The Golden Boy' (Mercury,
  Moran, Rice)
'Mr Bad Guy' (Mercury)
'The Great Pretender' (Malouf remix)
  (Ram)
'Love Kills' (Star Rider remix) (Mercury,
  Moroder)
'I Can Hear Music' (Larry Lurex, 1973
  single) (Barry, Greenwich, Spector)

'Goin' Back' (Larry Lurex, 1973 B-side) (Goffin, King)

'Guide Me Home' (piano version by Thierry Lang) (Mercury, Moran)

Disc two

'Love Kills' (Sunshine People radio mix) (Mercury, Moroder)

'Made in Heaven' (extended version) (Mercury)

'Living on My Own' (Egg remix) (Mercury)

'Love Kills' (Rank 1 remix) (Mercury, Moroder)

'Mr Bad Guy' (Bad Circulation version) (Mercury)

'I Was Born to Love You' (George Demure Almost Vocal mix) (Mercury)

'My Love Is Dangerous' (extended version) (Mercury)

'Love Making Love' (demo version)

'Love Kills' (Pixel82 remix) (Mercury, Moroder)

'I Was Born to Love You' (extended version) (Mercury)

'Foolin' Around' (early version) (Mercury)

'Living on My Own' (No More Brothers extended mix) (Mercury)

'Love Kills' (More Oder rework) (Mercury, Moroder)

'Your Kind of Lover' (vocal and piano version) (Mercury)

'Let's Turn It On' (a capella) (Mercury)

Release date
4 September 2006

Highest chart position on release
UK 6

BARCELONA: SPECIAL EDITION 2012

The special edition replaced the original synthesized backing with a full symphony orchestra, and also included a DVD featuring live performances of 'Barcelona', 'How Can I Go On' and 'The Golden Boy', plus three promotional videos for 'Barcelona'

Personnel
Freddie Mercury: vocals, piano
Montserrat Caballé: vocals

John Deacon: bass guitar
Mike Moran: keyboards

Additional credits
Barry Castle: horn
Deborah Ann Johnston: cello
Homi Kanga: violin
Laurie Lewis: violin
Pamela Quinlan: piano, backing vocals
Frank Ricotti: percussion
Madeline Bell: backing vocals
Dennis Bishop: backing vocals
Lance Ellington: backing vocals
Miriam Stockley: backing vocals
Peter Straker: backing vocals
Mark Williamson: backing vocals
Carol Woods: backing vocals

Additional orchestral credits
The Prague FILMharmonic Orchestra
David Garrett: violin
Naoko Kikuchi: koto
Rufus Taylor: drums

Cover art
Design: Richard Gray
Illustration: Matilda Beach

Tracks

Disc one
New orchestrated album
'Barcelona' (Mercury, Moran)
'La Japonaise' (Mercury, Moran)
'The Fallen Priest' (Mercury, Moran, Rice)
'Ensueño' (Mercury, Moran, Caballé)
'The Golden Boy' (Mercury, Moran, Rice)
'Guide Me Home' (Mercury, Moran)
'How Can I Go On' (Mercury, Moran)
'Exercises in Free Love' (Mercury, Moran)
'Overture Piccante' (Mercury, Moran)
'How Can I Go On' (bonus track feat. David Garrett) (Mercury, Moran)

Disc two
The best of the rarities and session outtakes
'Exercises in Free Love' (1987 B-side) (Mercury, Moran)
'Barcelona' (Freddie's demo vocal) (Mercury, Moran)
'La Japonaise' (Freddie's demo vocal) (Mercury, Moran)

'Rachmaninov's Revenge (The Fallen Priest)' (Freddie's demo vocal) (Mercury, Moran, Rice)

'Ensueño' (Montserrat's live takes) (Mercury, Moran, Caballé)

'The Golden Boy' (Freddie's demo vocal) (Mercury, Moran, Rice)

'Guide Me Home' (alternative version) (Mercury, Moran)

'How Can I Go On' (alternative version) (Mercury, Moran)

'How Can I Go On' (alternative piano version) (Mercury, Moran)

Disc three
album orchestral version
'Barcelona' (instrumental) (Mercury, Moran)
'La Japonaise' (instrumental) (Mercury, Moran)
'The Fallen Priest' (instrumental) (Mercury, Moran, Rice)
'Ensueño' (instrumental) (Mercury, Moran, Caballé)
'The Golden Boy' (instrumental) (Mercury, Moran, Rice)
'Guide Me Home' (instrumental) (Mercury, Moran)
'How Can I Go On' (instrumental) (Mercury, Moran)
'Exercises in Free Love' (instrumental) (Mercury, Moran)
'Overture Piccante' (instrumental) (Mercury, Moran)

Release date
3 September 2012

BOX SETS

THE SOLO COLLECTION 2000
Covers the whole of Freddie's solo career, and includes a set of interviews and a DVD comprising music videos and a documentary

Tracks

Disc one
Mr Bad Guy (1985)

Disc two
Barcelona (1988)

Disc three
The Great Pretender (1992)

'The Great Pretender' (Brian Malouf remix) (Ram)

'Foolin' Around' (Steve Brown remix) (Mercury)

'Time' (Nile Rodgers remix) (Clark, Christie)

'Your Kind of Lover' (Steve Brown remix) (Mercury)

'Exercises in Free Love' (Mercury, Moran)

'In My Defence' (Ron Nevison remix) (Clark, Soames, Daniels)

'Mr Bad Guy' (Brian Malouf remix) (Mercury)

'Let's Turn It On' (Jeff Lord-Alge remix) (Mercury)

'Living on My Own' (Julian Raymond remix) (Mercury)

'My Love Is Dangerous' (Jeff Lord-Alge remix (Mercury)

'Love Kills' (Richard Wolf remix) (Mercury, Moroder)

Disc four
The Singles 1973–1985

'I Can Hear Music' (Larry Lurex, 1973 single) (Greenwich, Barry, Spector)

'Goin' Back' (Larry Lurex, 1973 B-side) (Goffin, King)

'Love Kills' (original 1984 single version) (Mercury, Moroder)

'Love Kills' (original 1984 extended version) (Mercury, Moroder)

'I Was Born to Love You' (original 1985 extended version) (Mercury)

'Stop All the Fighting' (1985 non-album B-side) (Mercury)

'Stop All the Fighting' (1985 non-album B-side extended version) (Mercury)

'Made in Heaven' (original 1985 extended version) (Mercury)

'She Blows Hot and Cold' (1985 non-album B-side) (Mercury)

'She Blows Hot and Cold' (1985 non-album B-side extended version) (Mercury)

'Living on My Own' (1985 extended version) (Mercury)

'My Love Is Dangerous' (original 1985 extended version) (Mercury)

'Love Me Like There's No Tomorrow' (original 1985 extended version) (Mercury)

'Let's Turn It On' (original 1985 extended version) (Mercury)

Disc five
The Singles 1986–1993

'Time' (original 1986 single/album version) (Clark, Christie)

'Time' (original 1986 extended version) (Clark, Christie)

'Time' (original 1986 instrumental version) (Clark, Christie)

'In My Defence' (1986 album version) (Clark, Soames, Daniels)

'The Great Pretender' (original 1987 single version) (Ram)

'The Great Pretender' (original 1987 extended version) (Ram)

'Exercises in Free Love' (1987 non-album B-side) (Mercury, Moran)

'Barcelona' (original 1987 single version) (Mercury, Moran)

'Barcelona' (original 1987 extended version) (Mercury, Moran)

'How Can I Go On' (1989 single version) (Mercury, Moran)

'Living on My Own' (1993 No More Brothers extended mix) (Mercury)

'Living on My Own' (1993 radio mix) (Mercury)

'Living on My Own' (1993 club mix) (Mercury)

'Living on My Own' (1993 Underground Solutions mix) (Mercury)

Disc six
The Instrumentals

'Barcelona' (instrumental) (Mercury, Moran)

'La Japonaise' (instrumental) (Mercury, Moran)

'The Fallen Priest' (instrumental) (Mercury, Moran, Rice)

'Ensueño' (instrumental) (Mercury, Moran, Caballé)

'The Golden Boy' (instrumental) (Mercury, Moran, Rice)

'Guide Me Home' (instrumental) (Mercury, Moran)

'How Can I Go On' (instrumental) (Mercury, Moran)

'Love Me Like There's No Tomorrow' (instrumental) (Mercury)

'Made in Heaven' (instrumental) (Mercury)

'Mr Bad Guy' (instrumental) (Mercury)

'There Must Be More to Life Than This' (instrumental) (Mercury)

'In My Defence' (instrumental) (Clark, Soames, Daniels)

'The Great Pretender' (instrumental) (Ram)

Disc seven
Rarities 1

'Let's Turn It On' (a capella) (Mercury)

'Made in Heaven' (alternative version) (Mercury)

'I Was Born to Love You' (vocal and piano version) (Mercury)

'Foolin' Around' (early version) (Mercury)

'Foolin' Around' (original 1985 unreleased 12" mix) (Mercury)

'Foolin' Around' (instrumental) (Mercury)

'Your Kind of Lover' (early version) (Mercury)

'Your Kind of Lover' (vocal and piano version) (Mercury)

'Mr Bad Guy' (orchestra outtakes) (Mercury)

'Mr Bad Guy' (early version) (Mercury)

'There Must Be More to Life Than This' (piano outtakes) (Mercury)

'Living on My Own' (hybrid edit: early/ later versions) (Mercury)

'Love Is Dangerous' (early version) (Mercury)

'Love Me Like There's No Tomorrow' (early version) (Mercury)

'Love Me Like There's No Tomorrow' (second early version: extract) (Mercury)

'Love Me Like There's No Tomorrow' (third early version) (Mercury)

'Love Me Like There's No Tomorrow' (live take) (Mercury)

'She Blows Hot and Cold' (alternative version featuring Brian May) (Mercury)

'Gazelle' (demo) (Mercury)

'Money Can't Buy Happiness' (demo) (Mercury)

'Love Makin' Love' (demo) (Mercury)

'God Is Heavy' (demo) (Mercury)

'New York' (demo) (Mercury)

Disc eight
Rarities 2

'The Duet (The Fallen Priest)' (extract from Garden Lodge tape) (Mercury, Moran, Rice)

'Idea (Barcelona)' (extract from Garden Lodge tape) (Mercury, Moran)
'Idea (Barcelona)' (second extract from Garden Lodge tape) (Mercury, Moran)
'Barcelona' (early version: Freddie's demo vocal) (Mercury, Moran)
'Barcelona' (Freddie's vocal slave) (Mercury, Moran)
'Barcelona' (later version: Freddie's vocal only) (Mercury, Moran)
'La Japonaise' (early version: Freddie's vocal only) (Mercury, Moran)
'La Japonaise' (a capella) (Mercury, Moran)
'Rachmaninov's Revenge (The Fallen Priest)' (early version) (Mercury, Moran, Rice)
'Rachmaninov's Revenge (The Fallen Priest)' (later version: Freddie's demo vocal)
'Ensueño' (Montserrat's live takes) (Mercury, Moran, Caballé)
'The Golden Boy' (early version: Freddie's demo vocal) (Mercury, Moran, Rice)
'The Golden Boy' (second early version: extr.) (Mercury, Moran, Rice)
'The Golden Boy' (a capella featuring gospel choir) (Mercury, Moran, Rice)
'Guide Me Home / How Can I Go On' (alternative versions) (Mercury, Moran)
'How Can I Go On' (outtake: extract) (Mercury, Moran)
'How Can I Go On' (alternative piano version) (Mercury, Moran)
'When This Tired Old Body Wants to Sing' (late night jam) (Mercury, Moran)

Disc nine
Rarities 3
'Rain' (Ibex, live 1969) (Lennon, McCartney)
'Green' (Wreckage, rehearsal 1969) (Mercury)
'The Man from Manhattan' (Eddie Howell, 1976) (Howell)
'Love Is the Hero' (Billy Squier, 12" version 1986) (Squier)
'Lady with a Tenor Sax' (Billy Squier, work in progress 1986) (Squier, Mercury)
'Hold On' (Freddie Mercury and Jo Dare, 1986) (Mercury, Mack)
'Heaven for Everyone' (Cross version: Freddie vocal 1988) (Taylor)

'Love Kills' (rock mix) (Mercury, Moroder)
'Love Kills' (instrumental) (Mercury, Moroder, Keenan)
'The Great Pretender' (original demo) (Ram)
'Holding On' (demo) (Mercury)
'It's So You' (demo) (Mercury)
'I Can't Dance / Keep Smilin'' (demo) (Mercury)
'Horns of Doom' (demo) (Richards)
'Yellow Breezes' (demo) (Mercury, Moran)
'Have a Nice Day' (fan club message) (Mercury, Moran)

Disc ten
The David Wigg Interviews
1979, London
1984, Munich (part one)
1984, Munich (part two)
1985, Wembley
1986, London
1987, Ibiza (part one)
1987, Ibiza (part two)
1987, Ibiza (part three)

Disc eleven
The Video Collection (DVD)
'Barcelona' (live version) (Mercury, Moran)
'The Great Pretender' (single version) (Ram)
'I Was Born to Love You' (Mercury)
'Time' (Clark, Christie)
'How Can I Go On' (Mercury, Moran)
'Made in Heaven' (Mercury)
'Living on My Own' (Mercury)
'The Golden Boy' (Mercury, Moran, Rice)
'The Great Pretender' (extended version) (Ram)
'Barcelona' (Mercury, Moran)
'In My Defence' (2000 re-edit) (Clark, Soames, Daniels)
'Guide Me Home' (Mercury, Moran)

Disc twelve
The Untold Story (DVD)
Spice Island Dawn
Strange Discipline
Culture Shock
The Draftsman of Ealing
Musical Awakenings
Love of My Life
Bacchus and Aphrodite

Butterflies and Peacocks
A Day at the Opera
My Kind of Towns
Last Days

Release date
23 October 2000

SINGLES

'I Can Hear Music' / 'Goin' Back' (as Larry Lurex) *(29 Jun 1973, DNC)*
'Love Kills' / 'Rotwang's Party' *(10 Sep 1984, UK 10, US 69)*
'I Was Born to Love You' / 'Stop All the Fighting' *(8 Apr 1985, UK 11, US 76)*
'Made in Heaven' / 'She Blows Hot and Cold' *(1 Jul 1985, UK 57)*
'Living on My Own' / 'My Love Is Dangerous' *(2 Sep 1985, UK 50)*
'Love Me Like There's No Tomorrow' / 'Let's Turn It On' *(18 May 1985, UK 76)*
'Time' / 'Time' (instrumental) *(6 May 1986, UK 32)*
'The Great Pretender' / 'Exercises in Free Love' *(23 Feb 1987, UK 4)*
'Barcelona' / 'Exercises in Free Love' *(26 Oct 1987, UK 8)*
'The Golden Boy' / 'The Fallen Priest' *(24 Oct 1988, UK 83)*
'How Can I Go On' / 'Overture Piccante' *(29 Dec 1988, UK 95)*
'Barcelona' (re-release) / 'Exercises in Free Love' *(27 Jul 1992, UK 2)*
'In My Defence' / 'Love Kills' *(30 Nov 1992, UK 8)*

SOURCES, PICTURE CREDITS AND ACKNOWLEDGEMENTS

QUOTE SOURCES

All interviews quoted are the author's own, unless stated below.

6 'I mean, why …' FM interview, *Queen: From Rags to Rhapsody* documentary, 2015 **9** 'It would be …' FM interview, David Wigg, 1987 **10** 'I thought, I'm …' FM interview, *Queen: From Rags to Rhapsody* documentary, 2015 **16** 'Mercury isn't my …' FM interview, *Melody Maker*, December 1974 **16** 'Have I got …' FM interview, Julie Webb, *NME*, April 1974 **20** 'Those hands were …' Derrick Branche interview, *This Is the Real Life*, David Minns & David Evans, Britannia Press, 1992 **22** 'For a boy …' Jer Bulsara interview, *Freddie Mercury: Lover of Life, Singer of Songs*, EMI Music, DVD, 2009 **22** 'England's the place …' Jer Bulsara interview, *The Times*, 2 September 2006 **25** 'The thing I …' FM in *Killer Queen*, Brian May, Mick Rock and Mary Austin, Genesis Publications, 2003 **27** 'The biggest influence …' Brian May interview, *Perspectives: Freddie Mercury Saved My Life, with Alfie Boe*, ITV, May 2014 **28** 'It's surprising, really …' FM in *Killer Queen*, May, Rock and Austin **30** 'Freddie's role in …' Brian May interview, *Face to Face with Rick Wakeman*, August 2013 **31** '[Hendrix] is my …' FM interview, Scott Cohen, *Circus*, April 1975 **39** 'It was the …' FM in *Killer Queen*, May, Rock and Austin **39** 'If there were …' Roger Taylor interview, Danny Scott, *Sunday Express*, November 2014 **39** 'We took it …' Brian May interview, Neil McCormick, *Daily Telegraph*, 9 May 2011 **45** 'We all dressed …' Mike Grose interview, *Queen in Cornwall*, Rupert White, Antenna Publications, 2011 **45** 'Freddie wanted us …' Mike Grose interview, *Queen in Cornwall*, White **46** 'The name was …' FM in *Killer Queen*, May, Rock and Austin **47** 'We used to …' Roger Taylor interview, Ben Mitchell, *Q*, March 2011 **48** 'Freddie's personality was …' Mary Austin interview, David Wigg, *Daily Mail*, 30 March 2013 **48** 'Freddie's role in …' Brian May interview, Neil McCormick, *Daily Telegraph*, 9 May 2011 **50** 'And it was …' FM in *Killer Queen*, May, Rock and Austin **51** 'Freddie stood at …' Danny Baker, *Going to Sea in a Sieve: The Autobiography*, Weidenfeld & Nicolson, 2012 **52** 'I'm very intricate …' FM interview, Caroline Coon, *Melody Maker*, 21 December 1974 **54** 'We're a sitting …' FM interview, Julie Webb, *Melody Maker*, 12 March 1974 **54** 'I knew they'd …' Zandra Rhodes interview, Hilary Alexander, *Daily Telegraph*, 9 February 2011 **55** 'I did some …' Zandra Rhodes interview, Hilary Alexander, *Daily Telegraph*, 9 February 2011 **59** 'God, the agony …' FM in *Killer Queen*, May, Rock and Austin **59** 'There can be …' *Melody Maker* review, Queen, Rainbow Theatre, London, April 1974 **62** 'We have this …' FM in *Killer Queen*, May, Rock and Austin **65** 'For me, it's …' FM interview, unknown source, 1985 **65** 'They were outraged …' Roger Taylor interview, *Mojo*, August 1999 **65** 'Can't wait …' FM interview, *NME*, 4 November 1974 **69** 'It's the most …' FM interview, *Sounds*, 31 January 1976 **69** 'There was no …' Brian May interview, Mark Savage, *BBC News*, 29 October 2015 **69** '"Bohemian Rhapsody" didn't …' FM interview, *NME*, 18 June 1977 **70** 'I'm woken up …' Brian May interview, *Blender*, February 2002 **70** 'The whole group …' FM in *Killer Queen*, May, Rock and Austin **72** 'I think people …' FM interview, *NME*, 18 June 1977 **72** 'Freddie was a …' Brian May interview, *Blender*, January 2002 **72** 'I do think …' Brian May interview, Mark Savage, *BBC News*, 29 October 2015 **72** 'A lot of …' FM in *Killer Queen*, May, Rock and Austin **73** 'You can feel …' review of *A Night at the Opera*, Phil Sutcliffe, *Sounds*, 20 November 1975 **74** 'I thought it …' Roger Taylor interview, Ben Mitchell, *Q*, March 2011 **74** 'I was disappointed …' Mary Austin interview, *Daily Mail*, 30 March 2013 **74** 'I didn't realise …' Roger Taylor interview, Rick Fulton, *Daily Record*, 1 November 2013 **76** 'Little things spark …' FM in *Killer Queen*, May, Rock and Austin **76** 'I know he …' David Minns, *This Is the Real Life*, Minns & Evans **76** 'He had to …' David Minns, *This Is the Real Life*, Minns & Evans **76** 'Freddie gave me …' Eddie Howell interview, KRO Dutch radio, 2014 **78** 'It was a …' Mary Austin interview, *Freddie Mercury – The Untold Story*, Regno Unito Films, 2000

78 'All my lovers …' FM interview, unknown source, c. 1984 **81** 'Darlings, we're the …' FM interview, unknown source, c. 1975 **82** 'I hate pockets …' FM in *Killer Queen*, May, Rock and Austin **85** 'Let's face it …' Roger Taylor interview, *Cream*, April 1978 **85** 'It was anarchy …' John Reid interview, *Queen: Days of Our Lives* documentary, 2011 **86** 'I think I …' FM interview, *Queen: Days of Our Lives* documentary, 2011 **86** 'I would have …' FM interview, Tony Stewart, *NME*, June 1977 **89** 'We were all …' Brian May, Absolute Radio interview, August 2011 **89** 'What do you …' FM interview, Tony Stewart, *NME*, June 1977 **91** 'Elton's a good …' FM interview, *Freddie Mercury: The Definitive Biography*, Lesley-Ann Jones, Hodder, 2012 **92** 'We received an …' Peter Straker interview, *This Is the Real Life*, Minns & Evans **92** 'Things went very …' Brian May interview, *Queen: Days of Our Lives* documentary, 2011 **97** 'It was Freddie …' Roger Taylor interview, Jon Wilde, *Uncut*, March 2005 **97** 'Fred was gazing …' Roger Taylor, Absolute Radio interview, August 2011 **97** 'Every cycle shop …' Peter Hince, *Queen Unseen: My Life with the Greatest Rock Band of the 20th Century*, John Blake Publishing, 2011 **97** 'You have to …' FM in *Killer Queen*, May, Rock and Austin **98** 'Most of my …' FM in *Killer Queen*, May, Rock and Austin **98** 'Had boys following …' Brian May interview, Mick Wall, *Q* magazine, Queen special edition, 2005 **98** 'I sleep with …' FM interview, c. 1986, *The Show Must Go On: The Life of Freddie Mercury*, Rick Sky, Citadel 1997 **99** 'One of the …' Robert Hilburn, *Los Angeles Times*, November 1978 **99** 'There was a …' Hince, *Queen Unseen* **100** 'I'm a man …' FM in *Killer Queen*, May, Rock and Austin **103** 'It's not Mozart …' FM interview, *Melody Maker*, May 1981 **104** 'I'd like to …' FM interview, David Wigg, 1979 **107** 'We could all …' Roger Taylor interview, *Classic Rock*, January 2015 **107** 'After finding out …' FM interview, *Evening News*, October 1979 **108** 'What was a …' FM, source unknown, c. 1980 **108** 'His queerness, like …' Barney Hoskyns, *Glam! Bolan, Bowie & the Glitter Rock Revolution*, Faber & Faber, 1998 **112** 'If people ask …' FM in *Killer Queen*, May, Rock and Austin **112** 'When I look …' FM interview, David Wigg, 1987 **112** 'He immediately stated …' Hince, *Queen Unseen* **112** 'One man grows …' Roger Taylor interview, Ben Mitchell, *Q*, March 2011 **117** 'Although Freddie might …' Peter Freestone, *Freddie Mercury: An Intimate Memoir*, Omnibus, 1998 **118** 'I really do …' FM in *Killer Queen*, May, Rock and Austin **118** 'Whenever I watched …' FM interview, source unknown, c. 1985 **121** 'It's a precarious …' FM interview, *Melody Maker*, May 1981 **121** 'Fred was the …' Roger Taylor interview, Ben Mitchell, *Q*, March 2011 **122** 'His music, first …' Freestone, *Freddie Mercury: An Intimate Memoir* **123** 'The word "gay" …' Brian May interview, Queenonline, 28 March 2011 **123** 'I think *Hot Space* was a mistake …' Brian May interview, Paul Elliott, *Sounds*, October 1989 **123** 'I think [*Hot Space*] was way ahead …' FM interview, source unknown, c. 1985 **125** 'One of the …' Giorgio Moroder interview, IamMusicTV, May 2015 **129** 'I love nightlife …' FM in *Killer Queen*, May, Rock and Austin **131** 'Fred's lyrics came …' Roger Taylor interview, *Queen: From Rags to Rhapsody* documentary, 2015 **131** 'With Roger and …' FM interview, Mary Turner, *Off the Record*, Westwood One radio, 1984 **132** '"It's OK for …"' Hince, *Queen Unseen* **135** 'Queen come across …' FM interview, Mary Turner, *Off the Record*, Westwood One radio, 1984 **135** 'The *Led Zeppelin II* …' review of *The Works*, Parke Puterbaugh, *Rolling Stone*, 12 April 1984 **135** 'This guy, in …' Brian May interview, Queenonline, 29 March 2011 **135** 'Freddie was desperately …' David Mallet interview, *I Want My MTV: The Uncensored Story Of The Music Video Revolution*, Rob Tannenbaum & Craig Marks, Dutton Penguin 2011 **139** 'In America they …' FM interview, Simon Bates, BBC Radio 1, 1985 **139** 'In those days …' Roger Taylor interview, *Queen: Days of Our Lives* documentary, 2011 **139** 'Over here people …' Brian May interview, Queenonline, March 2011 **139** 'An enormous sum …' Jim Beach interview, *The Great Pretender* documentary, 2012 **139** 'On balance [the South Africa trip] …' Roger Taylor interview, *Queen: Days of Our Lives* documentary, 2011 **139** 'If I wanted …' FM interview, David Wigg, 1984 **143** 'Of course we're …' FM interview, David

Wigg, 1984 **143** 'For an offshoot …' Walter Yetnikoff interview, *Freddie Mercury – The Untold Story*, DVD 2000 **145** 'Queen smoked 'em …' Dave Grohl interview, source unknown, 2005 **146** 'Freddie was unique …' Lady Gaga interview, source unknown, 2011 **149** 'We were all …' FM interview, David Wigg, 1985 **150** 'Honestly, it's a …' FM interview, *BBC News*, July 1985 **150** 'It wasn't a …' Roger Taylor interview, *Queen: Days of Our Lives* documentary, 2011 **152** 'I find even …' FM in *Killer Queen*, May, Rock and Austin **152** 'Queen were absolutely …' Bob Geldof interview, Phil Sutcliffe, *Q*, March 1991 **153** 'I got a …' FM interview, David Wigg, 1985 **153** 'I thought about …' Russell Mulcahy interview, *A Kind of Magic* promotional video, 1986 **153** 'We had to …' FM interview, *A Kind of Magic* promotional video, 1986 **155** 'I like to …' FM interview, *Melody Maker*, May 1981 **155** 'He said, "You …"' Brian May, *Absolute Greatest* audio commentary **155** 'As chic as …' review of *A Kind of Magic*, *The Times*, September 1986 **155** 'I don't know …' FM interview, *A Kind of Magic* promotional video, 1986 **156** 'Freddie's sense of …' Brian May interview, Jon Hotten, *Classic Rock*, April 2014 **156** 'Freddie and I …' Roger Taylor interview, Ben Mitchell, *Q*, March 2011 **160** 'Freddie said something …' Brian May interview, Jon Hotten, *Classic Rock*, April 2014 **162** 'All the costumes …' FM interview, David Wigg, 1987 **165** 'I have lived …' FM interview, David Wigg, 1987 **166** 'He was still …' Elton John interview, *The Great Pretender* documentary, 2012 **169** 'Most of the …' FM interview, Rudi Dolezal, press kit for 'The Great Pretender', 1987 **170** 'She has that …' FM interview, Nick Ferrari, *Sun*, 19 July 1985 **170** 'She jokes and …' FM interview, Adrian Deevoy, *Q*, December 1988 **171** 'His technique was …' Montserrat Caballé interview, *Freddie Mercury: A Kind of Magic* documentary, 2006 **172** 'I was extremely …' FM interview, David Wigg, 1987 **172** 'He tried to …' Peter Freestone interview, Carmine Pascuzzi, Mediasearch, 2009 **172** 'He never, ever …' Peter Freestone interview, *The Great Pretender* documentary, 2012 **172** 'Oh *do* fuck off!' FM interview, Adrian Deevoy, *Q*, December 1988 **176** 'We made a …' Brian May interview, Paul Elliott, *Sounds*, October 1989 **176** 'Four artists trying …' Brian May interview, Neil McCormick, *Daily Telegraph*, 9 May 2011 **177** 'From now on …' FM interview, source unknown, 1987 **177** 'It was OK …' FM interview, source unknown, 1989 **177** 'Somewhere out there …' review of *The Miracle*, Kim Neely, *Rolling Stone*, September 1989 **178** 'He only asked …' Roger Taylor interview, Ben Mitchell, *Q*, March 2011 **179** 'I said, "Fred …"' Brian May interview, *Rolling Stone*, April 2013 **179** 'Songs like "The Show Must Go On" …' Brian May interview, *Rolling Stone*, July 2014 **181** 'He never seemed …' Brian May interview, *Guitar World*, July 2015 **181** 'He thought we …' Peter Paterno interview, *Freddie Mercury: The Definitive Biography*, Lesley-Ann Jones, Hodder, 2012 **181** 'What is astounding …' review of *Innuendo*, *The Times*, 1 February 1991 **181** 'The middle eight …' Brian May interview, BBC Radio 1, December 1995 **182** 'The disease killed …' Freestone, *Freddie Mercury: An Intimate Memoir* **182** 'I was about …' Roger Taylor interview, Ben Mitchell, *Q*, March 2011 **182** 'He lived life …' Brian May, Happy Birthday FM Google blog, September 2011 **185** 'I don't expect …' FM interview, David Wigg, 1987 **186** 'I'm trying to …' Adam Lambert interview, *Classic Rock*, January 2015 **189** 'I lost somebody …' Mary Austin interview, David Wigg, *Daily Mail*, 22 January 2000 **189** 'It was almost …' Freestone, *Freddie Mercury: An Intimate Memoir* **189** 'He protected us …' Jer Bulsara interview, Angela Levin, *Daily Telegraph*, 8 September 2012 **193** 'We were grieving …' Roger Taylor, *Absolute Greatest* audio commentary, 2009 **193** 'I found myself …' Mary Austin interview, David Wigg, *Daily Mail*, 31 March 2013 **193** 'He didn't want …' Mary Austin interview, David Wigg, *Daily Mail*, 31 March 2013 **194** 'Freddie Mercury sang …' Robert Plant interview, *The Freddie Mercury Tribute Concert*, DVD, 2013 **196** 'I didn't want …' Brian May interview, Queenonline, March 2011 **196** 'Sometimes there was …' Brian May interview, *Guitarist*, July 1998 **196** 'A more-than-worthy epitaph …' review of *Made in Heaven*, *Sunday Times*, 26 November 1995 **197** 'It's a lovely …' Brian May interview, Ben Mitchell, *Q*, March 2011 **197** 'I don't wish …' John Deacon press statement, published in the *Sun*, 21 April 2001 **198** 'There's never going …' Adam Lambert interview, Nick Hasted, *Classic Rock*, January 2015 **198** 'Adam is the …' Brian May interview, Nick Hasted, *Classic Rock*, January 2015 **202** 'Until you buggers …' FM interview, David Wigg 1984 **202** 'I don't give …' FM interview, David Wigg 1987 **202** 'A man who …' David Bowie interview, *Rolling Stone*, January 1992 **202** 'I never had …' Axl Rose interview, Corey Levitan, *Circus*, September 1992 **202** 'The greatest frontman …' Dave Grohl interview, NPR Music, April 2011 **202** 'In short, a …' Lady Gaga interview, Dailyrecord.co.uk, November 2009 **202** 'I didn't really …' Roger Taylor interview, Dailyrecord.co.uk, November 2013 **202** 'I miss his …' Brian May interview, *Q*, March 2008 **205** 'Freddie was fully …' Brian May, Happy Birthday FM Google blog, September 2011

Overleaf: Rainbow Theatre, London, 1974.

PICTURE CREDITS

Every effort has been made to trace and acknowledge the copyright holders. We apologise in advance for any unintentional omissions and would be pleased, if any such case should arise, to add appropriate acknowledgement in any future edition of the book. Please note below all sources for copyright associated where applicable with the images used.

t: top; b: bottom; r: right; l: left; c: centre

Robert Alford: 1, 72, 73, 80, 113l; **Getty Images:** 2–3, 134, 160l, 160r, 177 (Dave Hogan); 6–7 (Andrew Putler); 11, 147, 192–3, (Phil Dent); 16 (Archive Photos/Harvey Meston); 19 (Gamma Keystone); 26, 29r, 32, 34, 36, 37, 46 (Mark and Colleen Hayward); 39, 51, 60, 83tr, 86, 87, 93, 99 (Michael Ochs Archives); 54l (Redferns); 64 (Ian Dickson); 66 (Shinko Music/Koh Hasebe); 67, 90, (Erica Echenberg); 78–9 (LIFE/Terence Spencer); 84 (Lex Van Rossen); 88–9 (Richard E. Aaron); 91, 113r (Hulton Archive); 96, 102, 110–11 (Steve Jennings); 109 (Colin Davey); 117 (Jack Garofalo); 120 (Rob Verhorst); 122 (LIFE); 123t (Keystone); 129l (Kevin Mazur); 129r (Larry Marano); 138 (Steve Wood); 144 (Phil Dent); 151, 152 (Peter Still); 153t (Georges DeKeerle); 161 (Brian Rasic); 173 (Terry O'Neill); 194t (Mick Hutson); 195t, 224 (Michael Putland); 197l (Dave Benett); 197r (Andrew Cowie); 198t (Peter Pakvis); 198b, 199 (Christie Goodwin); 203 (Ebet Roberts); **Photo © Mick Rock 1974, 2016:** 8, 40, 44, 47l, 48–9, 53, 55, 56–7, 58, 204–5; **Rex Shutterstock:** 9 (Ilpo Musto); 20l (Martin Moxter); 68, 69, 194b (Andre Csillag); 130, 157, 168, 174–5, 176t, 178t, 190–91 (Richard Young); 140l (Rob Walls); 143 (Gill Allen); 154 (Philip Dunn); 188 (Associated Newspapers); 202 (SIPA/Nivière/Chamussy) 119; **Scope Features:** 12; **Dinodia Photo Library:** 15l, 18b; **Adrian Morrish:** 15r, 23t, 23b, 24, 25l, 25r; **Alamy:** 17t (Angus McComiskey); 21 (V&A Images); 75t (Tracks Images); 105r, 206 (John Henshall); 133 (Freddie Jones); 184 (Danuta Hyniewska); 196t (Phil Jones); **123RF:** 17r; **Bruce Murray:** 18t; **iStockphoto:** 20 inset, 20c, 196 inset; **Topfoto:** 22; **Royal Borough of Kensington and Chelsea Library:** 29l; **Renos Lavithis:** 31l; **John Garnham:** 33t; *Bolton Evening News:* 35; *Oxford Mail:* 38; **Art Archive:** 52l (Tate Gallery London/Eileen Tweedy); **Steve Emberton:** 70–71, 74t; **Photo © Peter Hince, www.peterhince.com:** 76, 94–5, 98, 100–101, 106, 108, 116, 118l, 156; **Corbis:** 77t (Martyn Goddard); 187 (Reuters); **Barry Plummer:** 85; **Mirrorpix:** 92, 127tl, 131l, 136–7, 140–41, 148, 200–201; **Photosets/Brannon Tommey:** 114–15; **Photoshot:** 124, 135 (LFI); 164, 183 (LFI/Simon Fowler); 170, 179t (UPPA); **Richard Young:** 128, 132t, 142, 150, 158–9, 162–3, 169l, 171; **PAimages:** 167 (Edward Hurst/Empics Entertainment); 180 (All Action/Empics Entertainment); **John Frost Newspapers:** 189

Memorabilia
Mark Blake: 30; **Queenconcerts.com:** 33bl, 33br; **Ferdinando Frega/QueenMuseum.com:** 43, 63; **Private Collection:** 63l, 63c, 75b, 77b, 83bc, 83bl, 97, 112l, 112r, 117 inset, 118r, 127tr, 127br, 127bl, 132b, 153b, 155, 169r, 176bl, 176br, 178b, 186; **Alamy:** 83bl (CBW); 139 (DWD Media); **Courtesy of Epiclectic:** 123br

We would like to give special thanks to Peter Hince and Mick Rock for the supply of photographs from their archives. Further examples can be seen in Peter Hince's *Queen Unseen: My Life with the Greatest Rock Band of the 20th Century* (John Blake Publishing, 2011/Music Press Books, 2015) and Mick Rock's *Killer Queen* (with Brian May and Mary Austin, Genesis Publications, 2003) and *Classic Queen* (Omnibus Press, 2007).

ACKNOWLEDGEMENTS

Many thanks to Colin Webb, Sally Claxton, James Hodgson and Joanne Rippin at Palazzo Editions, and to my agent Rupert Heath. Thanks also to Phil Alexander, Dave Brolan, Dave Everley, Ben Mitchell and all at *Q*, *Mojo* and *Classic Rock* magazines, and to Queen's publicist, Phil Symes.

This book contains material from interviews conducted by myself with Queen's Brian May and Roger Taylor for *Mojo* and *Q* between 1998 and 2014, plus my original interviews from between 2005 and 2015 with John Anthony, Roy Thomas Baker, Mike Bersin, Chris Chesney, Patrick Connolly, Peter Hince, Paul Humberstone, Ian Hunter, Gary Langan, Reinhold Mack, Aubrey Malden, Mark Malden, the late Bob Mercer, Barry Mitchell, Mike Moran, Adrian Morrish, Bruce Murray, Mick Rock, Subash Shah, the late Norman Sheffield, Chris Smith and John Taylor. Extra special thanks to Peter Hince for invaluable information and advice.